Palgrave Studies in P

**Series Editors**
Ludger Helms
University of Innsbruck
Innsbruck, Austria

Gillian Peele
University of Oxford
Oxford, UK

Bert A. Rockman
Purdue University
West Lafayette, USA

Palgrave Studies in Political Leadership seeks to gather some of the best work on political leadership broadly defined, stretching from classical areas such as executive, legislative and party leadership to understudied manifestations of political leadership beyond the state. Edited by an international board of distinguished leadership scholars from the United States, Europe and Asia, the series publishes cutting-edge research that reaches out to a global readership. The editors are gratefully supported by an advisory board comprising of: Takashi Inoguchi (University of Tokyo, Japan), R.A.W. Rhodes (University of Southampton, UK) and Ferdinand Müller-Rommel (University of Luneburg, Germany).

More information about this series at
http://www.palgrave.com/gp/series/14602

Jon Herbert · Trevor McCrisken
Andrew Wroe

# The Ordinary Presidency of Donald J. Trump

palgrave
macmillan

Jon Herbert
Keele University
Staffordshire, UK

Andrew Wroe
School of Politics and International
Relations
University of Kent
Canterbury, UK

Trevor McCrisken
University of Warwick
Coventry, Warwickshire, UK

Palgrave Studies in Political Leadership
ISBN 978-3-030-04942-3          ISBN 978-3-030-04943-0    (eBook)
https://doi.org/10.1007/978-3-030-04943-0

Library of Congress Control Number: 2018965228

This Palgrave Macmillan imprint is published by the registered company Springer Nature Switzerland AG
The registered company address is: Gewerbestrasse 11, 6330 Cham, Switzerland

*To our children:*

*Nathan and Adam*
*Kate, Josh, Henry, Ben and Will*
*Albert and Alice*

# Acknowledgements

Many people contribute to the writing of a book, not just the authors. The book's central thesis received a particularly strong grilling at the UK Political Studies Association American Politics Group's annual conference at the University of Oxford in January 2018. The "peace through strength" argument of the foreign policy chapter received helpful comments and suggestions when presented at the BISA US Foreign Policy Working Group conference at Liverpool John Moores University and at a joint workshop in Oxford between the Miller Center of Public Affairs at the University of Virginia and the Rothermere American Institute, both in September 2018. The book is much stronger as a result of those interrogations.

We would like to thank all those that have read parts or the whole of the manuscript and/or listened to us discussing Mr. Trump ad nauseam for the past two years. These include Ivan Wroe, Tom Watts, Rubrick Biegon, Edward Ashbee, Tom Wraight, Ben Gannon, Jon Parker, Michael Tappin, the anonymous Palgrave reviewer and other colleagues in our departments at Keele, Warwick and Kent. We would also like to thank Rob Singh who was instrumental in getting this project off the ground. Amanda Gosling requires special thanks, not only for reading the manuscript several times, but also for contributing to the statistical analysis in Chapter 4.

Coauthoring with two other people brings with it various challenges, including how to make sure you're not undoing the good work that one of your colleagues has just spent hours drafting. We have genuinely enjoyed working with each other, however, and each of us believes this book is stronger throughout for our combined energy, dedication and, hopefully, insights.

The staff at Palgrave Macmillan have done a sterling job in guiding this book to publication. Ambra Finotello, Palgrave's editor on our side of the pond, was extremely enthusiastic about the project and picked it up. Michelle Chen then took control on the American side and has displayed exquisite professionalism in the face of our sometime tardiness. John Stegner has guided the manuscript through the production process with equal professionalism. Thank you for answering our many queries with good grace and for your steady hand on the production tiller.

Each of our families deserves a special mention, not least for their patience as we spent many hours away from them watching Trump's presidency unfold, scratching our heads as we tried to figure out what it all meant, and writing and rewriting the chapters of our book. Rebecca Elliott, Jackie Clarke and Amanda Gosling can have us back now, as can all our children to whom we have dedicated this book.

While everyone above has helped make the book better than it would otherwise have been, we alone, of course, are responsible for its limitations.

October 2018
Jon Herbert
Trevor McCrisken
Andrew Wroe

# Contents

# 1

# Introduction: The Ordinary Presidency of the Extraordinary Donald J. Trump

"Today, I stand before the United Nations General Assembly to share the extraordinary progress we've made. In less than two years, my administration has accomplished more than almost any administration in the history of our country…. So true." Donald J. Trump address at 73rd Session of the United Nations General Assembly Annual General Debate in New York City, September 25, 2018.

Donald J. Trump has a very high opinion of himself and elicits the most extreme opinions in others. Almost no one is coolly objective on the man or his presidency. Some regard him as a disruptor and outsider who has challenged the cozy status quo of entrenched special interests and a corrupt political system that served the elites not the masses. In this view, he speaks truth to power on behalf of the millions of forgotten, downtrodden and economically insecure Americans whose jobs disappeared or are being threatened by a globalized marketplace in goods, services and the means of production. Trump has also rallied these "left-behinds" in the face of an alleged immigrant tide that is submerging traditional American values and culture, proliferating crime and threatening national security. He has, his cheerleaders argue,

© The Author(s) 2019
J. Herbert et al., *The Ordinary Presidency of Donald J. Trump*,
Palgrave Studies in Political Leadership,
https://doi.org/10.1007/978-3-030-04943-0_1

broken the mold of American politics by constructing a new winning election coalition of God-fearing, culturally conservative, white working-class voters and by remaking the Republican Party in his image. The rock-solid backing of party supporters, and especially its activists, instils fear, respect and discipline in the Republican congressional caucus, which has been harnessed to achieve a string of ground-breaking policy triumphs on the economy, tax cuts, deregulation, immigration, security and more. His challenge to the established order extends beyond America's shores and includes his attacks on globalist international organizations such as the United Nations, NATO and the International Criminal Court as well as hated multinational environmental and trade agreements including the Paris Agreement on Climate Change and the Trans-Pacific Partnership. According to his admirers, he has succeeded in his pledge to Make America Great Again at home and abroad.

To Trump's supporters, his outsiderness, populism, nationalism, America First patriotism and rebellious disruption are celebrated in themselves and held up as reasons for his many extraordinary accomplishments. To his detractors, however, these characteristics are precisely what they fear. They see a deeply flawed character wholly unsuited to the job of president—mendacious, narcissistic, quickly bored and distracted, misogynistic and ethnocentric, thin skinned and easily provoked, stunningly ill-informed yet utterly convinced of his own brilliance and intelligence. They believe he is incapable of remedying his ignorance in part because he does not recognize it and further because he cannot assimilate new information into his long-fixed worldview. His character flaws interact with his politics in most unappealing ways: An unapologetic racist playing on the base fears of vulnerable citizens, offering simplistic yet dangerous solutions to inordinately complex public policy problems; a bombastic, undiplomatic ignoramus lumbering across the world-stage upending decades-old and even centuries-old alliances and the international organizations that America built and which have sustained its dominance, all while cozying up to dictators and demagogues and affronting supposed friends and allies.

Perhaps even worse, according to critics, is Trump's complete disdain for democratic institutions, structures and processes. At stake, they argue, is nothing less than America's constitutional democracy itself.

Anyone or anything that threatens, even minimally, Trump's status and power is roundly attacked in the most vicious terms. His assaults on an inquisitive and robust media holding power to account are emblematic of the way Trump deals with any democratic opposition: They are belittled and delegitimized. He will trash anything and anyone that stands in his way. He puts his own ends before the democratic health of the United States. This is not an America First presidency, but a Trump First presidency. The media is thus labeled the "enemy of the American people" and the journalists who staff it are "horrible, horrendous people" promulgating "fake and disgusting news" based on "fictional" anonymous sources. Investigating the internal deliberations of government is "unpatriotic" and puts people's lives at risk. The freedom of the press to write whatever it wants is "disgusting…and someone should look into it" and libel laws need "opening up" to allow Trump and others to sue more easily. No institution or individual, save his immediate family, seems safe from Trump's democracy-threatening invective.

While these two views of Trump are polar opposites, they share a common assumption: that Trump's presidency is extraordinary. In the one view, it is extraordinarily good; in the other, extraordinarily bad; in both, extraordinarily different from any previous presidency. This book challenges these assumptions. The argument here and in the following pages is that Trump may well be an extraordinary individual, but that his is nonetheless an ordinary presidency. Before setting out what this seemingly counter-intuitive claim means, it is important to be clear about what it does not mean. This book does not claim that Trump is an ordinary *president*, but rather that his *presidency* is ordinary. Indeed, in the history of the United States, it is unlikely that there has been a more unusual, unorthodox, unconventional, unordinary president. On practically every criterion, Trump is an extraordinary man and an extraordinary president. It would be futile to argue otherwise, and readers will not find that argument made here.

To understand how and why Trump's presidency is ordinary it is useful to think about the way he approaches and executes this most difficult of jobs—what we call the methodology of the president—and to contrast this with the outcomes or accomplishments of his presidency. It is common and useful in many walks of life to contrast style and substance, process and policy, words and deeds, rhetoric and action, and promises made and promises kept. It is useful here, too. In each of these binary pairs, it is the former that speaks to Trump's methodology and underpins his extraordinariness. In style, process, words, rhetoric and promises made, Trump is a most extraordinary president. But in substance, policy, deeds, action and promises kept, Trump's presidency is not extraordinary. Indeed, it is ordinary—largely conventional, orthodox and conservative, rather than revolutionary or radical. Consider this assessment by Peter Baker, the *New York Times* White House correspondent and respected Trump watcher, at the end of the president's first year in office:

> [Trump] has spent much of his first year in office defying the conventions and norms established by the previous 44 [presidents], and transforming the presidency in ways that were once unimaginable. Under Mr Trump, it has become a blunt instrument to advance personal, policy and political goals. He has revolutionized the way presidents deal with the world beyond 1600 Pennsylvania Avenue, dispensing with the carefully modulated messaging of past chief executives in favor of no-holds-barred, crystal-breaking, us-against-them, damn-the-consequences blasts borne out of gut and grievance. (Baker 2017)

Baker's conclusion that Trump has reinvented, even revolutionized the presidency is, however, almost wholly based on an analysis of style, tone and process, on the way that Trump approaches issues and speaks to Washington, America and the world. There is no question that he is extraordinary in these respects—that is, in his methodology—but they are not good criteria on which to judge a president. All presidents to some extent or other are different in their approach and presentation, and there is no single, accepted best way of *being* president. What presidents can be judged on and compared on is their record of achievements and outcomes. In judging Trump, therefore, we instead draw on Richard Neustadt's classic argument that presidential leadership is ultimately a question of how far a president is able to influence or engender the *outcomes* of government (Neustadt 1990, 4). It is our contention that for all his attempts at shaking up the system and smashing convention, Trump's presidency is and will be relatively ordinary in its public policy outputs and their wider consequences.

But what does it mean to say Trump's presidency is ordinary in its outputs? How does one know ordinary when one sees it? The term ordinary is used here in two different but related ways. First, Trump's presidency is ordinary in that its outcomes are limited in number and scope. Trump simply has not achieved very much in policy terms. He has struggled to pursue his agenda in Congress, even though his party enjoyed unified control of both the executive and legislative branches during the first two years of Trump's presidency. His efforts to circumvent the legislative process and effect change via executive orders and other administrative actions have fared little better. The image of Trump penning his signature on a newly minted executive order is a familiar one, but those orders—at least the important ones—more often than not have been blocked and overturned in the federal courts. Trump's policy achievements look meager compared with the confident promises he made that change would come quickly and easily. They look meager next to his and his aides' grandiose claims about their successes once in office: "The President of the United States has accomplished more in just a few weeks than many Presidents do in an entire administration" said special political adviser Stephen Miller, while Trump himself bragged "I've done more in 500 days than any president has ever done in their first 500 days." More surprising than the laughter of his fellow leaders at the 2018 UN General Assembly when Trump repeated a version of his standard brag—quoted in the epigraph to this chapter—was that they did not laugh longer and harder. They also look meager when lined up next to the accomplishments of America's truly great presidencies: Washington's, Jefferson's, Lincoln's, F. D. Roosevelt's and perhaps Jackson's. But these presidencies are outliers. Their successes are not normal. They are the extraordinary presidencies. Meager is normal, meager is ordinary, especially in the post-Watergate era when presidents face additional constraints on their influence. In not achieving much of consequence, Trump falls within the parameters of presidential ordinariness.

If the first way in which Trump's presidency is ordinary is that its outputs are meager but average, the second way is that the few policy achievements that Trump can genuinely lay claim to for the most part are pretty mainstream Republican ones rather than the radical departures he promised on the campaign trail. The populist insurgent who hijacked the Republican Party in the primaries has followed a policy agenda in office that is largely in tune with his party colleagues at the other end of Pennsylvania Avenue, even though he has frequently attacked their leadership. When Trump pursues policies that can be thought of as outside the Republican mainstream, the initiatives usually end in failure, are reined in by Congress or the courts, or self-adjusted to greater orthodoxy by the administration itself. Tax and immigration reform are exemplars of the two types. The 2017 tax cut is the signature domestic policy achievement of Trump's first two years in office. It is not the biggest tax cut in American history, as he has claimed repeatedly. It is more ordinary than that, perhaps scraping into the top ten depending on the economic assumptions underpinning the calculations. More importantly, the biggest winners in terms of dollar reductions in tax are big business and America's richest families—people like Trump himself—not the ordinary hardworking Americans of limited and precarious means that Candidate Trump talked about protecting and helping while on the campaign trail. It is the hedge fund managers and Mar-a-Lago members who are smiling most broadly. There is nothing in the legislation to worry the plutocrats and business interests that donate large sums to the Republican Party. What's more, as we will detail in Chapter 4, the American public seem to recognize the true nature of the tax cut since it is approved of by less Americans than any similar tax reduction in the last 40 years and is even less popular than two major tax *hikes* during that period.

Conversely, when Trump challenged Republican orthodoxy on immigration—or at least one very influential strand of it—he failed to make any legislative progress. While it is true that anti-immigration and particularly anti-illegal immigration voices are slowly getting louder in the Republican Party, the pro-immigration chorus still easily out-sings them. The Republican congressional caucus is dominated by a pro-business wing that promotes a flexible and cheap labor force abetted by generous levels of immigration. Few pro-business Republicans would today openly support *The Wall Street Journal's* proposal for a constitutional amendment that "there shall be open borders," but a solid majority oppose Trump's plans to build a border wall with Mexico, to return Dreamers (who entered the United States illegally as children but were given legal protection from deportation by President Barack Obama) to the status of illegal immigrants and to reduce the level and change the composition of legal immigration. Despite the centrality of immigration to Donald Trump's presidential campaign, his populist and national-ist agenda remains largely unfulfilled and opposed by elites in his own party.

Similarly, in foreign policy, despite Trump's promises to put America First and disrupt international alliances and his penchant for insulting foreign leaders, especially allies, Trump has adopted the mainstream Republican strategy of seeking "peace through strength" and largely pur-sued the same policies and priorities as previous administrations, albeit with a very different style and attitude than his immediate predecessor. For example, while he has been more than willing to berate publicly his NATO allies for their apparently insufficient burden sharing, he is far from the first US president to do so and he shows no serious signs of withdrawing from the common defense alliance which continues to play a significant role in defense and security planning, including in strategy documents such as the Nuclear Posture Review. As we argue in Chapter 8, even his seemingly most extreme and extraordinary projec-tion of power and rhetorical saber-rattling with North Korea has oper-ated within the bounds of a common Republican approach of upping the ante in order to negotiate from a perceived position of strength. The ideas behind Trump's foreign policy approach are very orthodox in their view of how states interact on the international stage and to date most of his achievements in foreign affairs have been very modest, which is a scorecard in keeping with the track record of many post-World War II presidencies that have found it very difficult to deliver big wins and have suffered several major setbacks in their adventures overseas. Despite all the bluster and the over-confident claims of success, Trump's foreign policy has been fairly ordinary.

Finally, even Trump's election to the White House was pretty ordi-nary in terms of the nature of the vote cast for and against him. Again, this claim is not to be confused with thinking that his campaign was ordinary. Far from it. His victory in the Republican primaries was utterly extraordinary and unexpected and the nature of his general election campaign broke many conventions and received wisdom about what works and what does not. His messaging, rhetoric, outsiderness, approach to campaigning, the inexperience of his campaign team and tribulations during the campaign (particularly the Access Hollywood "hot mic" tape) all defy the tag of ordinariness. But the vote that turned out for him as the Republican candidate was nothing out of the ordinary. Republicans voted for him as their candidate and Democrats voted for Hillary Clinton as theirs in similar proportions to previous presidential elections. Yes, Trump won a bigger slice of the working-class vote than Romney four years earlier, but the movement of less educated Americans into the Republican camp is far from a new phenomenon and Trump did not win more of them than would be expected given the historical trend. And despite the prominence of immigration and other racialized issues in the campaign—such as Trump calling Mexicans rapists and criminals, equating Muslim immigration with threats to national security and appearing to reach out to white voters more generally—there was little notable redistribution of vote choices by race or ethnicity compared with the previous presidential election.

So, we have a president with few significant successes under his belt—whatever his own view about his greatness—and what few accomplishments he can lay claim to are mostly standard Republican fare. In this sense, the presidency of Donald J. Trump is ordinary. But how did we get here? How can the presidency of what seems to be the most extraordinary president in American history have descended into ordinariness?

The answer is fairly straightforward. First, as all students of American politics know, the Founding Fathers designed a system to constrain ambitious and potentially dangerous leaders. A president must share his constitutional powers with others and as Neustadt (1990, x) said: "to share is to limit." All presidents must work within constitutional structures that separate and constrain. The structure limits presidential agency. That is normal. That is ordinary. That is the American system. Of course, some presidents do manage to effect great change, to leave their mark on the US, and these are generally regarded as the great presidencies. But Washington, Lincoln and FDR were afforded opportunities for greatness by the times in which they lived. During times of crisis—war, insurrection, a depression—power flows to the center, to the executive branch, which presidents can utilize to introduce long-lasting and deep-seated reforms. However, while the opportunity presented by crisis increases the chance of presidential success, it does not guarantee it. In their efforts to lead and govern, let alone make history, US presidents must take opportunities when they present themselves and then utilize their political skills to achieve results (Edwards III 2012). These skills, as Neustadt tells us, amount primarily to the president's ability to bargain with and persuade other office holders of the merits of his ideas, legislation or course of action. Not all presidents can or do. Barack Obama's chief of staff, Rahm Emanuel, famously observed that "You never want a serious crisis to go to waste," but his boss is accused of doing exactly that by critics on the left. Their complaint is that Obama was offered a huge opportunity to remake America's financial system and even social fabric in the wake of the global financial crisis of 2008, but instead propped it up and saved it. He bailed out the banks that instigated the crisis at a cost of hundreds of billions of dollars to American taxpayers; failed to hold to account individual bankers for their misconduct; and ultimately offered only the most tepid of reforms, which actually strengthened the financial status quo. But unlike Obama, Trump has not yet had the opportunity for action that a crisis presents and without one his opportunity for greatness, for success on a historical scale, is seriously constrained.

Trump also governs during deeply polarized times, in which politicians from the opposition party are loath to support presidential initiatives. Reaching across the aisle to build a bipartisan coalition in Congress, once common, is now most uncommon. And with special interests better organized and funded than ever and, following the Supreme Court's *Citizens United* decision, able to spend unlimited amounts on political campaigns, they can more effectively protect their entrenched interests and defend against threats from reform. The political system is increasingly sticky or "thick" in the words of presidential historian Stephen Skowronek (1997). In other words, it is more difficult to navigate and to bend to one's will if you are the president today. There are fewer opportunities for persuasion and persuasion is generally less effective. There is less leeway for action and thus for success. In this thick, sticky Washington soup (one could even call it a swamp) of entrenched interests with partisanship at its postwar high and challenging congressional math, Trump's is a most difficult task.

So, Trump's ordinariness is partly explained by constitutionally fixed and limiting structures of power and also by the time and environment in which he governs. But the second part of the explanation for his presidency's ordinariness is the president himself. Simply put, Trump is just not very good at the job of being president. He has not been able to drain the swamp. He has not been able to cut through the established practices, let alone rules and regulations, that determine outcomes in US politics, nor even in international relations where those restrictions are perhaps looser. He claimed that being president would be "easy" and that he would win so much that people would get bored of winning. But there have not been many wins and he has made the job look almost impossible at times. He has done so in part because of his personality and character—he does not have the personal attributes required to make the office work for him—but also in part because of his presidential methodology, which was defined above as the way he approaches and executes the job. Some examples: Trump made key staffing decisions based as much on looks and personal loyalty as on experience, competence and ideology; he seems immune or uninterested in the cabals fighting a civil war around him and has allowed and even encouraged the White House to descend into a permanent state of chaos; he is happy to switch positions on a dime; he runs a personal public relations and outreach operation via Twitter; and he has settled on a self-defeating bargaining strategy—which we call 'hostage politics'—as his main method of leveraging policy successes.

This is an extraordinary list of methodological malpractice. Not only does it seriously hinder the president's pursuit of his policy goals because he cannot persuade others to do what he wants them to do, but it also opens up a policy space into which others sprint in an effort to dominate the agenda, which is a key reason why Trump's few policy successes have been largely mainstream Republican ones, not nationalist, populist or particularly disruptive. These problems are of Trump's own making. Indeed, some observers may find it ironic that it is precisely the president's methodological extraordinariness and the exceptional nature of his personality and character that help to render his presidency ordinary.

The goal of this book is to make a persuasive case that Trump's presidency is ordinary and to explain why it is so. Chapter 2, however, begins the task by setting out the opposite case. It presents the arguments made by the president himself, his supporters and critics, as well as more neutral commentators that Trump's presidency *is* extraordinary. We do this in the interests of objectivity but also to set out the case against which we are arguing. Chapters 3 and 4 present the evidence for ordinariness. We show that the vote for Trump was close to historical precedents in terms of who voted which way and why and that the president has not realigned or even de-aligned the long-standing attachments that American voters have to the Republican or Democratic parties. We also analyze the record of Trump's presidency in terms of its policy achievements, demonstrating as outlined above that he has enjoyed few policy successes, and that the few "wins" he has had are largely mainstream Republican ones. If Chapters 3 and 4 present *evidence* for ordinariness, Chapters 5, 6 and 7 turn to explaining *why* the Trump presidency is ordinary. These arguments were outlined very briefly above but the three chapters explore in depth the complex interactions between the president's personality and character, his methodology or approach and in particular his legislative, media and public strategies, and the political system and structures of power in which he operates.

The final substantive chapter takes a different turn. The previous chapters focus heavily on Washington and domestic politics. Chapter 8's focus is foreign policy and international affairs. These have their own chapter because the making of foreign policy and the president's role in international relations is different from that in the domestic sphere. For one thing, presidents have more leeway for action and more power in international affairs, including issues of trade, as Aaron Wildavsky (1966) showed half a century ago. Congress is generally more deferent in foreign affairs, so presidents are more likely to be able exert influence and demonstrate difference from their predecessors. For another thing, the distinction between policy, process and outcomes is less clear in foreign affairs than in domestic politics. In the domestic sphere, a president can have a "policy"—perhaps a carefully or not-so-carefully considered document on environmental protection or the status of a certain class of immigrant—but it remains just words and of no import until approved by Congress or put into effect via a formal and legal process of executive action. In the foreign sphere, the policy can become self-executing without a legal process. Other nations may respond to these words or presidential tone with actual actions, perhaps striking new alliances, building up their armed forces, or even launching a preemptive attack. Words and tone are much more consequential in foreign affairs than domestic matters. Nonetheless, our argument remains the same despite the more difficult terrain of international politics and trade: Even in foreign matters, the Trump presidency does not deserve to be called extraordinary. Instead, it is rather ordinary.

# References

Baker, Peter. 2017. "For Trump, A Year of Reinventing the Presidency." *New York Times*, December 31.

Edwards III, George C. 2012. *The Strategic President: Persuasion and Opportunity in Presidential Leadership*. Princeton: Princeton University Press.

Neustadt, Richard. 1990. *Presidential Power and the Modern Presidents: The Politics of Leadership from Roosevelt to Reagan*. New York: The Free Press.

Skowronek, Stephen. 1997. *The Politics Presidents Make: Leadership from John Adams to Bill Clinton*. Cambridge, MA: Belknap Press.

Wildavsky, Aaron. 1966. "The Two Presidencies." *Trans-Action/Society* 4: 7–14.

# 2

# A Trump Revolution?

When Donald Trump descended the escalator into the gilded atrium of Trump Tower on New York's 5th Avenue to announce his candidacy for the presidency of the United States on June 16, 2015, few seasoned observers believed that he could win. At best, his campaign was seen as a novelty. To some, it was a joke. The following year confounded the conventional wisdom on electoral politics as Trump achieved the extraordinary feat of winning the Republican Party's nomination. Six months later, President-elect Trump was preparing for office after an unexpected victory over Democratic candidate Hillary Clinton.

There followed a period of frenzied speculation as to how a Trump presidency would unfold. Observers had spent the best part of eighteen months attempting to understand the Trump phenomenon, generating a range of ways to comprehend how he and his interactions with the political system were different. Most acknowledged the extraordinary nature of Trump's victory, but extended debates developed over the ways in which he was unusual and what the impacts of those differences would be once he was in office.

© The Author(s) 2019
J. Herbert et al., *The Ordinary Presidency of Donald J. Trump*,
Palgrave Studies in Political Leadership,
https://doi.org/10.1007/978-3-030-04943-0_2

In this chapter, those differences are explored in terms of titles that Trump earned during his campaign and transition and has, according to many observers, carried with him into the White House. Trump was and is seen, variously, as an outsider, disruptor, nationalist, populist and insurgent. While these descriptions of the Trump phenomenon overlap in certain respects, each is conceptually distinct and each, in their own way, suggests that Trump's presidency is extraordinary. This chapter presents evidence which is in opposition to the book's main argument that Trump's is an ordinary presidency. It is important to be transparent, to set out all sides of the argument, but we also want to establish the case that we will be arguing against. In many ways, what is presented here is the "conventional wisdom" about the Trump presidency. And the conventional wisdom is that it is unconventional. So much so, indeed, that it can be labeled extraordinary. Subsequent chapters tackle the conventional wisdom head-on, presenting contrary evidence and arguments to make the case that Trump's presidency should be viewed as ordinary. For now, however, we make the case in favor of extraordinariness.

## 1    Trump the Outsider

Trump came to the 2016 campaign with no experience of political office, presenting himself as an outsider offering to fix politics in Washington. The outsider campaign is a regular feature of presidential election contests. Recent candidates as diverse as Jimmy Carter, Ronald Reagan, Bill Clinton, George W. Bush and Barack Obama have emphasized their distance from, and opposition to, a demonized politics-as-usual within the Washington Beltway. Presidential candidates trade on public distrust of politicians and political institutions to portray themselves as agents of change intent upon confronting an interest-dominated, out-of-touch capital.

Trump's outsider campaign, however, was a particularly virulent strain of the type. He presented himself as the anti-politician. Assisted by never having held elected office or even run for office before, Trump argued that he was a true outsider. He emphasized that his campaign was not funded by special interests, arguing that his personal wealth freed him from the malign networks of US politics. He touted his lack of commitment to either party, repeatedly attacking both Republican and Democrat leaders, although he contrasted himself in particular to the highly politicized and polarizing character of his extremely experienced opponent. Unlike Hillary Clinton, he argued, as a successful businessman, television personality and true independent, he could resist the constraints imposed by normal party and interest politics in Washington and truly represent his supporters.

The candidate's outsider status was a particular achievement given the tensions inherent to any outsider candidacy. Any realistic attempt to win the presidency demands that a candidate secure a major party nomination. Thus, he or she must become an insider, playing to party concerns and compromising their outsider appeal. Trump resolved this problem in an unusual way, maintaining his individual status by mounting a hostile takeover of the Republican Party nomination.

Conventional wisdom suggests that political party elites control their own nominating processes. The McGovern-Fraser reforms of the 1970s appeared to allocate the power of choice to rank-and-file members of the parties, but influential work by Marty Cohen and his co-authors popularized the idea that party elites had regained control of the nominating process. They argue that while rank-and-file party supporters formally choose the nominee in primary contests, party elites still control the process behind the scenes in an "invisible primary" in the year or so leading up to the first formal caucus and primary elections. Power lies with the party's broad "coalition of interests" which includes national, state and local elected officials, the leaders of various organized interests such as unions, business and religious groups, and other civil society organizations and pressure groups, unpaid but committed activists that staff the ground game and the mega-donors and the fundraisers with huge donor networks (Cohen et al. 2008, 15–18). These party insiders mobilize during the invisible primary to dissect and narrow down the field, rally around a particular candidate, and persuade rank-and-file voters to back their choice in the following public primaries.

This analysis points to one particularly important factor in determining who wins the nomination: endorsements by elective officeholders and especially officeholders from a different faction than the candidate. Endorsements send a signal to other officeholders and rank-and-file supporters about which candidates are acceptable and electable. Each endorsement helps engender more and slowly a favored candidate emerges. Even if these insiders cannot agree on a candidate during the invisible primary, they can veto the unappealing ones: "parties resist candidates who are unacceptable to important members of the coalition, even when those candidates are popular with voters" (Cohen et al. 2008, 339). In such cases, insiders do not choose the nominee, but essentially present voters with a list of insider-backed candidates from which they make their selection.

Republican Party elites clearly regarded Donald Trump as an unappealing candidate who should be vetoed. No Republican official in the House, Senate or any governor's mansion offered Trump support through the entire "invisible primary" period (Bycoffe 2016). Instead, elected officials queued up to condemn Trump, attempting to rally support behind other candidates in a deliberate, well-funded and thoroughly Republican "Anyone-but-Trump" strategy. For example, Republican Senator Lindsey Graham, who had previously said that choosing between Trump and opponent Ted Cruz was akin to choosing between being shot or poisoned, announced for Cruz in March 2016 because "we have to rally around Ted Cruz as the only way to stop Donald Trump" (Philips 2016). Even after Trump had wrapped up the nomination, Graham refused to endorse him. He was not alone. High-profile Republicans such as Jeb Bush and even previous Republican nominee Mitt Romney generated headlines through dramatic public interventions in the Anyone-but-Trump campaign. The Our Principles Political Action Committee (PAC) was established in January 2016. It was funded primarily by the Ricketts family, prominent Republicans and co-owners of the Chicago Cubs and staffed by alumni of Jeb Bush's and Mitt Romney's campaigns. Our Principles spent nearly $25 million in its failed attempt to "dump Trump." Other anti-Trump PACs included the Never Trump PAC and Republicans for Hillary PAC.

There were many reasons for this antipathy to the outsider. First, and most obviously, was Trump's overt hostility toward the elite of the Republican Party. Trump portrayed himself as the scourge of the

Washington establishment, including leaders of his party. As he pursued the party's nomination, he trash-talked the party he campaigned to lead. Second, there were serious questions about Trump's potential as a party leader. Republican elites saw themselves as participants in a vicious, zero-sum battle with the opposing Democrats. Trump's record of switching his affiliation from party to party underlined his outsider status and did not inspire Republican confidence. As recently as 2004, he had told Wolf Blitzer on CNN that "in many cases I probably identify more as a Democrat" (Laderman and Simms 2017, 67). He appeared to lack ideological convictions to tie him to the party's policy positions. His attacks upon party leaders hardly suggested a loyalty or perceived need to prioritize the Republican Party's concerns. His promises of bipartisanship and presentation as the "Art of the Deal" negotiator seemed to suggest someone who would not look to protect his party, its ideology or its elite. It often appeared that Trump simply found the Republican Party nothing more than a useful foil to advance his own interests.

Trump's victory marked an extraordinary upending of the conventional wisdom of political scientists, essentially that party elites determine who the nominee will be. In 2016, they did not. The prospect was, therefore, of a president entering office with fewer ties to his party than recent predecessors. Indeed, Trump might be at war with his own party's leadership, but therefore free of the constraints that loyal partisanship might impose. This situation posed important questions on how the president might try to get his legislative agenda passed and his executive actions tolerated, and what opportunities there were for a new form of outsider politics conducted from the Oval Office.

## 2     Trump the Disruptor

As a candidate Trump disrupted electoral politics through his character, campaigning techniques and policy. He refused to follow the conventions, instead making his own rules. His rejection of classic conservative positions suggested he would offer a radical new policy agenda at the expense of conservative orthodoxy. New issues would feature at the top of this president's political agenda, particularly trade and immigration. He also offered the prospect of a disruptive presidency determined to "drain the swamp" of Washington politics, begging questions as to how his form of disruption might work as an approach to the very different challenges of governing, rather than campaigning. The same techniques might be brought to the Oval Office, or perhaps Trump could bring different forms of disruption to the different challenges of holding and exercising power.

He refused to follow the normal conventions and patterns of electoral politics. Some observers, noting an obvious association with Trump's background, drew parallels between Trump's campaign and the management concept of disruption. Entrepreneurial "disruptors" enter markets and upend them with unconventional behavior (Williams 2016). Just as Netflix, Apple, Amazon and Uber usurped market leaders, Trump's entry into the political market undermined the position of established politicians. Disruptors reject the conventional behaviors of producers in the market, recognizing that the normal approach to the market is already finely honed. An improved service is offered, often as a function of technological innovation. The main challenge for such a market newcomer is to draw customers' attention to the distinctive strengths of the product. Such a disruptor makes an initial impression, but then experiments to increase market share, often stepping back promptly from failures and remaining open to new ideas.

The parallels to Trump's campaign were obvious. His approach involved a wide range of innovations that defied conventional understandings of what was required to win the Republican Party's nomination. Observers drew attention to different aspects of Trumpian disruption, with varying degrees of faith to the management concept. These included claims that his character was unlike that of mainstream politicians, that he was developing a different kind of campaign machine and that his policy positions were disruptive. Some observers found it hard to take the former reality TV star and businessman seriously as a politician. His character drew special attention: Many of Trump's behaviors did not match expectations of a presidential personality. While there is not a generic correct presidential personality, Trump appeared to contravene expectations that voters regularly look for certain core characteristics in presidential candidates. Candidates rated as competent (using ratings such as intelligent and knowledgeable) and as effective leaders are likely to thrive. Integrity, often measured on the basis of whether a candidate is seen as sincere, moral or honest, and appearing empathetic, through showing compassion and caring about voters' situations, also help. Some studies emphasize drive, expressed through variables such as strength, hard work, determination, and courage and other traits such as thrift, reasonableness and humility (Kinder 1983, 1986; Funk 1996, 1999; Benoit and McHale 2003).

Much of Trump's public persona did not fit these templates. He did not appear knowledgeable; indeed, his handling of political issues suggested a deep inexperience. Basic interview questions led to rambling, incoherent answers that betrayed an unfamiliarity with the issues. He made highly controversial and disruptive statements but then backtracked, such as his suggestion that women should be punished for having an abortion. His simplification of complex policy questions, presenting them as easily resolved, suggested a lack of understanding of those issues. Little evidence suggested that Trump could deliver effective, or even barely competent, leadership.

It was hard to defend Trump's personal integrity. His refusal to share his tax returns, as every presidential candidate had done since the mid-1970s, hinted at financial misconduct or perhaps a desire to avoid demonstrating he was not as rich as he claimed. Harassment cases from a series of women suggested an alternative form of unacceptable or even criminal behavior; the open microphone Access Hollywood tape in which he bragged of groping women moved discussions from the twice-divorced Trump's colorful personal life into issues of alleged sexual assault. It seemed unlikely that Christian conservatives, for example, would find Trump a sympathetic, or even tolerable, character.

Neither was Trump an obviously empathetic or compassionate candidate. He showed a clear willingness to express emotions that lie outside the usual range present in presidential performance; indeed, he seemed to revel in the expression of anger and intolerance. Both in person and through his much used Twitter account, Trump's rhetoric involved unprecedented personal attacks on enemies. Political opponents were branded with nicknames ("Lyin' Ted" Cruz, "Crooked

Hillary" Clinton, "Low energy" Jeb Bush) and exposed to withering abuse. Groups were also the focus of his ire, including enemies such as the media (labeled as "fake news") and conservative "losers" such as the Club for Growth and Bill Kristol of the *Weekly Standard*. Rude, crude and provocative, Trump seemed to delight in creating conflict and division, conducting a campaign that often seemed to be a series of personal battles rather than a coherent effort to win an election. Trump expressed concern for the plight of those on low wages, some who had lost their jobs and victims of some forms of crime, so expressing empathy was not beyond him, but much of the campaign seemed driven by his anger and personal vitriol.

Nor was Trump blessed with obvious humility. His braggadocio was rare for a presidential candidate. His speeches were often self-aggrandizing; Trump's acknowledgment of his own genius was highly unusual ("I have the best words"; "I'm the Ernest Hemingway of 140 characters"; "My I.Q. is one of the highest—and you all know it!"). His onstage preening and posing as he received applause from crowds exuded arrogance. Trump speeches often focused on personal slights he perceived, suggesting that the campaign was much more about him than it was about anyone who might vote for him.

Not only did Trump offer a different type of character, but he abandoned the standard means of managing a presidential campaign. He broke unofficial rules of campaign behavior, rules that, of course, only exist because they are believed to lead to victory. Trump barely maintained a professionalized campaign apparatus; his campaign staff seemed small and amateurish and was characterized by high turnover and few respected consultants. He also performed poorly in the money-raising stakes and refused to spend much of his own fortune. His speeches were rambling and unfocused leaving his campaign messaging unclear. Some of his statements seemed calculated to alienate certain groups. By classic indicators, Trump's campaign did not look serious. Subsequent accounts have not suggested that any of these apparent weaknesses were fronts for a highly disciplined and focused operation functioning away from the cameras—what you saw and heard was all there was (Lewandowski and Bossie 2018).

However, Trump did conduct a personal strategy to deliberately disrupt campaign politics as usual, by mounting an alternative form of campaign focused on his public performance and the media. Rather than relying on party organizations, most of which seemed likely to side with establishment candidates, or even a team of expert political consultants targeting paid media, Trump developed an extraordinary relationship with the media that he exploited to great advantage. His ability to generate attention was crucial, which he achieved through a combination of communication content and technique. Trump delivered a series of unusual behaviors which allowed him to dominate and define media coverage of the 2016 contest. Even when that coverage was negative, and it often was, it still worked for Trump because he was the center of attention—a place that he clearly craved—and first his Republican primary opponents and then Hillary Clinton were left scrambling for media coverage.

Trump's communication broke conventions and disrupted the opportunities of other candidates. His character garnered many stories in its own right, but Trump's performance as a candidate offered many other subjects for news coverage as well with his lack of focus, his untruths and outlandish promises, and his pursuit of the politics of conflict.

As opposed to the traditional message discipline of his competitors touting their theme of the day or week, in public Trump drifted off script, apparently onto whatever subject was on his mind at the time. Trump was, as Jamieson and Taussig (2017) claim in their analysis of Trump's rhetorical signature, "spontaneous and unpredictable." As Trump spoke off-the-cuff, both on the stump and in interviews, he sabotaged any attempt to highlight a particular issue, especially given his tendency to air personal grievances from the microphone. Unpredictability was not without costs: Some regarded Trump's lack of focus as broader than a rhetorical issue as, in many commentaries, "unpredictable" acted as a euphemism for "unstable." Its benefits, however, were extensive. Every Trump event was potentially newsworthy and worth (often live) coverage.

Trump's media-friendly but exaggerated rhetoric led to unrealistic promises. He pledged that "the crime and violence that today afflicts our nation will soon, and I mean very soon, come to an end ...safety will be restored." In healthcare, Trump promised "Everybody's going to be taken care of much better than they're taken care of now." Those covered under Obamacare could "expect to have great healthcare. It will be in a much simplified form. Much less expensive and much better… lower numbers, much lower deductibles." Promises to generate a miracle solution to the ongoing healthcare problems in the US, achieving lower costs, better quality and universal coverage, and to end crime, were credibility-stretching, or perhaps preposterous. While journalists wrote of the unrealistic promises, their audiences received a clear demonstration of the issues Trump thought important, enabling a connection with those potential voters.

The candidate's presentation of political arguments suggested a troubled engagement with the concept of truth. In a practice that Jamieson and Taussig (2017) call "evidence flouting," Trump regularly made exaggerated claims from the stump, such as his statements that murder rates were at the worst level for 45, or sometimes 47, years. Media stories highlighting factual inaccuracies again served to nonetheless communicate Trump's concerns. When he repeated the inaccurate information, or denied having misrepresented anything, further media stories reinforced the effect.

Trump's communication also defied convention in his approach to building coalitions of voters. Where many presidential candidates attempted to build a coalition by coaxing an aggregation of different groups to be supportive, Trump was a wilfully and deeply divisive candidate. Much of his campaign appeared a calculated, systematic effort to drive specific groups of voters away from him and his party. Condemning "political correctness," Trump employed language that had traditionally been regarded as not only outside the mainstream of American politics, but as wholly unacceptable. His presidential announcement speech denounced Mexican immigrants as rapists and criminals. Later speeches referred to "bad hombres" and repeatedly connected Hispanics with gang violence. His attitude to women was reflected in an allocation of "marks out of ten" for the looks of an opposing female candidate and his fat-shaming of former Miss Universe Alicia Machado. His alleged reference to Machado as

"Miss Housekeeping" offered a seamless interweaving of racism and sexism. He disgusted many observers with his impressions of a disabled reporter. Repeatedly, Muslims were portrayed as a terrorist threat. Trump marked out a clear position as a divisive, highly controversial candidate.

The Republicans' main review of their 2012 defeat, known as the "Growth and Opportunity Project", had highlighted the perilous state of the party in the face of demographic change and emphasized a particular need to win Hispanic votes. Trump offered the antithesis of this proposed inclusivity, seeming intent upon alienating an entire generation of Hispanics from Republicanism in one campaign, and many other groups in American society along with them. Elected members of the Republican elite felt this especially keenly as they tried to respond to media questions on each new Trump outrage. Should they stand by each racist statement of their party's chosen candidate, even though they might be outraged by the comments themselves? How would a forthright disavowal affect voting patterns in their district? Some Republicans consciously distanced themselves from Trump, while others performed linguistic contortions to avoid giving direct answers (Liu and Jacobson 2018). Trump's disruption even established a dynamic by which stories about other politicians were in terms of their responses to Trump's brand of conflict politics.

Trump combined his onstage rants and ramblings with a stream of insults and abuse from his Twitter feed. His unprecedented use of Twitter appeared to enable him to manipulate the media's agenda if not at will, then at least frequently. Immediate media attention for his confrontational and provocative tweets allowed Trump to time his intervention in the news cycle. He moved campaign communication strategy away from its traditional prime-time focus and could compete with potentially damaging stories by initiating another Twitter conflict. This incessant media attention on his Twitter account also spread his 140 character rants to a much broader audience than simply those potential voters who were users of the social media platform, ensuring also that each ephemeral interjection had a far longer shelf life than could occur within the Twittersphere itself.

The content of Trump's communication often appeared calculated to shock. He had spent much of his career building brands by considering how to get media coverage, judging that even critical coverage was better than no coverage (Trump 1987). He had developed a sharp instinct for how to create stories in order to earn media attention. Trump undoubtedly understood the appeal of conflict and controversy to journalists competing for market share. He may enjoy confrontation as a matter of personal style (one journalist describes him as having a "sweet tooth for chaos"), but was also aware of its practical advantages to him. The angry outbursts, misrepresentations and conflicts provided a narrative for much of the campaign, each Trump breach of convention adjudged to warrant further news headlines.

Trump was aided by a media simultaneously repelled and fascinated by an unprecedented candidacy. By covering his campaign rallies and public speeches in detail, reproducing his Tweets, and in effect acting as complicit influences in lending credibility to his self-proclaimed seriousness, the media became part of the Trump phenomenon. These successes compensated for the limitations of Trump's campaign machinery and fund-raising. He lacked paid television advertising, but media-Quant, which considers advertising rates to value candidates' media coverage, estimated that Trump won $4.96 billion of free media coverage in his final year of campaigning (Harris 2016). Volume of coverage was one dimension of his success, but Trump could claim other achievements. In a crowded Republican field, other candidates, with more conventional strategies but limited name recognition, could not establish themselves amid the storm of Trump stories. The disruptor changed the rules for other players as politics could not carry on as usual in Trump's presence. He highlighted the issue concerns he wanted to be associated with and that he judged germane to his potential voters. Furthermore, coverage of his unconventional behavior served to highlight his outsider credentials as something other than a run-of-the-mill politician. His notoriety as a forthright reality television presenter on *The Apprentice* from 2004 to 2015 helped reinforce his outsiderness.

While Trump disrupted the mechanisms of campaigning, he also challenged his party's traditional policy positions. As prominent Republican journalist Peggy Noonan commented:

[Republicans] think…that his support is all about anger, angst and theatrics. That's part of the story, but the other, more consequential part has to do with real policy issues… Mr. Trump has functioned… as the great disrupter. He brags that he has brought up great questions and forced other candidates to face them and sometimes change their stands - and he has. He changed the debate on illegal immigration. He said he'd build a wall and close the border and as the months passed and his competitors saw his surge, they too were suddenly, clearly, aggressively for ending illegal immigration. Mr. Trump touched an important nerve in opposing the political correctness that has angered the American people for a quarter century. He changed the debate when he asked for a pause in Muslim immigration until America 'can figure out what's going on.' In the age of terror, that looked suspiciously like common sense. … [Trump became] the party's 2016 thought leader. (Noonan 2016)

As Noonan describes, Trump disrupted an established pattern of behavior among Republican candidates that focused on particular forms of agreement and division within the party. Yes, his various policy declarations were mixed and often contradictory: How was one to read a president who suggested that he was for the Iraq War before he was against it? Research unearthed many specific policy positions he had taken that conservatives did not find persuasive. For example, Trump had supported a ban on assault weapons, suggesting an undesirable flexibility on second amendment issues. His positions on LGBTQ rights smacked more of New York liberalism than social conservatism. As Noonan identifies, his views on free trade and the role of international institutions seemed to orient against the liberal internationalism that guided most mainstream Republican approaches to foreign policy. Some of Trump's statements suggested an expanded role for the government, such as choosing specific industries to promote and protect. He did follow Republican orthodoxy by advocating the repeal and replacement of Obamacare, although with little personal enthusiasm and suggestions that the federal government should foot the bill for universal care. He also promised to appoint conservative judges and to re-establish law and order in a way that sat comfortably with many conservatives, but nevertheless, Trump failed key ideological litmus tests.

Furthermore, during the campaign, the New Yorker's willingness to reverse positions suggested a lack of commitment to any of them. This concern was magnified by Trump's presentation as a pragmatic, goal-oriented businessman, rather than a redoubt of ideological conviction. Trump was regarded by many on the right as less than a true conservative and with good reason. When conservative activist David Bossie introduced then right-wing political documentary producer Steve Bannon to Trump in August 2010, ostensibly to test the waters on a possible presidential run, they talked about his "problems on issues." The biggest was Trump's "very pro-choice" track record on abortion. Trump responded enthusiastically but in a way that would horrify true conservatives: "That can be fixed. You just tell me how to fix that. I'm–what do you call it? Pro-life. I'm pro-life, I'm telling you" (Woodward 2018, 3). To intellectual conservatives in 2016, Trump appeared an anathema, posing major challenges to established party and conservative movement positions. *The Weekly Standard*, a keeper of the conservative flame, explained why Trump did not deserve conservatives' votes (Cost 2016; Kristol 2016). *National Review*, another august publication of the right, published a scathing "Against Trump" edition with this emphasis (February 15, 2016). Again looking like an outsider, the "great disruptor" seemed to represent an unlikely combination of the wrong principles and no principles.

Trump's disruption, however, was deeper than to simply cross conservative principles. Just as the party had some agreed positions, it had acknowledged areas of disagreement. The movement was not uniform, but a coalition of groups characterized by certain familiar tensions over key policy positions and priorities. There were agreed territories on which the battle for a nomination might be fought, often reflecting tensions between different elements of the party coalition. A candidate might prioritize a socially conservative agenda, primarily targeting the support of Christian Republican voters. Others might emerge as the "business" candidate. A sophisticated strategic game usually ensued with candidates trying to aggregate groups' support, all seen through the lens of the primaries schedule.

Noonan identified Trump's bold disruption of choosing different venues for conflict within the party. In discussing immigration policy, most presidents and candidates either avoided the issue or sought a "grand bargain" to build a compromise between anti-immigrant positions that emphasized the need for border security and providing routes to citizenship and a labor supply for businesses. In contrast, Trump transmitted talk-radio populism to the stump with tales of murderous illegal immigrants and terrorists with easy access to the homeland. Few candidates and officeholders had questioned the virtues of free trade, for example, since the third-party Ross Perot campaigns of the 1990s. Trump's tales of free trade's failures offered a radically different explanation of Middle America's economic difficulties, in defiance of Republican beliefs on how the economy should be run.

Noonan's characterization of Trump as Disruptor, however, only credits Trump as using disruptive techniques to change the issue agenda for Republican primary candidates. His disruption was far broader than her primary season analysis suggested. Trump was not just challenging Republican norms but presenting a nationalist alternative to establishment politics in a form that questioned core American values as well.

# 3   Trump the Nationalist

Writing in *The National Interest*, Robert Merry argued that the best way to understand Trump's choice of issues and policy positions was to consider him a nationalist:

> Just about every major issue that this super-rich political neophyte has thrown at the elites turns out to be anti-globalist and pro-nationalist. And that is the single most significant factor in his unprecedented and totally unanticipated rise. (Merry 2016)

In campaigning, Trump returned to the same core themes, revealing a relatively consistent, profoundly nationalist understanding of the world and the position of the US and Americans within it. He described the US as in crisis, at home and abroad. His explanations for these crises involved condemnations of internationalism, of openness to international influences, and to ideas of global interdependence while his proposed remedies were rooted in an America First approach based on a nationalist viewpoint. In making these proposals, Trump challenged a series of core values and even national narratives that had been widely accepted.

Trump portrayed a profoundly divided and insecure United States. He described a US under attack from a series of hostile forces at home. In Trump's account, terrorism, drugs and gang warfare stalked the American streets. Basic law and order had failed, allowing "chaos in our communities... the attacks on our police and the terrorism of our cities threaten our very way of life." Americans confronted "poverty and violence at home." Trump also identified an economic crisis. Highlighting joblessness, low wage growth and the demise of US manufacturing, Trump described a US suffering chronic economic insecurity.

Abroad, Trump considered the US as weak and disrespected. He outlined a series of national humiliations. Allies exploited US weakness, accepting US foreign aid but then acting against US interests. Enemies were emboldened by this weakness, allowing other powers to assert themselves at American expense. Trump focused particularly on the Middle East. Iraq was "in chaos." Iran had been allowed to increase its power, the Obama administration negotiating "the worst deal in history" and so facilitating that rise and putting the Iranians "on the path to nuclear weapons." In Syria, weak US policy had led to US embarrassment over Obama's "red lines" on the use of chemical weapons, civil war and a refugee crisis. Egypt had been "lost" to the radical Muslim Brotherhood. Libya was "in ruins," and the attack on the US consulate in Benghazi represented a further dishonor. Most of all, the rise of ISIS (also known variously as Islamic State, ISIL and Daesh) had been allowed, presenting a threat to US security. Indeed, he even claimed Obama had "founded" ISIS. After fifteen years of war in the Middle East, thousands of lives lost and trillions of dollars spent, "the situation is worse than it has ever been before. This is the legacy of Hillary Clinton [who had been Secretary of State during Obama's first term]: death, destruction, terrorism and weakness."

Trump's campaign performances involved many patriotic declarations of love for country, and of his country's potential, but the core of his approach was this description of a deep national crisis in the face of threats at home and abroad. The nation's weakness, inability to command respect and damaged pride were central themes. The crisis, in both economic and security terms, was captured by Trump's plaintive "Why don't we win anymore?" during his announcement speech. A weak America incapable of victory in Iraq, Afghanistan or against ISIS was evidence of US failure. Not winning anymore also spoke to the experiences of those who had lost their industrial jobs or good salaries to, in Trump's explanation, global economic competition. A great nation had stopped winning, leaving many Americans unsafe and struggling economically. The US was "like a third world country," hence the need to Make America Great Again.

Trump's explanation of this crisis, or "this American carnage" as he would later call it in his Inaugural Address, consisted of two parts. First, he regarded the US as confronting a series of enemies. Second, the advances of these enemies had been facilitated by US weakness; Trump blamed core assumptions underpinning US policies that had left the US vulnerable. The crisis was a function of America's pursuit of globalism, in economic and foreign policy, and its failures to pursue security at home due to a tolerance of diverse cultures and mass immigration.

Trump outlined a nationalist worldview in describing the situation of the US and ordinary Americans. According to Trump, country and people faced a series of highly competitive, harsh environments. Trump described a Hobbesian world of conflict and chaos, involving every player furthering their own interests at the expense of everyone else. It was not hard to imagine how a man schooled in New York real estate markets might understand the world this way. Mostly, these conflicts were presented in terms of specific enemies. These contests were fundamental to Trump's definition of America and Americans. Using standard techniques of nationalist rhetoric, Trump portrayed America and Americans in a series of competitions described as simple binaries: America vs China, America vs Terrorism, Americans vs Muslims, Americans vs Illegal Immigrants and Americans vs Gangs. Multiple "others," both beyond American borders and within, provided enemies against which his community of Americans could define and defend themselves.

On the world stage, as discussed further in Chapter 8, Trump lined up a series of enemies. The US faced threats from familiar opponents such as China and North Korea, but Trump expanded the cast of demons to include exploitative allies. The cross-border threats were slightly more complex. Trump described an America under assault from illegal immigrants. He blamed illegal immigrants for America's drug and crime problems, particularly highlighting the role of criminal gangs. The gangs that he described as bringing lawlessness to the American streets, including attacking law enforcement officers, were Hispanic. At rallies, he told and retold stories of families who had lost a loved one to crime by illegal immigrants. As terrorist attacks in the US and abroad seized the headlines, Trump gave substantial attention to the terrorist threat. Here, as Trump described it, the threat was Muslim. Where President Obama had refused, despite political pressure, to use terms such as "radical Islamic terrorism," Trump embraced the language, unconcerned as to whether or not it might offend the majority of Muslims. A key feature of Trump's rhetoric was its lack of precision, sometimes targeting not specific individuals or gangs, but entire demographic groups. He did little to distinguish between Americans and non-Americans, appearing to attack people for their religious or ethnic identity. For example, his indiscriminate demand in December 2015 for a "total and complete shutdown of Muslims entering the US" did not distinguish between those with the right to come into the United States and those without. His repeated labeling of "bad hombres" seemed to cover all Hispanics in a racist slur. Amid his rhetorical unpredictability and eccentricities, Trump often portrayed the cultural "other" as a key source of America's apparent woes.

By emphasizing the ethnic and religious natures of the division, Trump portrayed an American society divided against itself. His narrative did not always focus on race directly, finding proxies such as economics in the form of jobs flowing to other countries and crime and terror imposed by illegal immigrants, but it was hard not to notice that those Trump regarded as a threat were not Caucasian. This form of construction was unnervingly redolent of extreme right political parties in Europe, Trump speaking consistently in terms that implied the need to "protect the sanctity of one's own ethnos" (Heinisch 2003, 95). Merry, analyzing Trump's campaign, noted that:

Nationalists believe that any true nation must have clearly delineated and protected borders, otherwise it isn't really a nation. They also believe that their nation's cultural heritage is sacred and needs to be protected, whereas mass immigration from far-flung lands could undermine the national commitment to that heritage. (Merry 2016)

The aggressive encroachment of these other nations, races and faiths, Trump argued, warranted a need to protect the nation.

Trump's central claim was that the US needed to recognize the contests in which it was embroiled and to prioritize their prosecution at the expense of other priorities underpinned by other values. His phrase America First represented the need to recognize, focus on and win these competitions in the hostile world. One of Trump's most important promises was, therefore, to win again. As is argued in greater detail in Chapter 8, this position included a commitment to projecting strength. Enemies had been able to generate an American crisis by exploiting flawed policies and principles, which left the US weak and vulnerable. The lost nation would be restored through strength and an unbinding of American power and progress from the flawed policy assumptions that restrained them.

Trump's declaration that, "Our plan will put America First. Americanism not globalism will be our credo," reflected a potential reordering of priorities in government business that could inform policy in many areas. America First connected a number of Trump's values and ideas and held the potential to be an organizing principle underpinning his approach to many policy areas. The slogan had a dubious history, given its association with American fascist sympathizers during the 1930s, but Trump rightly calculated that the link was, in electoral terms, an irrelevance nearly a century later (while perhaps enjoying the offense its use might cause to the liberal intelligentsia). Instead, America First represented a new nationalist focus for policy. This nationalist approach challenged existing assumptions in domestic, economic and foreign policies.

Trump blamed US internationalism for his country's weakness. Enemies advanced in the face of American weakness, whether ISIS, Iran or China, betraying a failure of the international order. Rather than recognizing that the US had gleaned substantial advantages from the post-World War II order of alliances, organizations and agreements, Trump attacked the costs of the system and the limits it imposed on US power. Subsidizing the international order, through foreign aid and payments to sustain international organizations such as UN and NATO, looked like a waste of money to Trump. He was particularly incensed by so-called allies that received US support but then refused to back US interests and to pay their share of defense costs. His scathing criticisms strongly echoed Republican neo-isolationists of the mid-1990s, but with the addition of Trump treating the Iraq war as an extension of the internationalist system and another set of costs imposed on the US. Not only had the US people underwritten this system through their taxes and willingness to serve in the military, but they had been left vulnerable to terrorist attacks. Trump also offered a sovereignty argument common to many nationalist narratives. Trump argued that working with allies and international organizations had compromised the ability of the US to pursue its own interests, as US conduct was constrained by international law, diplomatic sensitivities and international opinion.

Trump's alternative, in the most literal form of America First, suggested that the US should prioritize its own interests by challenging and potentially abandoning the internationalist system and confronting rather than engaging with its enemies. American blood and treasure would not be committed to maintenance of the liberal international order and America's leadership role within it. American troops would only be committed when clearly in the US interest and therefore rarely. Preserving American security might be grounds for international involvement, but there would be no more Iraq or Afghanistan defeats. Commitment to international organizations, such as what he characterized on the campaign trail as the "obsolete" NATO, would be reduced, and the US would pursue its own interests regardless of over-sensitive allies or some notional higher moral standard of conduct in line with international law. US sovereignty, strength and resolve would be restored, allowing the US to choose when to express its power. Unbound, and with Trump's promised revival of the US military, the US would be able to confront enemies from a position of strength, whether in military terms (ISIS) or economic (China), rather than perceived US weakness being exploited by them.

Trump also wanted to change policies to address the domestic crisis he had identified. As noted above, Trump discussed Muslims and Hispanics in America as threats, whether as terrorists or criminals. While he emphasized illegal immigrants as his primary concern, he was often less specific. Most politicians shied away from labeling security threats in general racial or religious terms that characterized millions of unthreatening people, immigrant and citizen alike, as terrorists, criminals and enemies. Trump's explanation dismissed this approach as political correctness that embraced and excused the very people who threatened Americans' security. As mentioned above, Trump delighted in using the label "radical Islamic terrorism" and calling out opponents for failing to use it, as it demonstrated his willingness to recognize what he saw as the Muslim nature of the threat, while the "politically correct" refused to associate faith and threat.

Trump wished to develop policies without being bound by values of diversity and political correctness. He focused on the failings of the immigration system, arguing that the deeply flawed system left borders permeable, allowing terrorists and criminals to enter the country. Instead, he argued for strong measures to identify and evict potential threats. Defense against the outsiders required defense of sovereignty with deportation of illegal immigrants, regardless of economic impact or the breaking up of families. Policies on asylum needed reform; Trump lambasted policies that allowed immigrants, particularly Syrian refugees, entry to Western nations. Proposals for tighter border control included, of course, a wall on the Mexican border. Addressing crime would also be eased, Trump argued, by prioritizing security over political correctness. "Stop-and-search" policing, dependent upon racial profiling, had been thoroughly condemned by minority communities and was of dubious constitutional status, but Trump advocated it. The restoration of sovereignty argument would also have significant repercussions in addressing the terrorist problem. Shedding of the shackles of international opinion would stop the US compromising its own security arrangements to prevent terrorism. Under Trump, it would be legitimate, indeed virtuous, to pursue "extreme vetting" of immigrants, to reintroduce the now-banned practice of waterboarding to interrogate terrorist suspects or keep the detention camp at Guantanamo open. Through a determination to support policing, especially through strengthened protection of police officers and a restoration of the War on Drugs, Trump pledged to address the country's crime, drug and terrorist problems.

Just as US internationalism was a central feature in Trump's explanation of US weakness abroad, it underpinned his explanation of US economic difficulties. Internationalism, in the form of economic globalization, had established a network of trade deals on terms that disadvantaged Americans. Specifically, US trade deals had, according to Trump, been made by weak-minded negotiators who had allowed the exposure of American workers to unfair competition. Jobs and investment had flowed out of the country, and American manufacturing industries had been destroyed. The US economy had not been able to thrive in the face of these deals and a decaying infrastructure.

Trump's America First approach proposed to replace globalization with economic nationalism. The pursuit of American economic interests would involve a refusal to compromise American domestic interests in trade policy. He promised to renegotiate trade deals, considering trade a means to an economic end rather than, for example, as part of a foreign policy designed to engage other nations and encourage peaceful economic development. He directly challenged the idea underpinning US support for globalization that mutual exchange of goods and services benefited Americans. Trump would abrogate foreign trade agreements that he believed had been poorly negotiated by his predecessors at the expense of American interests, such as NAFTA, and he would negotiate better deals. He threatened to impose tariffs on incoming goods to protect American industry and promised a resulting boom in American manufacturing. Trump pledged to stop both outsourcing of jobs and outflows of investment capital by American companies. He would even look to repatriate their funds. His economic nationalism extended to commitments to revive specific industries, notably manufacturing and coal, and his promise of substantial investment in the nation's infrastructure to support economic development. This approach, he promised, would return jobs to the US and, borrowing a phrase from President Reagan, Make America Great Again.

Across foreign, economic and domestic policy, Trump challenged existing policies with alternatives based in a nationalist understanding of the world and what he perceived to be the plight of his country. His proposals, he argued, if implemented, would involve fundamental changes in presumptions about American society, economics and America's place in the world. Trump was challenging established positions on neoliberalism, internationalism and exceptionalism.

While such an approach sat at odds with Trump's long-nurtured brand as a symbol of free market excess, Trump's economic nationalism stood in opposition to the standard neoliberal rhetoric of competition, markets and global free trade. Indeed, his explanation of US economic problems questioned the very nature of the free market. Where a belief in free trade had become conventional, as had the belief that the US had gained enormously from international trade networks, Trump presented these values as threats and decried their effects. His blaming of trade deals for lost jobs and poor wages suggested that the free market, at least as lived out in 2016, was not a "fair" system, but one marred by unfair trade deals. His policy proposals contradicted a series of neoliberal dogmas: The principles of free movement of goods, capital and labor so central to globalization all seemed under threat from America First approaches. Tariffs challenged free trade in goods. Trump's promise that US companies would repatriate funds seemed like a threat to use federal government power to control the investment decisions of private companies. Promises to defend certain industries also defied free market assumptions. Nor did Trump suggest that easy movement of labor was to be encouraged with his proposals for less permeable borders. America First seemed to involve fundamental shifts in presumptions about how the American economy should work and its engagement with the rest of the world.

Trump also refused to present himself as a believer in American exceptionalism. He did not accept claims of the American political system's superiority. His criticisms identified deep flaws, and he even drew its legitimacy into question when stating that he would not accept the election results it produced, unless he won. Nor did he accept that the system was worth propagating beyond US borders. The idea of the US as a "shining city on a hill," providing a democratic model for other nations to follow and taking a special role in the world promoting democratic values, was not part of his worldview. Rather than recognizing that the US had gleaned substantial advantages from the post-World War II order, Trump proposed that the US should not be guaranteeing allies' security, arguing that the liberal international order was a ruse that simply allowed the American people to foot the bill for achieving only American weakness.

Finally, Trump challenged established national narratives on culture, race and immigration in the US. America's image as a "nation of immigrants" has never been merely a description of changing demographics but an embodiment of political ideals. Immigrants have been absorbed (in greater or lesser numbers and with more or less hostility, depending on historical period) on the assumption that the newcomers would, if they worked hard, have the opportunity to further themselves and in doing so contribute to and assimilate into the United States. While discussions over multiculturalism had posed questions about the degree and nature of assimilation, the basic assumptions of e pluribus unum remained intact. America provided an opportunity for redemption for those that arrived at its shores and would unify a people diverse in ethnicity, religion and culture through progress. To maintain this creed, the US retained a certain openness, or at least a tolerance, of those arriving in the US. David Brooks, framing his analysis in biblical terms that highlighted the forgiveness and redemption implicit in the established narrative of assimilation, suggested that "Trump and [presidential adviser Steve] Bannon have…their own creed, which is anti-biblical. The American story they tell is not diverse people journeying toward a united future. It's a zero-sum struggle of class and ethnic conflict" (Brooks 2016).

Trump's identification of threats as racial and religious served a nationalist narrative very well, but framed Americans' choice over their future in terms that rejected the traditional understanding of American development. The America First approach presented a negative juxtaposition of American diversity, tolerance and international engagement with the security and economic well-being of most Americans, with Trump very clear as to which priorities Americans should emphasize.

The "Trumpism" of the 2016 campaign, perhaps best captured in the phrase America First, appeared to amount to a genuinely radical agenda underpinned by a nationalist worldview that challenged assumptions of the existing order. A Trump presidency, therefore, appeared it would herald an imposition of nationalist policies. The political agenda would change sharply, at least in contrast with the previous eight years under Obama, to focus on immigration, law and order, remaking America's economy and its role in the international system based on these new principles. It promised to be genuinely different.

## 4   Trump the Populist

A different reading of Trump's campaign was to see him as a populist. Trump developed a narrative within which he was the populist tribune of the people ready to replace an incompetent and corrupt establishment. Brooks' criticism above notes the presence of "class warfare" in Trump's appeals; Trump aimed much of his vitriol at an elite in American society who had either forgotten or exploited the mass of Americans who he wished to represent.

In his nationalist understanding of an American crisis, Trump held certain values as being responsible for the nation's problems, chief among them being internationalism and political correctness. Trump left no doubt as to whom he blamed for the predominance of these values and, therefore, for his country's crisis. The perpetrators and beneficiaries of this system were the American elites who had taken over and corrupted the US political system. Trump identified a dominant elite that combined all the main political institutions, the media and corporate leaders as a group of establishment interests, without reflecting of course on the easily reached conclusion of his detractors that he was part of that elite himself. These elites, Trump argued, had failed to recognize the nature of the competitions and threats their country faced. Elites were unwilling to stand up to the nation's enemies and allowed the US to be exploited by allies. They had negotiated the unfair trade deals that had destroyed American jobs and left the US weak and vulnerable.

Trump in his Inaugural Address on January 20, 2017, described a political system captured by a combination of special interests and politicians that he referred to as the "establishment." Although for years, Trump had claimed that every politician was an incompetent, Obama was singled out as "perhaps the worst president in the history of the United States!" (Twitter, August 2, 2016). In the more malevolent, conspiratorial version of this narrative, Trump claimed during his nomination speech on July 21, 2016, at the Republican National Convention that elites served their own interests, having "rigged our political and economic system for their exclusive benefit." Corruption was "at a level never reached before in our country" as politicians allegedly "put their personal agendas before the national good" (Trump 2016). On occasions, both versions were deployed concurrently:

> I have no patience for injustice, no tolerance for government incompetence, no sympathy for leaders who fail their citizens. When innocent people suffer, because our political system lacks the will, or the courage, or the basic decency to enforce our laws – or worse still, has sold out to some corporate lobbyist for cash – I am not able to look the other way. (Trump 2016)

Globalism and the tolerance of diversity masked behind a conspiracy of political correctness served elites' well-being and covered up their failure to protect the American people while they reaped their rewards from an open economy. This explanation justified Trump's relentless take-no-prisoners assault on party elders and other candidates. Hillary Clinton, of course, would become the ultimate symbol of the system's failings, her wrongdoing symbolized by her use of an unofficial e-mail server during her service as Secretary of State and the contents of leaked e-mails revealing questionable campaign practices.

The real victims of this conspiracy were ordinary Americans. Elites' exertion of power, to pursue their own interests through government policies, had occurred at the expense of the American people. Confronted by unfair trade deals and high taxes to sustain a liberal internationalist foreign policy, US workers suffered joblessness and poor pay. Left vulnerable in lawless communities confronting gangs, illegal immigrants, drugs and terror, according to Trump the American people had been exploited by an establishment that would rather fund foreign wars than address domestic problems.

Many elements of Trump's narrative were familiar, however. The idea of a government captured by special interests dated back at least as far as the 1970s. The suggestion that politicians should be labeled incompetent or corrupt had a much longer vintage. Each was a familiar attack playing on the public's widespread distrust of Washington, the political class and both parties. He interwove three familiar brands of populism, in each case identifying an elite operating against the great mass of the American people. An economic elite exploited American workers while benefitting from free-trade agreements, echoing the populism of the "robber barons" era. Trump echoed Reagan's anti-government populism by arguing these elite interests had captured the political system, corrupting it to act against the people's interests. Furthermore, Trump described a cultural dimension to this elite dominance. Sounding now like Nixon and subsequent culture warriors, he railed against a cultural elite that told Americans how to think about issues such as race and crime and even how to speak. The establishment became the locus of these combined evils, offering Trump a punch-bag that was rooted in long traditions. He aligned all of these populist strands in one candidate.

Trump cast himself in the classic role in populist rhetoric, as the representative of the people against the elites. He was:

> determined to deliver a better life for the people all across this nation that have been ignored, neglected and abandoned... These are the forgotten men and women of our country and they are forgotten, but they're not going to be forgotten long. These are people who work hard but no longer have a voice. I am your voice. (Trump 2016)

His relentless abuse of the establishment allowed Trump to present himself as the only candidate telling the electorate a deeper truth about the corrupt political system. He promised to act against "entitled" political, economic and cultural elites, which were embodied in the persona of Hillary Clinton on the campaign trail. During his Inaugural Address, in a classic populist formulation, Trump identified the group he wished to promote to power.

Today, we are not merely transferring power from one administration to another, or from one party to another but we are transferring power from Washington, D.C., and giving it back to you, the people. (Trump 2017)

Obligingly, the elites attempted to strike back. As Trump flouted the conventions of candidate performance, highlighted new issues that had received little attention and adopted policy positions that no establishment politician would brook, the criticism of Trump was intense. However, establishment cries of "foul" merely served to confirm Trump's message. Trump's chosen guises as populist outsider and anti-politician were reinforced and allowed the candidate to talk to supporters at rallies of the elites' loathing of him and, by extension, of those supporters and their concerns. Trump drove a wedge between voters and the elite; the very breaks with convention that encouraged party elites to reject him offered reasons for the mass to embrace him.

Like many populists before him, Trump claimed a unique connection to the people which allowed him, and he alone, to pose as their champion and solution to the nation's problems. This claim was sustained, to a degree, by the rise of Trump's base of voters. After his initial announcement speech won him attention, dramatic mass rallies generated enthused crowds joining in with Trump chants such as "build the wall" in celebration of his lack of political correctness. As the invisible primary developed, Trump's poll numbers climbed. Trump's many alleged flaws, at least in terms of conventional candidates, seemed to have a clear counter-balancing gain; Trump, his message, or both, appealed to large numbers of Republican voters. He had found an appeal that differentiated him from the large Republican field in the primaries and then set him completely apart from Hillary Clinton in the presidential campaign itself.

Trump claimed, persistently, that he was mobilizing a new force in US politics, even echoing Nixon's suggestion that he was awakening a new "silent majority" of voters (Twitter, August 21, 2015). His appeal to certain demographic groups, those with fewer educational qualifications and whites with lower-to-middle incomes, especially suggested that Trump, with his anti-elite rhetoric, had identified a populist fault line based on class. Combined with his outsider's rejection of both parties and claims to be challenging politics as usual, questions arose as to whether his populism was reaching new voters, drawing in independents or attracting Democrats. Certainly, it became accepted that Trump had built a base of loyal Trump voters within the Republican electorate.

Very much in the spirit of a populist leading the people against elites, Trump gleefully claimed a direct relationship, through social media, with this newly mobilized group of voters. Twitter, he claimed, allowed a close relationship with his base. Early in his presidency, he tweeted: "The Fake News Media hates when I use what has turned out to be my very powerful Social Media - over 100 million people! I can go around them" (June 16, 2017).

Trump the populist managed to mobilize a base within the Republican Party against its own elites. Returning to the The Party Decides thesis, the outsider was able to bypass the mechanisms that would normally have given party elites the power to marginalize his candidacy. Rather than depending on local party organizations or a cabal of familiar Republican campaign consultants, Trump's populist appeal amplified by the likes of arch-conservatives Steve Bannon and David Bossie (Green 2017; Woodward 2018) and channeled through a genuinely original media campaign, proved its capacity to overcome the conventions of the primary process. He mobilized the mass of the party against the elite who rejected him.

Trump's victory over Hillary Clinton allowed him to reinforce his populist message, partly through the power of its surprise and partly through his successes in Midwestern states that were supposed to constitute the "blue firewall" guaranteeing Democratic victory. As Trump took office, therefore, many speculated that he represented a newly mobilized, virulently anti-establishment movement. He seemed to promise dramatic change both on behalf of, and powered by, the people, or at least his base. The primary question seemed to be the degree of change his movement could impose.

## 5     Trump the Insurgent

The most dramatic interpretation of Trump's impact suggested that the changes would be extraordinary. A fortnight after Trump took office, *The Economist* (February 4, 2017) described Washington as being "in the grip of a revolution… onward [the new president] and his people have charged, leaving the wreckage of received opinion smouldering in their wake." Trump the insurgent was apparently leading revolutionary forces against the political system.

For *The Economist*, some of the revolution was simply the matter of Trump extending his disruptive campaign style into the early days of his presidency. His "chaos seems to be part of the plan." However, the new president's style also pursued "the politics of conflict," treating it as "a political asset," especially with Steve Bannon now appointed chief strategist and Stephen Miller as senior policy adviser and speech-writer (Green 2017; Woodward 2018). Trump would continue to act decisively, picking his fights for political advantage. Conflict demonstrated the disrupting and overthrowing of the forces Trump claimed to oppose. Ignoring experts and "blow[ing] up norms of good governance" from the beginning provided useful symbols of Trump bringing change.

*The Economist*'s declaration of a Trump insurgency, though, actually understated the nature of the president's declared goals; his pledges of change were often at the systemic level. During his campaign, he made repeated, clear declarations of a break with the status quo. In his speech accepting the Republican Party nomination, for example, he declared that, "things have to change and they have to change right now." Clearly, articulating his desire to overthrow political elites in Washington amounted to a plan to change the power structure in Washington. The elite would have to be replaced, as would policies informed by their failed presumptions. His promises to shake up Washington and to "drain the swamp" identified the locus of power and spoke to an attack upon established governing arrangements. The base was to be mobilized against the elites to bring the people to power in the form of their representative and tribune, Donald Trump. That was the simple plan: The role of Washington power structures in a Trump presidency was to be swept away.

Trump's rhetoric suggested that his presidency would dominate the US political system. Questions of a governing coalition and the likelihood of either party accepting his new ideas and policies were all subsumed under the assertion that Trump would deliver strong leadership as the people's sole agent. He talked of the presidency as though he believed he could arrive in Washington and the city would respond to his command. Indeed, leadership would be "easy", he claimed. Trump identified new sources of power to sustain his presidency. First, his personal skill set would transform the status of the office. Previous incumbents of the office, he believed, had not been competent enough to use the position effectively. Trump would translate his business skills, where he had triumphed amid hostile competition, to win similar battles for the American people in the political environment. His growing momentum in the campaign, despite experts' declaration of its impossibility, helped to generate a sense that Trump personally might have the capacity to lead the system in new and unexpected ways; if he could beat the electoral rules, why should governing be different? His innovative means of communicating, both in person and via social media, suggested potential for a different form of leadership. Second, Trump's connection with his voting base was presented as a personal mandate. Trump saw himself as leading a popular insurgency, the force of which would allow him to sweep away opposition.

The exaggerated character of Trump's assault upon the establishment was unusual. Both his range of targets and the fervent nature of his expression stood out as Trump appeared incapable of finding any redeeming feature of the existing system. He ably identified a series of foils for his "Trump vs the World" approach, rejecting the establishment's elected representatives, narratives, norms, practices and even their facts. However, his disdain for everything Washington amounted to more than a dislike of policies or elites; observers noted Trump's attacks on the institutions that, he argued, sustained elite power. Trump's attacks upon the system included a rejection of basic US democratic norms.

Since the founding, US politicians have emphasized, with a degree of reverence, the legitimacy of the democratic system under which they govern. Trump, by contrast, questioned the legitimacy of that system and its institutions. His attacks on the mainstream media were an integral part of his campaign. Labeling their output "fake news," Trump cast the media not as "the fourth estate" holding politicians accountable and acting as bastions of free speech, but as part of the grand elite conspiracy against the people. As private organizations, media companies have an ambiguous status as institutions necessary to maintain democracy. The federal courts, however, do not. After an unfavorable ruling in the Trump university case—which he settled for $25 million after being sued by former students for fraud—Trump launched a verbal assault on the presiding Judge Gonzalo Curiel, claiming his behavior was, "a disgrace. It is a rigged system … This court system, the judges in this court system, federal court." Not only was the integrity of the individual judge impugned, but the entire court system was "rigged." Trump was perfectly willing to reject the legitimacy of institutions integral to US democracy, suggesting that anything that obstructed his aspirations was unjustifiable.

Trump also jeopardized the system's legitimacy when he initially refused to commit his support to any winner of the campaign for the Republican nomination unless it was him and then threatened to run as an independent if he was not selected. Subsequently, he made the even more extraordinary claim that he would only accept the result of the November election if he was victorious. He projected a conspiracy theory of US politics in which the people and Donald Trump were victims of marginalization by an elite-dominated system. In this context, ignoring the constraints of that system would be not a breach of constitutional principle, but a warranted assertion of the people's power. This position was, of course, consistent with his position as the challenger to an establishment that would do anything to prevent him from winning office and so reinforced his image as the outsider.

A presidential candidate claiming that he would lead the political system hardly presented an exceptional conceit, but Trump seemed to believe that electoral victory would issue him the authority to overrule all other players in the political system. This was more than the normal tendency of presidents to enhance the power of the Chief Executive (Moe 1985; Rudalevige 2006). Trump seemed to have an authoritarian streak, an impression magnified by the respect he expressed for authoritarian leaders in other countries, such as Russia's President Vladimir Putin. Comments suggesting that Trump only possessed a cursory grasp of the Constitution did not encourage observers to believe that he would be bound by the revered document's prescriptions either. Instead, Trump seemed to offer a personalized concentration of power in the Oval Office to allow him to dominate the political system.

The perception of threat was widespread. Many elected officials including a substantial number of Republicans decried Trump's authoritarian impulses. Some perceived a genuine threat to the democratic institutions of the US, including the Constitution's guarantees both of individuals' rights and the checks and balances integral to the federal government. Evidence of authoritarian voting practices suggested that the Trump base might tolerate such behavior (Hetherington and Weiler 2009; MacWilliams 2016). *The Economist* (February 4, 2017) noted nervously that "America's democratic system might struggle to contain a despot."

As a populist, Trump suggested he would dismantle the power of elites. Considering him as an insurgent begged questions as to which political institutions he might attack and how. At the core of the election winner's presumptions about the US political system lay a powerful presidency as an engine of leadership; many of Trump's pronouncements indicated an intolerance for any opposition to the power of a Trump White House. The most nervous of observers worried for the future of American democracy.

# 6 Conclusion

Trump's 2016 campaign invited a series of different readings. The outsider candidate emphasized that he was not beholden to other players, including his own party's leadership. His nationalist campaign promised a radical new agenda, focused on trade, law and order, economic rebuilding and immigration. Classic conservative policy positions and long-established bipartisan positions and values would be challenged. Whether Trump could remain so unbound once trying to impose policy changes despite Congress' legislative, budgetary and oversight powers was unclear. Trump the disruptor seemed likely to bring a different style of presidency. While some speculated that he might behave in a more "presidential" manner, it seemed likely that this president's character would be unlike that of any predecessor. His desire to make his own rules seemed unlikely to disappear altogether: Would the disruptor also bring new techniques of governance as he had new techniques of campaigning? Given Trump's populist claim to a new base as a source of legitimacy, his ongoing relationship with his voters would surely be an important part of his attempts to lead. Trump, and his base, might prosecute class war against the establishment elite. A peasant march on Washington, complete with pitchforks, was a commonly deployed allusion. The insurgent Trump and his revolution might even undermine key democratic institutions in an empowering of the presidency. Observers read the Trump phenomenon in very different ways, but they were agreed on one thing: Trump's would not be an ordinary presidency.

This book challenges the thesis that Trump's presidency would be extraordinary. The next two chapters present evidence for the proposition that Trump's presidency is indeed ordinary. Chapter 3 focuses on the 2016 presidential election and the structure of party support in America. It shows how the vote for Trump was fairly ordinary in terms of the people that voted for the Republican candidate and the reasons why they did so. Chapter 4 then turns to Trump's policy achievements. It shows that Trump's successes are few and far between, as is the case for most contemporary presidents. But where Trump has enjoyed policy "wins" as he likes to call them, they have not in the main been disruptive, populist, insurgent or nationalist in character. Instead, they are best regarded as mainstream Republican successes.

# References

Benoit, William L., and John P. McHale. 2003. "Presidential Candidates' Television Spots and Personal Qualities." *Southern Communication Journal* 68 (4): 319–334.

Brooks, David. 2016. "The Week That Trump Won." *New York Times*, October 30.

Bycoffe, Aaron. 2016. "The Endorsement Primary." *fivethirtyeight.com*, June 7. https://projects.fivethirtyeight.com/2016-endorsement-primary/.

Cohen, Marty, David Karol, Hans Noel, and John Zaller. 2008. *The Party Decides: Presidential Nominations Before and After Reform.* Chicago: University of Chicago Press.

Cost, Jay. 2016. "Why Neither Hillary Nor Trump Deserve My Vote." *The Weekly Standard*, September 10.

Funk, Carolyn L. 1996. "The Impact of Scandal on Candidate Evaluations: An Experimental Test of the Role of Candidate Traits." *Political Behavior* 18 (1): 1–24.

Funk, Carolyn L. 1999. "Bringing the Candidate into Models of Candidate Evaluation." *Journal of Politics* 61 (1): 700–720.

Green, Joshua. 2017. *Devil's Bargain: Steve Bannon, Donald Trump, and the Storming of the Presidency.* New York: Penguin Press.

Harris, Mary. 2016. "A Media Post-mortem on the 2016 Presidential Election." *mediaQuant.net*, November 14. https://www.mediaquant.net/2016/11/a-media-post-mortem-on-the-2016-presidential-election/.

Heinisch, Reinhard. 2003. "Success in Opposition—Failure in Government: Explaining the Performance of Right-Wing Populist Parties in Public Office." *West European Politics* 26 (3): 91–130.

Hetherington, Marc J., and Jonathan D. Weiler. 2009. *Authoritarianism and Polarization in American Politics.* Cambridge: Cambridge University Press.

Jamieson, Kathleen Hall, and Doron Taussig. 2017. "Disruption, Demonization, Deliverance, and Norm Destruction: The Rhetorical Signature of Donald J. Trump." *Political Science Quarterly* 132 (4): 619–650.

Kinder, Donald R. 1983. "Presidential Traits." Report to the NES Board of Overseers, Center for Political Studies, University of Michigan.

Kinder, Donald R. 1986. "Presidential Character Revisited." In *Political Cognition*, edited by Richard R. Lau and David O. Sears. Hillsdale, NJ: Lawrence Erlbaum.

Kristol, William. 2016. "Donald J. Obama." *The Weekly Standard*, April 29.

Laderman, Charlie, and Brendan Simms. 2017. *Donald Trump: The Making of a World View*. London: I.B. Tauris.

Lewandowski, Corey R., and David N. Bossie. 2018. *Let Trump Be Trump: The Inside Story of His Rise to the Presidency*. New York: Center Street.

Liu, Huchen, and Gary C. Jacobson. 2018. "Republican Candidates' Positions on Donald Trump in the 2016 Congressional Elections: Strategies and Consequences." *Presidential Studies Quarterly* 48 (1): 49–71.

MacWilliams, Matthew. 2016. "Who Decides When the Party Doesn't? Authoritarian Voters and the Rise of Donald Trump." *PS: Political Science & Politics* 49 (4): 716–721.

Merry, Robert W. 2016. "Trump vs. Hillary Is Nationalism vs. Globalism." *The National Interest*, May 4.

Moe, Terry M. 1985. "The Politicized Presidency." In *The New Direction in American Politics*, edited by John E. Chubb and Paul E. Peterson. Washington, DC: The Brookings Institution.

Noonan, Peggy. 2016. "The GOP Establishment's Civil War." *Wall Street Journal*, January 8.

Philips, Amber. 2016. "Why Even Lindsey Graham Might Be a Ted Cruz Voter Now." *Washington Post*, March 2.

Rudalevige, Andrew. 2006. *The New Imperial Presidency: Renewing Presidential Power After Watergate*. Ann Arbor: University of Michigan Press.

Trump, Donald J. 1987. *Trump: The Art of the Deal*. New York: Random House.

Trump, Donald J. 2016. "Full Draft: Donald Trump 2016 RNC Draft Speech Transcript." *Politico*, July 21. https://www.politico.com/story/2016/07/full-transcript-donald-trump-nomination-acceptance-speech-at-rnc-225974.

Trump, Donald J. 2017. "The Inaugural Address, January 20, 2017." The White House. https://www.whitehouse.gov/briefings-statements/the-inaugural-address/.

Williams, Luke. 2016. *Disrupt: Think the Unthinkable to Spark Transformation in Your Business*. 2nd ed. Old Tappan, NJ: Pearson.

Woodward, Bob. 2018. *Fear: Trump in the White House*. London: Simon & Schuster.

# 3

## Trump's Electoral Politics

The previous chapter highlighted that Donald Trump won the Republican presidential primary race with few endorsements from the party's big names, without spending much of his own or anyone else's money, without a professionalized campaign apparatus, with a set of policy positions that challenged mainstream Republican principles, by breaking many norms of campaign behavior and against the expectations of almost all experienced and professional observers of the political scene. It was by any measure an extraordinary and unexpected victory. But it was also the zenith of his disruption. Despite much talk of a populist uprising, his vote in the general election was fairly ordinary. Contrary to speculation and some preliminary empirical analyses, our original examination of both county-level and individual-level data shows the pattern of his support, particularly among white working-class voters, is consistent with trends observed over the last 40 years. And places most exposed to the process of deindustrialization did not swing heavily to Trump.

It is noteworthy that Hillary Clinton won more votes than Trump among Americans with an income of less than $50,000 per year. Only one-third of Trump voters earned less than $50,000 per year. Only

© The Author(s) 2019
J. Herbert et al., *The Ordinary Presidency of Donald J. Trump*,
Palgrave Studies in Political Leadership,
https://doi.org/10.1007/978-3-030-04943-0_3

one-quarter of white voters who voted for Trump had both an income of less than $50,000 *and* did not attend or graduate from college, which is a strong measure of being working class. The Latino vote for Trump did not collapse; he may even have won a larger share of the Latino vote than Mitt Romney four years previously. And there have been no discernable shifts in which political party individual voters identify with. Their allegiances seem very stable. Finally, while Trump certainly enjoys high approval ratings among self-identified Republican supporters, deeper analysis shows that most do not share his ideological and policy positions on the key issues.

In sum, America's polarized electorate continued to vote in habitual ways, driven by a psychological attachment to one or other of the two parties and by the standard set of concerns and issues. Trump's support was in many respects very conventional and essentially ordinary, despite the extraordinariness of his candidacy and his campaign. This chapter digs down into these details.

# 1     An Extraordinary Campaign

Chapter 2 collated the arguments in favor of the proposition that Trump's presidency is extraordinary and mold-breaking. One of the key reasons relates to the nature and success of his campaign to become the Republican Party's presidential nominee. Trump the outsider, populist, insurgent, disruptor and nationalist elbowed aside the best funded, best known and best connected candidates, wrestling the nomination from a shocked and disbelieving Republican elite. Equally stunned by his success were professional observers and interpreters of American politics—journalists, commentators and academics—who held to the orthodox reading that party elites decide primary outcomes. Trump's capture of the Republican presidential nomination defied all expectations, including his own, and in the process dashed theoretical models of candidate selection on the jagged rocks of populist outrage.

Trump's general election campaign against Hillary Clinton was equally extraordinary. Even the most hardened observers of electoral politics were left wide eyed and open mouthed by his promise to "lock her up"; the unparalleled verbal assaults when anyone opposed him, including those in his own party; the racially tinged attack on a Muslim Gold Star military family; the mocking of Republican Senator John McCain's war hero status; his threat to only accept the election result if he won; plus breaking all previously accepted standards of behavior and decorum. The release of the Access Hollywood hot mic tape on which Trump bragged about grabbing women's genitals threatened to blow his campaign up just one month before election day. Under enormous pressure to leave the race, Trump told the Wall Street Journal that "nobody has more respect for women than I do… I never, ever give up, [there] is zero chance I'll quit." The interventions of FBI Director James Comey over Hillary Clinton's use of a personal e-mail server while Secretary of State added further spice and intrigue, not least when he announced just 11 days before the election that he was reopening the investigation.

After this extraordinary election campaign, perhaps more outlandish and abnormal than any in American history and certainly than any in the television age, it is plausible to hypothesize that the nature of Trump's election victory was also extraordinary. Early commentaries pointed to how Trump forged a new electoral coalition, winning huge numbers of white working class left behind voters in key Rust Belt states with his economically and culturally populist campaign that married opposition to free trade and immigration with scathing attacks on the Washington "swamp" and global elites. Was the nature of his victory really as extraordinary as his campaign to secure it? The short answer is no. The long answer is a little more complex.

The broad outline of the idea that the white working class, and its men in particular, have been left behind economically is built primarily on the phenomenon of deindustrialization. In the mid-twentieth century, the American working class was employed largely in primary extraction industries such as coal mining, in factories that transformed the earth's ores and minerals into valuable products such as steel, and in assembly plants that constructed automobiles and household appliances among many other things. The work was often hard, dangerous or repetitive, but the pay was good and job security high, even for those that lacked a good education. It would not last. After adjusting for inflation, median yearly earnings of white men without a college degree fell by nearly one-fifth between 1975 and 2015 (Tankersley 2016). And while household incomes were not as badly hit, this is due to the growing incidence of people working multiple jobs and longer hours. The labor market no longer provides the kinds of jobs that the white working class had come to expect.

The reasons for this decline are complex and interwoven. Changes in technology have played an important role as automation decreased the demand for those doing routine tasks (see Machin 2008 for a survey), but it is globalization and particularly the role of government policy in encouraging it that is most relevant here. Trade reduces prices, increases the size of markets and encourages the spread of technological change. On the other hand, it exposes some domestic workers and domestic producers to increased competition. In the short run, therefore, it can create winners and losers. It is these losers that were targeted by the Trump campaign.

Previous administrations had acted on the assumption that the gain to the winners outweighed the loss to the losers and so encouraged freer movement of goods and capital. George H. W. Bush signed the North American Free Trade Agreement (NAFTA) in 1992 and Bill Clinton helped shepherd it through the congressional approval process with bipartisan support in 1993. Clinton also negotiated the terms for China's entry into the World Trade Organization (WTO), which formally occurred in 2001 during George W. Bush's presidency. Both presidents regarded China as a huge potential market for US goods and services.

Trump saw the world differently: Trade was a zero-sum game and America was losing. Announcing his intention to seek the Republican presidential nomination on June 16, 2015, he pledged to be the:

> greatest jobs president that God ever created... bring[ing] back our jobs from China, from Mexico, from Japan, from so many places. I'll bring back our jobs, and I'll bring back our money. Right now, think of this: We owe China $1.3 trillion. We owe Japan more than that. So they come in, they take our jobs, they take our money, and then they loan us back the money, and we pay them in interest, and then the dollar goes up so their deal's even better. How stupid are our leaders? How stupid are these politicians to allow this to happen? How stupid are they?

These early ideas were fleshed out more carefully one year later in a tele-prompted speech in Monessen, Pennsylvania on June 28:

> Our politicians have aggressively pursued a policy of globalization—moving our jobs, our wealth and our factories to Mexico and overseas. Globalization has made the financial elite who donate to politicians very wealthy. But it has left millions of our workers with nothing but poverty and heartache. When subsidized foreign steel is dumped into our markets, threatening our factories, our politicians do nothing. For years, they watched on the sidelines as our jobs vanished and our communities were plunged into depression-level unemployment.... This wave of globalization has wiped out our middle class. It doesn't have to be this way.

Trump proposed withdrawing from the signed but unratified Trans-Pacific Partnership (TTP) between the US and eleven Pacific Rim nations, renegotiating or withdrawing from NAFTA ("the worst trade deal maybe ever signed anywhere"), labeling China a currency manipulator, and promising 45% tariffs on China for dumping subsidized exports and stealing US intellectual property and 35% tariffs on imports by US companies who offshored production. In turn, Trump's campaign sought to highlight Hillary Clinton's support for NAFTA, TTP and other trade deals. She was the job-killing, trade-deal supporting establishment candidate who cared nothing about how globalization was hurting ordinary workers and in her own words wanted no less than "to put a lot of coal miners and coal companies out of business." Despite being taken out of context, Clinton struggled to explain her coal gaffe and also to parry attacks that she was part of the swamp that needed draining, not only due to her extensive Washington experience but also after being paid a minimum fee of $225,000 per one hour talk by the denizens of Wall Street for private speaking events. She was painted as an establishment figure and the de facto incumbent, while Trump was promoted as the outsider candidate and establishment foe, even though his story is far from a rags to riches one. He moved from elite schools, through kick-starter funding and bankruptcy swerving interventions from his wealthy businessman father, to his billionaire lifestyle in a gilded Louis XIV-style penthouse in his Fifth Avenue New York skyscraper that he had self-reverentially named Trump Tower.

Trump campaigned hard in traditional white working-class areas that were suffering economic adversity. He set up field offices in many Rust Belt counties with small-to-medium-sized cities that Republican candidate Mitt Romney had lost in 2012 and Clinton was neglecting in 2016 (Cohn 2016; Small 2016). He visited these states more often than recent Republican candidates and his opponent Hillary Clinton. And while Trump had much less money to spend on campaigning, and especially on advertising, than his opponent, he spent more of it (proportional to his overall spending) in the Rust Belt. Clinton, on the other hand, was accused of ignoring the Midwest, even by her Democratic colleagues. Her main contender for the Democratic nomination, Bernie Sanders, complained in a postmortem: "I am from the white working class, and I am deeply humiliated that the Democratic Party cannot talk to where I came from" (Thompson 2016). Sanders holds his Senate seat as a Democratic Socialist, and although he caucuses and generally votes with the Democrats, he was nonetheless highly critical of the party whose nomination he had tried to win. His critique of the party seems aimed particularly at the kind of politician he views Clinton as being: "Democrats are focused too much with a liberal elite, which is raising incredible sums of money from wealthy people in the upper middle class, but has ignored to a very significant degree the working class and the middle class and low-income people in this country" (Edsall 2016). Vice President Joe Biden, the self-styled everyman from hardscrabble Scranton, Pennsylvania, agreed: "You didn't hear a single solitary sentence in the last campaign about that guy working on the assembly line" (Edsall 2016).

Nate Cohn, election and data specialist at the *New York Times*, looked at the early numbers and on the morning after election night claimed definitively: "Trump won the presidency by riding an enormous wave of support among white working-class voters" (Cohn 2016). Cohn pointed to a plethora of Rust Belt counties full of white working-class voters that had swung from Obama to Trump, many by large margins, to deliver the states he needed to win. Trump took Rust Belt states of West Virginia and Indiana and the swing states of Ohio and Iowa. More remarkably Trump won the "blue-wall" states of Pennsylvania, Michigan and Wisconsin that had been Democrat since 1992, while Clinton held only Illinois and Minnesota.

## 2    An Ordinary Vote

"I love the poorly educated," Trump, February 24, 2016, after his Nevada primary win.

The conventional view, then, is a picture of an extraordinary campaign targeting left-behind voters in Rust Belt states with a message that blamed their ill fortune on globalization, free trade, uncaring liberal elites and more ominously on immigrants. If correct, it would seem to offer support to the notion that not only the campaign but the nature of the voting that secured Trump's election victory was extraordinary in that the reasons for his success and why people voted for him were notably different to those for his Republican predecessors. One way to address the question of the extraordinariness of Trump's victory is to see whether there is any evidence of a seismic break in the pattern of Republican support across different groups of people.

The first set of evidence comes from two National Election Exit Polls. The data are reported in the appendix. Here we just present the key points. Certainly, Republican presidential candidates enjoy a large electoral advantage among white voters (20 percentage points more than Democrats in both 2012 and 2016) but also suffer a larger disadvantage among non-white voters who are far more likely, especially if they are African American, to vote for Democrats. What matters for present purposes, however, is the extent of change across the two elections. The data show that Trump did not do any better than Romney among whites as a whole. Trump did improve his party's margin among white men by 4 percentage points, but more important are the effects of education and income.

Romney lost out to Obama among those at the top and bottom rungs of the education ladder but was relatively more popular with those in the middle. Trump, by contrast, did better among the less well educated. He beat Clinton by 5 percentage points among voters who at best graduated from high school, a shift of 11 points in favor of the Republican candidate between 2012 and 2016. Trump beat Clinton by 8 points among those with some college experience, a 9 point uptick on 2012. But Trump lost among college graduates and postgraduates, with the Republican vote share falling by 9 and 8 points, respectively. If these educational levels are combined, a similar story appears. Trump did 8 points worse than Romney among college graduates but 11 points better among non-college graduates. Some of the stereotyping of Trump's base, therefore, as being less well educated does have evidence to support it. The most highly educated voters, those who had completed a university-level degree, were more likely than in the previous election to vote for the Democratic candidate, while Trump appealed more than the last Republican presidential candidate to those voters who had no more than a high school education.

A similar change occurred with regard to income, where Trump made inroads at the lower end of the income distribution while losing voters at the top end. Among voters with a family income of less than $50,000 per year, Trump improved his vote over Romney by 10 percentage points, but he lost the same proportion of votes among those earning more than $100,000. Along with the education numbers, these changes offer sustenance to the argument that there was a shift to Trump among working-class Americans.

But what of Trump's appeal in particular to the *white* working class? One way to look at this is through the impact of educational attainment by race on voting. Trump's margin of victory over Clinton among whites who did not attend or graduate from college was a whopping 37 percentage points. Romney's margin over Obama among the same less educated white voters was 25 points. Thus, Trump's margin of victory over Clinton was 12 points better than Romney's over Obama. Conversely, Trump lost 11 points among better educated whites. These are significant differences and on their face support the proposition that there is something unusual, even exceptional, about the racial and class composition of Trump's electoral coalition—specifically that Trump's championing of the white working class was rewarded with large numbers of these voters supporting him at the polls. This, however, would be the wrong conclusion. To see why, one needs to look at the margins-of-victory among graduates and non-graduates when race is ignored. The increase in Trump's marginal advantage (vis-à-vis Romney) of 12 points among white non-graduates is almost matched by a marginal change of 11 points among all non-graduates. Similarly, Trump's 11 point decline (vis-à-vis Romney) among non-white graduates needs to be interrogated next to the 8 points decline among graduates of all races. The strong implication is that education is more important than race. Two other pieces of information back up this story: First, none of the over-time changes within the race categories are statistically significant, and, second, the size of the shift toward Trump was roughly equal among less educated whites and non-whites, at 12 and 10 points, respectively.

In sum, we have a situation where Trump made his biggest gains among the lower paid and less educated, and Clinton the opposite. These changing vote patterns across income and education, as well as race and gender, seem on their face to support the widely told story about Trump's campaign speaking successfully to working-class voters, especially male ones and not only white ones, threatened economically by globalization, trade, technological change and the contraction of traditional primary and manufacturing industries and who were attracted to Trump's strident cultural appeals on immigration and identity. However, while the above analysis provides a useful first look at the problem and identifies some interesting trends, it only looks back to 2012. Many electoral trends have deep roots. We need to go back further in time, beyond Romney, to see whether Trump started or accelerated his party's advantage among the white working class, and particularly white working-class men, or whether he is part of a trend started several presidential contests ago. Put differently, is Trump's advantage exceptional or ordinary given the historical trajectory?

Figure 1 plots the Republican share of the two-party vote for white men by level of education since 1976 using data from the publically available American National Election Studies.

The graph shows that white male college graduates have been moving away from the Republican Party for some time. The pattern for white male non-college graduates is less clear. While there is evidence of a leap in support in 2016, this is not larger than past changes. Also notable is that Trump won a smaller proportion of the white male non-college graduates than Ronald Reagan did in 1984.

Another set of evidence comes from a county-level analysis of voting behavior from 2000 to 2016 (Gosling and Wroe 2017). The key question asked in the analysis was "Did the swing to Trump occur more in counties that were more adversely affected by industrial change?" The

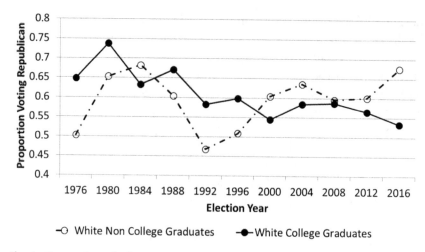

**Fig. 1** Proportion of white men voting Republican by education, 1976–2016

measure of industrial change used was the change in the proportion of the population in manufacturing. The analysis found that the relationship between deindustrialization and the vote for Republican presidential candidates disappears once education is taken into account. Broadly speaking, the counties most affected by deindustrialization have more lower educated people and this group is becoming more Republican over time.

In sum, there is no evidence of a large switch to Trump among the left-behind, whether one thinks about this group as poorly educated or poorly paid or having lost manufacturing jobs. Over time, the GOP is winning more strongly among these voters, but Trump has not accelerated the process. There seems nothing unusual or extraordinary about the coalition of voters that drove him to victory.

## 3    Other Evidence

Our conclusions in the section above are supported by analyses of individual-level survey data by other political scientists. Larry Bartels calculates that the state-by-state correlation between the 2012 and 2016 votes shows that there was almost no change at all in partisan voting patterns. Nine in ten Republican identifiers voted Trump and nine in ten Democratic ones voted Clinton, about average for a contest without an incumbent running. His conclusion is clear: "an extraordinary campaign has produced a remarkably ordinary election outcome, primarily reflecting partisan patterns familiar from previous election cycles" (Bartels 2016).

And despite talk of ongoing and longer-term realignment of working-class voters toward the Republican Party, a majority of all voters with a yearly family income of less than the national median of about $50,000 chose Hillary Clinton, not Donald Trump, to be their president. Trump ran 12 points behind Clinton among this group. Most of his support came instead from affluent voters. Nicholas Carnes and Noam Lupu (2017) estimate that both Trump's primary and general election support drew equally on low (less than $50,000), middle ($50,000–100,000) and high (more than $100,000) income groups, concluding in the *Washington Post* that "It's time to bust the myth: most Trump voters were not working class." So even if working class is defined very broadly as earning less than the median income, at least two-thirds of the Trump coalition was not part of it. It is true that a little more than two-thirds of Trump's general and primary voters do not have a college degree—another scholarly measure of what makes someone working class—but this is almost exactly the same proportion of all Republicans that do not have a college degree. "Far from being a magnet for the less educated, Trump seemed to have about as many people without college degrees in his camp as we would expect any successful Republican candidate to have," observe Carnes and Lupu. What's more, a clear majority of white Trump voters without college degrees had family incomes of more than $50,000 and 20% were in the $100,000-plus bracket. It certainly seems odd to label these relatively affluent Trump voters as working class simply because they did not graduate from college. Only 25% of Trump's white supporters in the general election had both an income below the median and also lacked a college degree (Carnes and Lupu 2017). The evidence to support the proposition that the so-called blue-collar billionaire had built a winning coalition based on a solid foundation of working-class whites is meager at best, despite the continuing popularity of this argument (see, e.g., Brownstein 2015, 2016a, b; Alberta 2016).

Some analysts argue that Trump's vote was driven by an underlying or even overt prejudice against certain minorities, such as Latinos, African Americans and Muslims. This is an intuitively reasonable hypothesis given the tone of Trump's primary and general election campaigns, and it has some support in the data (Ehrenfreund and Clement 2016; Schaffner 2016; Tesler 2016). But the question for us is not whether Trump's vote (and the vote against him) was driven in part by racial animosity, but whether its extent is unusual historically. Trump is far from the first Republican hopeful to build a primary campaign around fiery anti-immigration and especially anti-illegal immigration rhetoric—Pete Wilson, Pat Buchanan and even Bob Dole did just that in the 1990s (Wroe 2008). George W. Bush and Karl Rove may have striven to promote a more inclusive, immigrant-friendly message in the 2000s, but it was rejected by many congressional Republicans, other party elites and even more party activists. John McCain tacked to the right on immigration in 2008 after having pushed a liberal reform package in the Senate, and Mitt Romney promoted a stronger border and asked undocumented migrants to self deport in 2012.

Strikingly, however, Morris Fiorina's (2018) analysis of survey data that taps underlying racial prejudice of respondents shows that Trump voters were actually slightly less racist than Romney voters. Fiorina also debunks the argument that racism accounts for the defection of one-third of white Democratic voters to Trump; after all, these voters had previously supported a black presidential candidate over a white one in 2012. Moreover, Trump's Latino support did not collapse, as many observers predicted it would in the face of his anti-illegal immigration and anti-Mexico discourse. In the end, he polled at least as well as Romney, and likely a little better, especially among Latinas among whom he gained an impressive 9 points.

The associated argument that Clinton ignored the concerns of working-class voters in her 2016 campaign can also be challenged. A word-frequency analysis of all her primary and general election speeches demonstrates that the three things she talked most about were jobs, the economy and workers (Roberts 2016). Clinton herself (2017, 394–395) has sought to rebuff claims that she ignored the Midwest in particular. She highlights in her autobiography that in Pennsylvania she had 500 staff (120 more than Obama in 2012), made 25 campaign stops and spent 211% more than Obama on TV ads, while in Michigan she had 140 more staff than Obama and spent 166% more on advertising. While acknowledging it was a mistake not to visit Wisconsin during the presidential campaign, she argues that her 133 staff and $3 million on ads there was a big investment in a state that polls suggested was safely Democratic.

In the end, Clinton lost the Rust Belt states of Michigan, Wisconsin and Pennsylvania by the narrowest of margins. If just 40,000 people had voted for her rather than Trump across the three states, Clinton would have won. Further, the results in these states are not as shocking as has been suggested. Michigan has a history of supporting candidates from both parties. In the seventeen post-war presidential elections prior to 2016, it voted Republican eight times and Democrat nine. It also tends to vote with the winning candidate, having done so in twelve elections since the war and in seven of the nine prior to 2016. Wisconsin voted with the winning candidate in thirteen post-war elections prior to 2016, bucking the trend just four times. It voted Republican for Nixon in 1968 and 1972 and Reagan in 1980 and 1984. And while George W. Bush lost the state in 2000 and 2004, he did so by less than half of one percent of the popular vote both times. Bush Jr. trailed his Democratic opponents in Pennsylvania by larger margins than in Wisconsin, but still by only four points in 2000 and two-and-a-half points in 2004. And Pennsylvanians voted for Reagan twice and Bush Sr. in the 1980s. Democratic election strategists made a serious error in thinking these states were bankers for Clinton. History suggests that they should in fact be considered classic swing states, and Trump's victory there is far from unprecedented. This is not the stuff of political earthquakes. Fiorina's eloquent summary is worth quoting at some length:

Our country is not poised on the abyss of a race war, Civil War, or any other kind of domestic war. Nor are we sliding down a slippery slope toward fascism. Normal people—a.k.a the general public—continue to live their lives as they did before the election. The voters changed little between 2012 and 2016, although the small changes that occurred were critical for the outcome. Many of Trump's voters were not endorsing his draconian proposals so much as sending a message that they were unhappy with the direction of current policy. Finally, many if not most Americans thought that the parties had given them a historically poor choice. Believing that change was needed, just enough of them in the right places rolled the dice to send the candidate of the status quo down to defeat.

In sum, our own and others' assessment of the data discussed above offers little or no support for order-shattering claims that "2016 feels like an earthquake—a once-in-a-generation event that will remake American politics" (Lind 2016) or that Trump "redrew the electoral map, from sea to shining sea" (Gamio and Keating 2016). Yes, he attracted more working-class votes than recent Republican presidential candidates (whether class is measured by income or education), but not more than the trend over time would predict. The shift of working-class voters, especially white ones, from the Democratic Party to the GOP is an ongoing phenomenon. Trump did not accelerate it. Moreover, only a small proportion of his supporters were working class while a large majority enjoyed family incomes above the median. His election to America's highest office undoubtedly shocked many seasoned observers of the political scene but it was fairly ordinary in terms of who chose to vote, the way they voted and the reasons why they did so.

## 4     Trump, the Republican Party, and America

Many commentators have claimed that Trump has or is in the process of remaking American politics and, in particular, reordering Americans' attachments to the Democratic and Republican parties. The analyses presented above demonstrate that Trump did well among less educated citizens but also that the Republican Party's advantage among this group has been growing steadily over time. That Trump did better than Romney is no surprise given the historical trajectory. But voting is not the only indicator—or even the best indicator—of the landscape of

American politics. Political scientists have long distinguished between a one-off vote for a particular candidate at a particular point in time and a more deep-seated psychological attachment to a political party acquired via a long process of socialization. An individual's so-called party identification may not align with her vote choices in the short run. In the 1980s, for example, many voters chose Ronald Reagan over the Democratic alternatives (Jimmy Carter in 1980 and Walter Mondale in 1984) but nonetheless continued to think of themselves as Democrats and vote blue in congressional elections. Thus, while control of the White House oscillated between the parties in the post-war years, the Democrats locked down the House of Representatives for forty years between 1954 and 1994 in good measure because of their advantage in party identification.

Political scientists are especially interested in party identification because it is a window onto the nation's political substructure. Presidential elections are like volcanos—lots of fire and fury—but party identification is akin to the earth's tectonic plates: Incremental movements over time slowly remake the political landscape in important ways. We do not know for sure yet, but the changing demography of the United States may generate a new Democratic majority as the expanding and Democratic-leaning Latino population challenges the Republican-leaning white population's electoral dominance. Whites already constitute less than fifty percent of California's population and demographers predict America as a whole will follow by the middle of this century. But demographic change is sluggish and the political consequences far from certain. The Democratic Party's large advantage among Latino voters is a relatively recent phenomenon and may not persist if Republicans can switch post-Trump to a more inclusive discourse backed up by liberal immigration reform, such as that signed into law by Ronald Reagan in 1986 and that pushed, ultimately unsuccessfully, by George W. Bush in his second term. Both legislative efforts offered undocumented migrants, many of whom were Latinos, a path to legal residency and potentially citizenship. Bush and his top political adviser Karl Rove thought Latinos were natural Republican voters—hard-working, God-fearing, culturally conservative—but their efforts were thwarted by a coalition of conservative Republicans who thought the reforms too liberal and liberal Democrats who thought the reforms too conservative.

While the tectonic plates of America's party system generally grind slowly, they can be shifted by a seismic event of such magnitude—the Great Depression of the interwar years, for example—that the reordering of people's partisan allegiances is immediate and fundamental. Has Trump, the alleged populist disruptor, reordered or begun a process of reordering the American party system, perhaps if only on a smaller scale than Franklin D. Roosevelt? The answer appears to be no.

While there are undoubtedly important differences today in the issue positions of ordinary Democratic and Republican identifiers, there is also much overlap. Morris Fiorina and colleagues (2004) argued over a decade ago that the American public was not riven by a culture war and was not polarizing around hot-button issues, and that public opinion was still broadly centrist and moderate on most issues, contrary to much academic and media speculation. Even in the age of Trump, majorities of Republicans think that government should make sure everyone has access to good health care, provide a decent standard of living for people unable to work and regulate pollution and environmental hazards, all liberal positions more associated with the Democratic Party. Conversely, majorities of Democrats believe speaking English is essential for being a true American, that government should protect our borders to prevent illegal immigration, and even that government efforts to solve social problems are generally less effective than private efforts, all regarded as conservative positions more associated with the Republican Party (Bartels 2018, Table 1).

Of course, it could be that these fairly stable issue positions on the surface of American public opinion hide lots of movement underneath as previously Democratic supporters (less educated Americans, for example) switch to the Republican Party and previously Republican supporters (better educated Americans, for example) switch to the Democratic Party, thus "sorting" their partisan affiliation to better fit their positions on the issues (Fiorina et al. 2004). If Trump has helped sort the American electorate, it would provide considerable ammunition for those claiming that his is an extraordinary presidency. Bartels again crunches the numbers, examining shifts in party identification between 2015 and 2017, and concludes that: "the most striking fact...is that...partisan change was exceedingly rare." Only 3.9% of Democrats (including self-described independents who acknowledge that they "lean" Democratic) became Republicans and 5.2% of Republicans became Democrats. "The net effect of these shifts was to produce a tiny increase in the Democrats' partisan advantage, from 10.4% in 2015 to 10.7% in 2017. This remarkable partisan stability—stretching from the early stages of Trump's candidacy through the primary season, the general election campaign, and most of the first year of his singular presidency—is a testament to the strength of voters' partisan loyalties in the contemporary party system.... Thus, rather remarkably, there is no evidence in these data that Trump has alienated traditional Republicans" or won over Democrats (Bartels 2018, 12–13, emphasis in original). Data collected over a similar period by the Pew Research Center (2017a) show about twice as much inter-party mobility as the YouGov's Cooperative Campaign Analysis Project data analyzed by Bartels, but the headline is nonetheless one of "stickiness," not change. Those that did switch were more likely to be younger and less attentive to politics.

Another argument promulgated by Trump-is-extraordinary proponents is that he now dominates the Republican Party and is molding it in his image. In one respect, this is a fairly mundane point. Trump was chosen over all other alternatives to be the party's presidential nominee by rank-and-file voters in the GOP primaries, won the presidential election, and is now de facto head of his party. It would be odd if he was not its central figure, just as George W. Bush or Ronald Reagan "dominated" the party during their White House years. Relatedly, his is likely to be the most important single voice in most legislative debates because a bill needs his signature to become law (absent an unlikely override of his veto by two-thirds majorities in both chambers of Congress). But it would also be odd if there was not some conflict between the president and his fellow partisans in Congress. Parties are broad churches, even in an age of congressional polarization. Senator Bob Corker's description of the White House as an adult daycare center, Senator Jeff Flake's emotional anti-Trump retirement speech on the chamber floor and significant wavering over support for Supreme Court nominee Brett Kavanaugh, as well as Trump's Twitter tirades against Senate Majority

Leader Mitch McConnell, stand out as quite extraordinary and deliberate moments of high intra-party conflict and drama, but do not match the partisan political significance of Republican Senator Jim Jeffords' decision to abandon his party and caucus with the Democrats in the first year of George W. Bush's presidency (2001), handing them control of the chamber in the process.

In another respect, however, the point is not mundane but actually wrong. While the vast majority of Republicans approve of the job Trump is doing as president, data collected by Pew highlight just how few share Trump's core issue positions, whether one thinks about Republicans in the general public, registered Republican voters, or politically engaged Republicans. Based on in-depth interviews with over 5000 Americans in 2017, Pew identified four main Republican groups: core conservatives, country-first conservatives, market-skeptic Republicans and new era enterprisers. Core conservatives favor free trade and markets, low taxes and small government, think the US economic system is fair, are relatively pro-immigration, and lean libertarian on social issues. They are wealthy and more likely to have a college education than other Republicans. They don't have much in common with country-first conservatives, who are half as likely as core conservatives to have a college education and be financially comfortable. Country-firsters are most closely aligned with Trump positions on trade (less than 4 in 10 think America's involvement in the global economy is a good thing, compared to 7 in 10 core conservatives) and immigration (three quarters think immigrants are a burden on the US because they take jobs and housing compared to only 4 in 10 core conservatives). Country-firsters are not as positive about the US economic system as core conservatives but still about half think it is generally fair to most Americans. But even this modest level of support puts them well ahead of the market-skeptic Republicans, of whom just 5% agree it is fair. They are very wary of financial institutions and big business and would support increased taxes on them. Surprisingly, while they are almost wholly negative about the US economic system, they are more positive about the global economy than country-firsters. They are also more libertarian than core conservatives on cultural issues but not quite as pro-immigration. Finally, the new era enterprisers who are younger and less white are the most positive about the global and American economic systems, the most pro-immigration and culturally libertarian.

In terms of group size, country-first conservatives are the smallest of the four groups identified by Pew, constituting just 1 in 7 registered Republicans, while core conservatives are 1 in 3. Market skeptics and new era enterprisers each contribute a further one in four. And core conservatives are an even bigger segment of politically engaged Republicans at 44%, compared to country-firsters who constitute just 13%. So we have a Republican Party in which the largest group, core conservatives, share very few of the president's most basic policy positions. Conversely, the group closest to the president ideologically, country-firsters, is the smallest. Overall, a very significant minority, and sometimes a majority, of Republicans do not share the president's positions on international trade, immigration and the fairness of the US economic system (Pew 2017b). This is not a party whose supporters (especially the most engaged ones) are ideologically in step with their president.

Despite their ideological distance from the president, core conservatives were the most positive about Trump's job performance at 93% approval, compared to country-firsters at 83, market skeptics at 66 and new era enterprisers at 63% when quizzed in 2017. On the face of it, this may seem something of a puzzle, but this educated, wealthy and powerful group of free-market supporting Republicans have little to fear from Trump. As the next chapter shows, he has delivered big tax cuts for corporations and the wealthiest individuals, made an incoherent effort to disrupt the international trade system, failed to significantly tighten the immigration spigot and is no closer to building a wall at the US-Mexico border than he was on the first day of his presidency. If one cuts away the outer layers of bluster, populist rhetoric and administrative chaos and instead examines the inner core of substantive policy achievements, this superficially disruptive representative of the American people looks like a pretty ordinary Republican. The idea that Trump has captured the Republican Party and succesfully imposed his disruptive and populist anti-establishment ideology on it is not supported by the concrete policy outputs delivered during his first term. If anything, the party has coopted Trump.

# 5    Conclusion

Whether one thinks in terms of Americans' deep-seated psychological attachments to political parties or more short-term vote choices, the election of Donald Trump does not seem out of the ordinary. Even among the white working class, Trump did not win more votes than expected given the longer-term trend of this group toward the Republican Party. Conversely, despite running a campaign which many commentators thought was explicitly racist or ethically dubious at best, his Latino vote did not collapse. Indeed, exit polls and other returns suggest that he may have even won a larger proportion of Latino votes than the 2012 Republican presidential nominee, Mitt Romney. Finally, Pew's deep dive into the ideological composition of GOP supporters after the election highlights that most do not share Trump's core ideological positions, even though they say he is doing a good job.

All-in-all, the evidence presented in this chapter weighs heavily in favor of the Trump-is-ordinary argument. This is perhaps somewhat surprising given the brouhaha that surrounded Trump during the election campaign and has continued into his presidency, but the data are drawn from a multitude of reliable sources and analysts. One on its own may not make a convincing case, but they all point in the same direction. Each adds weight to the conclusions of the others.

Of course, the conclusion that Trump's election victory was fairly ordinary and that he has not remade the American party system is one thing. It may well be that once in office, Trump has put into effect some or all of the radical populist agenda he promoted on the campaign trail. The next chapter explores Trump's accomplishment to see if his presidency is extraordinary, even if his election was not.

# References

Alberta, Tim. 2016. "The 'Diploma Divide' Explains Why Iowa Looks Better for Trump Than New Hampshire." *National Review*, October 24.

Bartels, Larry. 2016. "2016 Was an Ordinary Election, Not a Realignment." *Washington Post*, November 10.

Bartels, Larry. 2018. "Partisanship in the Trump Era." Paper Presented to Center for the Study of Democratic Institutions, Vanderbilt University, February 7.

Brownstein, Ronald. 2015. "The Billionaire Candidate and His Blue-Collar Following." *The Atlantic*, September 11.

Brownstein, Ronald. 2016a. "The Parties Invert." *The Atlantic*, May 23.

Brownstein, Ronald. 2016b. "The Class Inversion of American Politics Accelerates." *The Atlantic*, July 26.

Carnes, Nicholas, and Noam Lupu. 2017. "It's Time to Bust the Myth: Most Trump Voters Were Not Working Class." *Washington Post*, June 5.

Clinton, Hillary Rodham. 2017. *What Happened*. New York: Simon & Schuster.

Cohn, Nate. 2016. "Why Trump Won: Working-Class Whites." *New York Times*, November 9.

Edsall, Thomas. 2016. "One Problem for Democratic Leaders Is Democratic Voters." *New York Times*, December 22.

Ehrenfreund, Max, and Scott Clement. 2016. "Economic and Racial Anxiety: Two Separate Forces Driving Support for Donald Trump." *Washington Post*, March 22.

Fiorina, Morris. 2018. "The Meaning of Trump's Election Has Been Exaggerated." *RealClearPolitics.com*, January 10. https://www.realclearpolitics.com/articles/2018/01/10/the_meaning_of_trumps_election_has_been_exaggerated__135968.html.

Fiorina, Morris P., Samuel J. Abrams, and Jeremy C. Pope. 2004. *Culture War? The Myth of a Polarized America*. New York: Longman Publishing.

Gamio, Lazaro, and Dan Keating. 2016. "How Trump Redrew the Electoral Map, from Sea to Shining Sea." *Washington Post*, November 9.

Gosling, Amanda, and Andrew Wroe. 2017. "De-industrialisation and the 2016 Presidential Election: A Spatial Analysis of Trump's Victory." Paper Presented at 2017 American Politics Group Conference, University of Leicester, January 5–7.

Lind, Michael. 2016. "This Is What the Future of American Politics Looks Like." *Politico*, May 22. https://www.politico.com/magazine/story/2016/05/2016-election-realignment-partisan-political-party-policy-democrats-republicans-politics-213909.

Machin, Stephen. 2008. "An Appraisal of Economic Research on Changes in Wage Inequality." *Labour* 22 (1): 7–26.

Pew. 2017a. "Partisan Identification Is 'Sticky,' But About 10% Switched Parties Over the Past Year." *Pew Research Center*, May 17. http://assets.pewresearch.org/wp-content/uploads/sites/5/2017/05/31163430/05-17-17-Longitudinal-partisanship-release.pdf.

Pew. 2017b. "Political Typology Reveals Deep Fissures on the Right and Left." *Pew Research Center*, October 24. http://assets.pewresearch.org/wp-content/uploads/sites/5/2017/10/31115611/10-24-2017-Typology-release.pdf.

Roberts, David. 2016. "The Most Common Words in Hillary Clinton's Speeches, in One Chart: They Weren't About 'Identity Politics'." *Vox*, December 16. https://www.vox.com/policy-and-politics/2016/12/16/13972394/most-common-words-hillary-clinton-speech.

Schaffner, Brian. 2016. "White Support for Donald Trump Was Driven by Economic Anxiety, but Also by Racism and Sexism." *Vox*, November 16. https://www.vox.com/mischiefs-of-faction/2016/11/16/13651184/trump-support-economic-anxiety-racism-sexism.

Small, Andrew. 2016. "Trump's Rust Belt Bet." *CityLab*, November 11. https://www.citylab.com/equity/2016/11/trumps-rust-belt-bet/507353/.

Tankersley, Jim. 2016. "How Trump Won: The Revenge of Working-Class Whites." *Washington Post*, November 9.

Tesler, Michael. 2016. "Views About Race Mattered More in Electing Trump Than in Electing Obama." *Washington Post*, November 22.

Thompson, Derek. 2016. "The Dangerous Myth That Hillary Clinton Ignored the Working Class." *The Atlantic*, December 5.

Wroe, Andrew. 2008. *The Republican Party and Immigration Politics: From Proposition 187 to George W. Bush*. New York: Palgrave Macmillan.

# 4

# Trump the Ordinary Republican

As a purported outsider, disruptor, nationalist, populist and insurgent, Trump promised dramatic change. While the previous chapter showed that the electoral support for Trump was not out of the ordinary, his election nonetheless portended a clash between the new president and the system he professed to loathe. The newcomer brought ideas and policies and a style and approach that would not sit comfortably with established ways of operating in Washington. Trump seemed to suggest that he would overthrow the governing orthodoxy and replace it with a new approach, but what form the clash would take and how it might be won or lost were anything but clear as he took office.

Most observers assumed that the Washington establishment would resist change, begging the question of whether the new but inexperienced outsider president had the capacity to deliver his promises. A lasting "Trump Revolution" would require the new president to establish a new governing coalition, corralling power to take over the executive branch and winning congressional support for changes to the law. Effectively, Trump promised a grand governing project that absorbed the challenges of evicting the existing elites and replacing them with his own power arrangements to allow him to establish his new policies.

© The Author(s) 2019
J. Herbert et al., *The Ordinary Presidency of Donald J. Trump*,
Palgrave Studies in Political Leadership,
https://doi.org/10.1007/978-3-030-04943-0_4

The record of Trump's presidency suggests he has not been successful. When Trump has tried to be bold, to implement his nationalist
agenda, to be disruptive and populist, and to challenge elite interests,
he has largely failed. It is certainly not the case that Trump's presidency
is inconsequential or has not generated any policy triumphs, but the
successes are few in number and limited in scope. Moreover, the limited successes that Trump has enjoyed look very much like mainstream
Republican ones. The 2017 tax bill and his two appointments to the
Supreme Court are classics of the type. Both Neil Gorsuch and Brett
Kavanaugh are solidly conservative jurists hued from America's most
exclusive and expensive prep schools and universities. And the biggest
beneficiaries of the tax bill are big business and America's wealthiest
individuals. The relatively modest tax cuts awarded to middle-income
earners are designed to decline year-on-year before being phased out
completely by 2025. This was necessary under congressional budget
rules in order to pay for the much larger and permanent cuts to corporation tax and other business benefits. The elite are doing very well in
Trump's America.

The idea that Trump is "draining the swamp" is fanciful. His language may still at times invoke the anti-establishment discourse of
his primary and general election campaigns, but underneath the
populist bluster is a fairly standard Republican president. Some congressional Republicans may call out Trump on his more divisive and
culturally inflammatory remarks, but they have rallied their votes
behind him where there is policy agreement. Where there is not and
where Trump has thus tried to circumvent Congress with his executive powers, he has found that other political actors and institutions have resisted his reform efforts. The courts, for example, have
blocked or at least severely constrained his immigration reforms
and his own bureaucracy continues to resist his attempts to deconstruct it. Trump's presidency may generate lots of fire and fury, but in
terms of policy outputs it is fairly ordinary. This chapter presents the
evidence.

# 1    The Congressional Agenda

The most notable aspects of Trump's early legislative forays were the paucity of significant successes and the degree to which he looked like an ordinary Republican president. While the first year is widely regarded as the period most conducive to presidential leadership of the legislative agenda, Trump did not establish a policy revolution or even a small rebellion. There were no wins on the priority agenda items of trade, immigration or infrastructure. Indeed, during his first year in office, no serious debate of major, presidentially backed legislation took place in Congress on any of these topics. Moreover, Trump's legislative record reflected an agenda that was ideologically consistent with many of his party's long-standing priorities.

The new president's first significant congressional victory was the confirmation of Neil Gorsuch to the Supreme Court. Gorsuch was selected from the conservative Federalist Society's list of vetted and approved judicial nominees. He would have been a mainstream choice for any recent Republican president and was widely welcomed by social conservatives. While Trump has loudly proclaimed Gorsuch's appointment as a significant "win," there was a good deal of luck involved as well as parliamentary smarts by other key players, especially Senate Majority Leader Mitch McConnell who manufactured the appointment opportunity for the new president to replace Justice Antonin Scalia who had died suddenly in February 2016. Much to the chagrin of Democrats, McConnell refused to hold hearings for President Obama's nominee Merrick Garland in 2016 because, McConnell argued creatively, the vacancy occurred in the final year of the president's term of office and thus the next president should fill the slot. Without a Democratic majority in the Senate, Garland's prospects stalled, shriveled and died. After Trump won the election, McConnell also changed the Senate's rules—employing the so-called nuclear option—to allow Gorsuch's nomination to proceed with a simple majority vote rather than the supermajority of 60 previously required to overcome a filibuster. Trump followed up Gorsuch's appointment with a swathe of conservative nominations to the lower courts. His supporters have claimed that this again represents a significant achievement but it is completely conventional for a Republican president.

Trump's luck was in again when Supreme Court Justice Anthony Kennedy resigned his post in July 2018, affording Trump a second opportunity to make an appointment to the land's highest court. If Gorsuch was a like-for-like replacement for Scalia, Trump's nomination of Judge Brett Kavanaugh will push the court in a more conservative direction. While the Senate confirmation process was anything but ordinary—the allegations of sexual assault made by Christine Blasey Ford, now a professor of psychology, who accused the nominee of attacking her in 1982 when she was 15 and he was 17, almost derailed his nomination—Kavanaugh is a mainstream Republican jurist who enjoyed a privileged upper-middle class upbringing in Bethesda, Maryland. He attended one of America's most exclusive and expensive schools—Georgetown Prep, where Gorsuch also went—and then one of its most elite universities, Yale. There is nothing swamp-busting on his resume, which even led some Republicans to oppose him initially. Former presidential candidate Rick Santorum accused Trump of having "bowed to the elite in Washington… He is the establishment pick. He is the Bush pick" (Johnson 2018). It is possible to argue either way whether two Supreme Court appointments less than two years into the job represent wins for Trump or just good luck or perhaps both. It is harder to make the case that Gorsuch and Kavanaugh are anything other than mainstream Republican choices in terms of their conservative positioning and elite backgrounds. The highly divisive controversy over the Kavanaugh appointment may yet prove damaging to Trump's presidency in the long term making it something of a Pyrrhic victory. If anything it has deepened the degree to which claims of inappropriate behavior and misogyny have followed Trump from the campaign trail to the White House, not least because he has also been accused of sexual misconduct by as many as 22 women and allegedly paid off a pornographic film actress, Stormy Daniels, to keep her from disclosing an alleged affair with him.

If the Senate's confirmation of Gorsuch was Trump's first notable congressional win, the first outright failure was healthcare. Trump was persuaded by House Speaker Paul Ryan that the repeal and replacement of the Affordable Care Act (ACA), widely known as Obamacare, should be the administration's first major legislative initiative. Its repeal had become a Republican *cause célèbre* since the original legislation's passage in 2010. As debate over the contentious issue of what, if anything, would replace it unfolded, Trump's legislative calendar was consumed by an agreed Republican priority and campaign staple, even if the party was not agreed on the direction it should take over the issue despite having nearly two presidential terms to think about it.

Trump followed the embarrassing collapse of healthcare reform with a focus on tax cuts. The Tax Cuts and Jobs Act of 2017 (TCJA) signed by President Trump on December 22, 2017, was undoubtedly a legislative win. Yet the tax reform bill protects the interests of big business and the wealthy at the expense of ordinary Americans. The bill is perhaps the least disruptive, least populist, least swamp-draining legislation imaginable. The law demonstrates that Trump is governing as a traditional Republican plutocrat, influenced by the same organized interests and economic ideology as his recent predecessors. It slashed corporate tax from 35 to 21% on a permanent basis. Real estate developers like Trump and his son-in-law Jared Kushner will benefit mightily from a last minute change to allow companies to use the "pass through" rules to reduce their tax. It rewards wealthy Americans with significant reductions in income tax and a doubling of the estate tax threshold. Only couples with assets greater than $22 million and individuals worth over $11 million will be subject to death duties. Changes to income tax also benefitted the richest the most. While tax rates fell across most groups by three to four percentage points—apart from the lowest rate which remained the same—those at the very top welcomed the biggest dollar reductions. Meanwhile, Americans in the bottom half of the income distribution don't pay federal income tax and thus did not receive any benefits from the tax cuts.

Trump's political strategist Steve Bannon tried to fight the populist corner, arguing in preliminary discussions that the top income tax rate should be increased, not decreased. According to Bob Woodward, Trump even suggested at one point in the discussions that the top income tax rate could go up to finance the cut in corporation tax. Chief economic adviser Gary Cohn reminded Trump: "You're a Republican. You will get destroyed if you take the top rate up" (Woodward 2018, 290). The idea was quickly dropped. The elites' taxes would not be going up on Trump's watch. Further, the reductions to income tax are tapered—and so get smaller each year—and will disappear by 2025 in order to meet budget reconciliation constraints on how much a bill can add to the deficit. Permanent cuts to both corporation and income tax would not have passed parliamentary muster, and so the law traded off both the size and permanence of the much vaunted middle-class tax cut in favor of significant and permanent cuts to corporations' tax bills and the tax returns of America's wealthiest individuals.

Perhaps even more deleterious for Trump's image as a defender of ordinary Americans, the carried interest loophole was not closed, thus allowing private equity and hedge fund managers, some of America's richest people, to continue to classify most of their income as capital gains and thus pay tax at a much lower rate than average Americans subject to income tax. Trump had promised to eliminate the loophole many times, including an August 4, 2016, speech in Detroit: "We will eliminate the carried interest deduction and other special interest loopholes that have been so good for Wall Street investors, and for people like me, but unfair to American workers." Economic adviser Cohn, former president and chief operating officer of Goldman Sachs and estimated to be worth $260 million, pushed hard for its elimination. Treasury Secretary Steve Mnuchin, former hedge fund manager and Goldman Sachs investment banker with an estimated net worth of $300 million, together with enough Republicans on Capitol Hill, wanted it preserved or were unwilling to take a stand in the face of fierce lobbying in its favor. Trump's complaint that he would definitely pay more tax under the new rules—it would "cost me a fortune… believe me"—is probably a considerable inexactitude. He was much more candid when he told his wealthy guests at his Mar-a-Lago club ($200,000 to join plus a $14,000 per year membership fee) the same day he signed the tax bill: "You all just got a lot richer" (Watson 2017).

And he even reminded the billionaire industrialist Koch brothers and major Republican Party donors that "[t]hey love my Tax & Regulation Cuts, judicial picks & more. I made them richer" (Twitter, July 31, 2018). Conservative columnist and author Ann Coulter exploded in fury at the failure to end the carried interest loophole, berating Trump on Twitter for not following through on a key election promise. The tax bill also incorporated a nullification of the Obamacare mandate that had required individuals to purchase, and some businesses to offer their employees, health insurance. While its effects will take some time to discern precisely, it clearly represents a relaxation of government intervention in the health marketplace and thus pleased most conservatives.

Not only was the one significant legislative win of Trump's first year a traditional, anti-populist, plutocratic measure, likely to increase the wealth and health inequalities that drove some people to Trump in the first place, but polls suggested a majority of Americans were unsupportive of the reforms, believing rightly that they would mainly benefit the rich and corporations. Indeed, the tax *cuts* were even more unpopular at the time of passage, with only 32% of Americans supporting them, than the infamous "Read my lips, no new taxes" tax *hike* imposed by George H. W. Bush in 1990 that was supported by 41% of Americans and Clinton's tax increase in 1993 that had 34% support. By stark contrast, Ronald Reagan's tax cut after entering office in 1981 garnered 51% approval and was only disapproved by 26% of Americans, whereas 46% of Americans disapproved of Trump's tax cut in 2017 (Enten 2017).

In sum, Trump followed a standard Republican agenda early in his presidency. His legislative achievements were relatively limited, but each could be seen as fitting comfortably with conservative beliefs. Of course, there was much disagreement within the conservative movement, as exposed by the dissension in Republican ranks over how to reform Obamacare, but Trump's agenda choices were conventional. On economics, reducing tax rates mirrored the early initiatives of the Reagan and George W. Bush administrations. His proposal brought together libertarian, small government and business wings of the movement. As usual among Republican tax reforms, this achievement was despite the hesitancy of budget hawks who feared an increased deficit. Within the package, there was some more emphasis on corporate tax cuts than previous Republican reforms, but the main thrust was familiar. Equally, appointing socially conservative judges had been a standard Reagan and Bush activity and a core part of both of their legacies. The rolling back of government intervention in healthcare, most obviously represented by the negating of the individual mandate, sat very comfortably alongside the rhetoric of small government Republicans and at odds with Trump's own boast that he would deliver a better, more comprehensive healthcare plan than Obamacare and at a cheaper price.

Furthermore, the source of these substantive legislative achievements appeared to be the Republican Party's congressional leadership, not the Trump White House. The tax bill was largely conceived, written and driven by congressional Republicans, and its passage and other successes were marked by unmistakable patterns of partisan voting. All but 12 Republicans in the House, every Republican in the Senate and no Democrats voted for the tax bill. Gorsuch's confirmation in the Senate drew only three Democratic votes and that of every present Republican. Kavanaugh's nomination only succeeded because the slim Republican majority on the Senate Judiciary Committee and in the chamber held the party line. Overall, Republican legislators' support for their party's president has been solid. Dismal support scores among Democrats suggested that Trump followed the recognized trend toward a highly partisan presidency, where two tribes face one another in Congress with little capacity for cooperation. There were high profile disagreements within the Republican congressional party over healthcare and vocal complaints over Trump's style of leadership, but when it took final votes on Trump-supported legislation and nominations, his governing coalition looked very much like the Republican Party that had supported each of his Republican predecessors. Congressional politics seemed just as partisan as before. Trump had not established a new governing coalition to support his presidency, yet neither had he repulsed his party to the extent that they were willing to break ranks.

## 2    Executive Power

Just as Trump's successes in the legislature reflected his party's orthodoxy, so did many of his exertions of executive power. Presidents do not
lead through legislative initiatives alone. Close observers of power place
increasing emphasis on presidents' capacity to take executive action.
Few believe this action to be unbound, recognizing that Congress
and the Courts retain authority to constrain presidential assertions.
Furthermore, most regard executive action as lacking durability; the
capacity of a subsequent president to reverse the actions of their predecessors suggests that a legacy based on presidential instructions may be
short-lived. Nevertheless, presidents can do much to change the behavior of the federal bureaucracy and shape other actors' behavior through
the so-called administrative presidency based on executive rule-mak-
ing and other similar initiatives (Resh 2015). One of Trump's key targets, and one particularly exposed to executive action, was the federal
bureaucracy that he headed.

Trump had grandly claimed during the 2016 election campaign
that he'd "cut [the federal bureaucracy] so much your head will spin"
(quoted in Rein and Ba Tan 2017), and Bannon identified the "deconstruction of the administrative state" as a primary priority at the
February 2017 Conservative Political Action Conference. In Bannon's
thinking, the progressive left had grown the state by increasing the size
and reach of the regulatory agencies in the federal bureaucracy, often
without congressional approval, and smothered American business and
entrepreneurial spirit in unnecessary red tape. While Bannon argued
passionately against the spaghetti of agencies that allegedly entangle
American citizens and business, he was largely reiterating a longstand-
ing conservative argument about a bloated state that can be traced back
through Ronald Reagan to Barry Goldwater.

To begin the process of deconstructing the federal bureaucracy,
Trump quickly issued executive orders establishing general principles to guide his administration's approach. All new costs would
be offset by savings elsewhere, while for every new regulation issued
two would be withdrawn. The effect of these was partly theatrical

(one set of regulations does not necessarily have an equal impact to another, so withdrawing ten may have less impact than imposing one), but it did mark a clear direction. Furthermore, Trump appointed a series of agency heads with a record of disdain for the regulatory efforts of their agencies. Scott Pruitt as Attorney General of Oklahoma had spearheaded efforts to sue the Environmental Protection Agency (EPA), resisting a series of Obama-era regulations. Trump subsequently appointed Pruitt to head the very EPA he had opposed so strongly. This nomination won particular attention, but further serious questions were raised about the tensions between the missions of departments and the ideological leanings of many among Trump's selections. Betsy DeVos at Education, Ryan Zinke at Interior, Tom Price at Health and Human Services, Rick Perry at Energy and Ben Carson at Housing and Urban Development all faced questions over their competence to run departments given their antipathy to those department's missions.

Trump's broad guidance and the ideological fervor of many of his appointees triggered extensive efforts to reduce government regulation. Pruitt's campaign against climate change regulation, assisted by Zinke at Interior and Perry at Energy, won a great deal of media coverage. High profile efforts such as repealing Obama's Clean Power Plan, which had promised to limit emissions of greenhouse gases from power plants, and revising plans for fuel economy standards were matched by a series of other changes such as delays to new Waters of the United States regulations, easing the approval processes for new chemicals, and streamlining environmental reviews for infrastructure projects. Development and fossil fuel production were clearly prioritized in decisions to open more federal lands and offshore waters for drilling, shrinking the size of some national monuments, approving pipelines and moving to rescind rules on fracking. On June 1, 2017, Trump gave added impetus to these domestic actions by withdrawing US cooperation from the 2015 Paris Agreement on Climate Change, arguing it was "unfair" to the US and failed to effectively protect the environment. As he put it: "The Paris Accord would undermine our economy, hamstring our workers, weaken our sovereignty, impose unacceptable legal risks, and put us at a permanent disadvantage to the other countries of the world."

Deregulation also extended to the financial sector. The Trump administration proved consistently friendly to banks in its decisions, working to loosen the regulations imposed on the finance industry after the collapse of 2008. A series of efforts have been made to reduce the impact of the Dodd-Frank legislation of 2010, such as simplifying the "stress tests" of banks designed to better guarantee their longevity and stripping back the investigations and enforcement proceedings of the Consumer Financial Protection Bureau (CFPB). These efforts were enhanced by Congress' passage of the 2018 Economic Growth, Regulatory Relief and Consumer Protection Act, which slackened the regulation of smaller and medium sized banks by exempting them from stress tests. Action on labor issues also tended to favor business. The administration has weakened many workplace protections, such as mine safety inspection regimes and regulation of dangerous substances in the workplace.

Executive power was also deployed to pursue a sustained campaign to undermine Obamacare, much as would be expected of a Republican president given the party's devout opposition to it since its passage in 2010. Trump used executive power to shorten the period for enrollment in insurance programs through the ACA's exchanges. Funding for marketing programs designed to let people know of the opportunities available to them and to assist consumers in finding coverage was cut. In each case, these moves seemed likely to reduce enrollment. Trump also used executive power in October 2017 to eliminate a series of subsidies called cost sharing reductions. These CSRs had helped those on low incomes pay for healthcare costs when they needed treatment and provided a greater guarantee to insurers that those on lower incomes could be insured profitably. Furthermore, Trump changed rules to weaken the quality of basic plans around both the health benefits that insurance packages were obliged to offer and the consumer protections available. Presented as giving insurers and states greater flexibility, the administration downgraded the quality of plan mandated by the government.

How should these reform efforts be judged? Trump has undoubtedly used executive actions and the legislative process to undermine some aspects of Obamacare. However, much of the basic structure of the ACA remains intact, such as the health insurance exchanges, the presence of national standards for insurance plans, the main subsidies for consumers' premiums and the associated expansion of Medicaid. One reading of the modest changes confirms both aspects of what defines Trump's presidency as ordinary: On the one hand, they constitute a basic failure to fundamentally disrupt and reform the healthcare status quo and, on the other, the tinkering on the margins that has taken place is very much in a standard Republican direction. Similar deregulatory trends can be identified in agencies overseeing education, media and agriculture.

Trump had inherited an extraordinary opportunity rooted in his predecessor's own exertions of executive power. Many of Obama's later actions had been undertaken through executive action. Arguing that "we can't wait," he made notable changes in environmental, healthcare and immigration policy through orders to the bureaucracy on how to interpret and implement existing laws. In some respects, this was a logical response to a resistant Republican Congress, but Obama's use of executive power made his actions vulnerable to prompt reversal by an unsupportive successor. Obama grasped more power for the presidency in the short term, but simultaneously established the potential for the dismantling of his achievements by his successors. Trump grasped the opportunity to dismantle Obama's vulnerable regulatory legacy with glee and issued a series of executive actions to do so. Congressional Republicans spent much of the later Obama years condemning these actions and now supported their new president in his efforts to reverse the expansion of the federal government's regulatory grip. Of course, Trump's own executive actions will be vulnerable to reversal under the next presidency, again demonstrating the rather ordinary, business as usual nature of Trump's actions.

Alongside this deregulatory direction, Trump also pursued classic Republican means to shrink the size of government. On taking office, he announced a federal hiring freeze. First used in the Nixon administration, and to much greater effect by the Reagan administration, leaving posts vacant can disrupt the structures, and so the business of government, as well as reducing expenditure. The approach clearly delivered successes for Trump, although some Republicans expressed skepticism about his ability to lead departments in a conservative direction if he didn't appoint leaders. According to the *Washington Post*, Trump had managed to reduce the number of permanent federal government workers by 16,000 within his first eight months as president (Rein and Ba Tran 2017). While 16,000 was not many in the context of nearly two million permanent staff, Trump had engineered a reversal in a previous trend under Obama.

In sum, Trump has appeared decidedly Republican in his approach and actions. Deregulation and reducing the size and spending of government were consistent themes of Reagan's and both Bush administrations, echoing the desire to free the market to operate by reducing government intervention. Libertarians, business interests and small government advocates all embraced a radical policy first articulated in the 1980s. It might be argued that Trump was more committed to, or effective at delivering on, these concerns than his predecessors—doubts have been cast on both Reagan's and Bush's achievements as deregulators and tamers of government's size—but each made similar commitments to reducing government in their first years in office. In this respect, Trump toed the classic ideological line of the Republican Party.

## 3    Draining the Swamp

The most original feature of the deregulatory agenda was its public presentation. While the policy itself was standard Republican fare, Trump labeled these initiatives as "draining the swamp." The phrase was first used at a campaign rally on October 17, 2016, and he explained at a subsequent rally that he was initially unimpressed when an unnamed aide had suggested it to him, but changed his mind when the crowd responded enthusiastically. It quickly became a popular Twitter hashtag and meme and part of Trump's call-and-response routine along with "lock her up" and "build the wall." It slotted comfortably into his oratorical repertoire because it was at once theatrical and vague but also determinedly populist and disruptive.

During the 2016 campaign, Trump had articulated an unusual rejection of basic democratic norms. Since the Founding, US politicians have spoken of their political system with respect, emphasizing the legitimacy of the system under which they govern. Trump, in contrast, questioned this legitimacy, arguing that the system was rigged against the people and their potential tribune, himself. Various institutions of government felt the sting of his criticism, but Trump's verbal rejection of the establishment was all-encompassing, taking in politicians, interest groups, media, courts and many others. There was also a very clear condemnation of the role of money in politics in Trump's diatribes on corruption and the rigged system plus his public statements on (but not the practice of) refusing outside contributions to his campaign. Trump's campaign appeared to identify and promise to address fundamental imbalances in the political system. Even when Bannon grabbed attention with his claim that the Trump administration was embarking upon a "deconstruction of the Administrative State," readable as a wonk-translation of Trump's campaign pledge to "drain the swamp," his phrase carried similar implications of power and conspiracy, identifying a governing elite as merely one step away from the conspiracy theorists' all-powerful Illuminati.

Trump and his audience did not dwell much on the dissonance between his own elite status and swamp-draining promises, despite his candid admission in a GOP primary debate that as a businessman he contributed financially to "everybody" in the expectation that they would be "there for me" when he called. He expanded on the relationship at a campaign rally in Iowa: "I've given to everybody. Because that was my job. I gotta give to them. Because when I want something, I get it. When I call, they kiss my ass" (quoted in Fahrenthold and Helderman 2016). Trump the property developer made many campaign contributions to protect his business interests. For example, concerned that Florida's Attorney General Pam Bondi might pursue fraud claims against Trump University, he broke campaign finance rules by using his charitable foundation to donate $25,000 to her reelection campaign. Seeking to encourage Florida Governor Jeb Bush to relax his opposition to casinos, he held a $500 per head fund-raiser for him at his New York apartment. Wanting to persuade Palm Beach County commissioners to stop noisy planes flying over Mar-a-Lago, he set up a Political Action Committee to donate to noise-averse candidates in Palm Beach. Trump the candidate resourcefully sought to turn his murky involvement in the lobbying swamp to his advantage, arguing in his 2016 GOP convention acceptance speech that "Nobody knows the system better than me, which is why I alone can fix it."

If taken seriously as an agenda for reform, Trump's promise to drain the swamp would imply some large system-level repercussions, potentially including campaign finance reform to address interest group contributions, regulation of lobbying by interests, rules on redistricting to contain gerrymandering and other elements of the good governance agenda. Trump's actual response, however, has been very much more limited and self-interested. For example, he established a Presidential Advisory Commission on Election Integrity by Executive Order in May 2017, but this was intended to investigate his evidence-free claim that he would have won the popular vote and overcome Hillary Clinton's near three million vote advantage "if you deduct the millions of people who voted illegally." The Commission descended into chaos. States refused to respond to requests for data and legal battles broke out over the access to commission papers for its Democratic members. After little but political controversy and bad publicity for the president's unfounded claims of illegal voting, the Commission was disbanded in January 2018.

There is a multitude of other evidence in support of the claim that Trump's commitment to draining the swamp was purely verbal, particularly regarding entrenched special interests. Mick Mulvaney, Trump's own pick as interim head and avowed critic of the CFPB, unwittingly summed up the process neatly in an April 2018 speech before the American Bankers Association. Reminiscing about his pay-to-play days as a Republican member of the House of Representatives before being plucked out by Trump to head the White House Office of Management and Budget and then the CFPB, Mulvaney recalled the "hierarchy in my office in Congress. If you're a lobbyist who never gave us money, I didn't talk to you. If you're a lobbyist who gave us money, I might talk to you." Without irony, Trump's lieutenant reminded the mainly rich white men seated before him that lobbying was part of the "fundamental underpinnings of our representative democracy. And you have to continue to do it" in order to pressure members of Congress to diminish the power and independence of the CFPB, Mulvaney's own bureau set up to protect consumers and regulate financial institutions in wake of the financial crash in 2007–2008 (quoted in Thrush 2018).

Trump himself began playing by the same swamp rules he allegedly despised even before winning the presidency. He claimed to be so rich that he would not need to accept campaign contributions from special interests, but the notoriously parsimonious businessman had little interest in spending his own money either. After loaning, not gifting, his primary campaign $12 million, he closed his checkbook. His general election campaign took money from all-comers. The bundlers bundled, rich businessmen heaved open their wallets, SuperPACs spent wildly in support, and Trump attended fund-raisers where supporters each stumped up tens of thousands of dollars to be in the room. Trump continued to raise money from rich benefactors once in office. At one exclusive event organized by private equity mogul Stephen Schwarzman—paid $799 million in 2017 by his firm Blackstone Group—about two dozen super-rich business leaders paid $100,000 a head to hear Trump talk for 20 minutes at Schwarzman's palatial Manhattan triplex in December 2017 (Dawsey 2017; Kranish 2018). But not only was Trump taking the money, it also appeared that those making contributions had the president's ear. Schwarzman had considerable business interests in China and as chair of the President's Strategic and Policy Forum helped talk Trump out of his campaign promise to label China a currency manipulator (Kranish 2018). Hillary Clinton might well raise an eyebrow, given Trump's vicious criticism of her private speaker fees.

Just weeks after the $100,000 per head luncheon, Trump in a remarkable volte-face traveled to ground zero of the global economic swamp, the World Economic Forum in Davos, Switzerland. Both Barack Obama and George W. Bush avoided the event because they did not want to be seen cozying up to the world's most rich and powerful people. Trump has no such qualms and was warmly received by the free-trade touting globalists able to see past his fierce America First rhetoric and focus on the substantive tax cutting and deregulatory agenda. Goldman Sachs chief executive and previously vocal critic Lloyd Blankfein praised Trump's down-the-line support for Wall Street and its financial titans: "I've really liked what he's done for the economy, and I think he's gone out of his way to be very, very supportive of the system." Schwarzman was happy too, as the money was flowing and life was good for America's plutocrats: "You're making money and it's not real hard work." Trump made no mention of draining the swamp and the populist rhetoric was dialed down to near zero in his set-piece Davos address, arguing instead America "was open for business" and stressing that "America first doesn't mean America alone." Trump enjoyed the Davos party, and the Davos globalists didn't find his presence there too distasteful either.

Draining the swamp was a convenient campaign slogan, not a blueprint for government. Trump likely had no intention of trying to drain it once in power. Similarly, his empathy with his blue-collar constituency is largely verbal. He has not acted on the rhetoric. He has no experience of poverty or even a life less than wealthy. While he claimed to "love all people, rich and poor," he was flabbergasted that senior civil servants could get by on only a few hundred thousand dollars a year, and could not conceive of staffing his cabinet with people "with modest means... [I]n those particular positions I just don't want a poor person." Instead he wanted only "people that made a fortune," and he got them in the wealthiest cabinet in history. Rather than attacking entrenched and elite interests, Trump's draining of the swamp took its much more traditional Republican form, concentrating on reducing the size and cost of federal government and dismantling regulations. Rather than a radical populist, Trump is an ordinary Republican.

# 4    A Conventional Social Conservative

Trump's executive actions also indicated his willingness to pursue the traditional social conservatism associated with the Republican Party. His campaign declarations did not embrace all the fundamental tenets of social conservatism, with liberal statements on LGBTQ rights and gun control alongside a personal history of luxury, extramarital affairs and divorce that sat awkwardly alongside Christian traditions. Once in office, however, Trump has followed the party line of social conservatism. A month into his presidency, Trump indicated how he would govern on LGBTQ issues, revoking guidance that had forced public schools to allow students to use bathrooms that reflected their chosen gender identity. Obama had announced that transgender troops should be allowed to serve openly in the military, but Trump blocked such a move. The Department of Justice moved away from considering discrimination on grounds of gender a breach of the 1964 Civil Rights Act and therefore did not pursue prosecutions on this basis.

On crime and justice, Trump made a series of moves that fitted with the traditional Republican position of being "tough on crime." The Obama administration had emphasized the accountability of police authorities. Having identified systematic racial bias in police actions, Obama's Justice Department had used its prosecutorial leverage to persuade local departments to reform their practices. Trump, however, chose different priorities, dismantling the system of "consent decrees" that had underpinned the Obama approach and aligning himself with the Blue Lives Matter movement to emphasize his desire to protect the police. Once again, local police authorities were allowed to purchase surplus military equipment such as high-caliber weapons and armored vehicles. Being tough on crime included a restoration of "war on drugs" policies, such as a mandatory minimum sentence on non-violent and low-level drug offenders. Trump's Attorney General Jeff Sessions over-ruled the Obama-era instruction to federal prosecutors to give low priority to enforcement of the federal prohibition of marijuana sales. He also declared the need to increase the use of capital punishment in federal cases. The administration's belief in market solutions to problems was emphasized by the Department of Justice's moves to restore private provision of prisons.

Many of these policies had an unambiguous racial dimension, given the disproportionate number of black Americans represented within the justice system, confronting drug problems and suffering police violence. The administration also adopted conservative positions on a series of civil rights issues, delaying new fair-housing rules, rewriting the rules on investigations of civil rights abuses in schools and preventing new reporting requirements on pay levels by race and gender being imposed on large businesses. Perhaps most prominently, Trump quickly backtracked on his surprising promise to take a look at beefing up gun control after the Marjory Stoneman Douglas High School massacre. The intervention of the National Rifle Association and some pro-gun Republican Senators was swift and decisive. Trump quickly fell back in with the party line.

All-in-all, social and economic conservatives could see many reasons to celebrate the Trump administration. Despite Candidate Trump's apparent lack of commitment to conservative values during his campaign, the vast majority of President Trump's legislative and executive initiatives can be classified as thoroughly Republican. The above analysis, however, admittedly ducks away from the issues of immigration, trade and infrastructure. On the face of it, these sit outside the Republican Party's comfort zone by challenging its steady support of free trade, relative tolerance of immigration and rejection of big government programs. These issues have only been touched on above, but they will now be addressed in detail.

# 5    The Nationalist Agenda

The totemic populist promise of Trump's primary and general election campaigns was to take back control of America's borders and fix the allegedly broken immigration system. Trump would among other things build a "big, beautiful wall" and get Mexico to pay, ban Muslims from entering the United States at least temporarily, impose extreme vetting on other entrants, start deporting undocumented immigrants from day one, and remove all federal funding from so-called sanctuary cities and other jurisdictions that refused to hand over undocumented detainees to the immigration authorities. But at nearly every turn, the courts constrained executive power or at least subjected it to exacting judicial review on every aspect of the president's immigration policy.

Just five days into his presidency Trump issued Executive Order 13768 to follow through on his promise to defund sanctuary cities. That order has been subject to a series of judicial defeats, including in the US District Court of Judge William H. Orrick in November 2017, the 7th Circuit US Appeals Court in April 2018, and the 9th Circuit US Court of Appeals in August 2018. The efforts of Trump and then Attorney General Jeff Sessions remain immobilised in the judicial system and sanctuary cities remain largely unimpeded by executive action.

Two days after issuing his order to outlaw sanctuary cities and just one week into his presidency, Trump signed Executive Order 13769 to bar citizens of seven mainly Muslim countries—including at least initially US legal permanent residents—from admittance to the United States. The "Muslim travel ban" as it quickly became known was a bold statement of intent, following up a specific and hugely controversial campaign pledge "calling for a total and complete shutdown of Muslims entering the United States until our country's representatives can figure out what the hell is going on." Stephen Miller wrote the order in a sloppy manner without input from relevant federal agencies, key Cabinet members, senior White House staff, Republican senators or friendly interest groups. It ignited a maelstrom of confusion, protest, derision, accusations of overt racism and of course legal challenges (Shear and Hirschfield 2017a). Above and beyond its contents, the document is an extraordinary indictment of the innocence and ignorance of the principal figures at the heart of the new administration who were naïve and arrogant enough to believe that Trump's lurid campaign promises could be actioned simply by reformatting them as an executive order and adding the president's signature. That it was immediately ensnared in the courts surprised no-one but the president and his closest confidants. Trump even had to fire Acting US Attorney General Sally Yates, appointed by Obama but now serving Trump, who defied her boss by refusing to defend the order in court.

A second executive order (EO 13780) published March 16 to address the problems of the first was also quickly blocked in the courts. Even a third and much watered-down effort in the form of presidential Proclamation 9645, issued in September, was declared unconstitutional by a federal district judge in Hawaii. The Supreme Court, though, intervened in December to let the third version go into effect pending a Spring 2018 hearing, which found in the administration's favor. Ultimately the form of the travel ban approved by the Supreme Court was a shadow of its former self, but nonetheless represents a considerable shift in established policy and serves as a primary exhibit for the argument that Trump's presidency is not ordinary in its policy outputs. But proponents of the Trump-is-extraordinary thesis need to judge the evidence in the round. The travel ban is an outlier. It is one of very few policy successes and needs to be assessed next to his many failures. Moreover, and importantly, the federal courts have historically allowed presidents considerable scope to determine who enters the United States, and in this case, the Supreme Court ultimately followed precedent and ruled in the administration's favor. Further, while Trump has authoritarian and monarchial tendencies, his actions are subject to judicial oversight as per all presidents. The constitution checked and balanced presidential ambition and the travel ban had to be altered considerably to pass muster.

If the travel ban is an outlier, Trump's efforts to shut down the Deferred Action for Childhood Arrivals (DACA) program, an executive action introduced by Obama in June 2012, which protects "Dreamers"—undocumented children brought to the US by their parents or others—actually offers sustenance to the Trump-is-ordinary thesis. An executive order on September 5, 2017, would have killed the program in March 2018, but intervening legal action revived it, allowing those already enrolled to renew their legal status and continue to live, work and study without fear of deportation (Shear and Hirschfield 2017b; Liptak 2018). A further ruling by a Federal District Court in April 2018 required the administration to reopen the program to new applicants. Judge John D. Bates criticized the administration's "meagre legal reasoning" and called the decision to terminate "arbitrary and capricious" (Sacchetti 2018; Jordan 2018). Much to Trump's mounting anger, DACA remains operational.

While largely thwarted in the courts, Trump hoped that the Republican-controlled legislature would be more amenable in supporting his immigration agenda and particularly his key pledge to build the wall along the Mexican border. Trump and his advisers saw the 2018 spending bill as the most likely source of a win. He had dreamed of $50 billion for his wall, asked for $25 billion, and got $1.6 billion as he signed the $1.3 trillion omnibus spending bill into law on March 23, 2018. And this small pot had to be spent on projects already authorized under current law, with none of it available to finance the imposing wall prototypes on display near San Diego which Trump had visited just days earlier. Trump was furious and called the bill ridiculous. He railed against it, even Tweeting a veto threat. At the White House signing ceremony, he pointed to the 2000 or so pages sat imposingly on the table next to him and promised never to sign anything like it ever again. But he did sign, albeit casting a dejected, betrayed, defeated figure. Moments later the right-wing Twittersphere lit up in anger with Trump-booster Ann Coulter to the fore. "Congratulations, President Schumer!" she immediately mocked Trump by suggesting he may as well concede his position to Democrat Minority Leader of the Senate, Chuck Schumer. She followed up by mentioning impeachment. Breitbart News was scathing; Fox News commentators saddened and betrayed with Jesse Watters decrying: "This was a huge defeat for the president on his signature issue. It's really, really bad. There's no way to spin it." Coulter warned:

> He had absolute rock-solid locked us in on support because we thought we wouldn't be betrayed.… [We] stood by him through thick and thin and thought this was finally something different, finally we have a politician who is not going to lie to us… Former Trumpers should put the fear of God in him.… He's failing. (Bruni 2018)

In an effort to persuade his base that the administration was doing something, anything on immigration in the continued absence of his "beautiful wall," Trump and Sessions floated and sought to enact a series of increasingly radical interventions. Trump suggested via Twitter that some money allocated to the military in the spending bill could be instead used to help build the border wall. After all, "building a great Border Wall, with drugs (poison) and enemy combatants pouring into our Country, is all about National Defense" (March 25, 2018). Once this idea was firmly rebuffed, Trump immediately tried to spin the $1.6 billion as a down payment with the rest to follow soon and that work on the wall would start immediately. This was followed on March 28 by 4 Tweeted photos of a border fence under construction and an accompanying text referring to the "start of our Southern Border WALL!" The photos were not of a wall, but an existing fence undergoing repair and reconstruction. Trump's nerves frayed as Fox News and other conservative outlets picked up the story of a caravan of hundreds of mainly Honduran migrants heading through Mexico toward the US border.

The culmination of these perceived threats and real policy failures was a dramatic announcement by Trump made without consultation with key White House advisers that "Until we can have a wall and proper security, we're going to be guarding our border with the military. That's a big step. We really haven't done that before, or certainly not very much before" (Davis 2018). Since Trump did not seek advice and knew little beyond what he had seen on Fox News, he was not aware that under a Title 32 deployment (where the federal government finances but the state governors command the troops), the National Guard is not permitted to enforce immigration law, engage in law-enforcement activities such as arresting suspected undocumented migrants or even using surveillance equipment to look into Mexico. The Guard would only be allowed to act in a support capacity to Border Patrol agents by, for example, mending vehicles or repairing border roads. Moreover, both Presidents Bush and Obama had sent National Guardsmen to the border, as had various border-state Governors. Indeed, Bush had sent 6000 in 2006, compared with Trump's 4000. Trump was following a well-established precedent of appearing to act decisively while changing little on the ground. Sending the military to the border was an act born of weakness, a desperate ploy to send the signal to his base that the president is in charge, making a difference on this most important issue, but in effect largely posturing. Even allies in the fight to reduce immigration were critical of his approach and results. Executive director of the restrictionist Center for Immigration Studies Mark Krikorian observed: "Some of it is just the guy at the end of the bar yelling his opinions—his gut reaction is to say we've got to send the military" (Davis 2018; Fernandez 2018).

The most radical intervention, however, was the decision to implement a zero tolerance strategy at the border in the face of an increase in unauthorized crossings. Families crossing illegally would be separated, with parents jailed and their children effectively incarcerated elsewhere in the United States. A White House official revealed that "The thinking in the building is to force people to the table." But House Minority Leader Nancy Pelosi's deputy chief of staff Drew Hamilton was more forthright: "They are holding the kids hostage" (both quoted in Scherer and Dawsey 2018). Large swathes of the American public were horrified, however, as stories and particularly images of children in what appeared to be cages began to appear in the media in early June. As public anger built, the administration's response was incoherent and chaotic. Secretary of Homeland Security Kirstjen Nielsen said there was no policy to separate families. Trump falsely claimed that a Democratic law required the administration to separate families and Congress needed to change the law because he could not do it by executive fiat. Sessions offered both the most honest and the most disingenuous responses, acknowledging that the administration designed the policy to deter illegal border crossers but also quoting scripture to defend the righteousness of his government's position. White House Press Secretary, Sarah Huckabee Sanders, picked up the theme in a press conference, arguing "it is very biblical to enforce the law" even though no law required children to be taken away from their parents.

After weeks of protests and in the face of blanket criticism around the world, Trump capitulated and signed an executive order on June 20, 2018, to end family separation. But he did not apologize or even appear contrite as he wielded his pen—"I didn't like the sight or feeling of families being separated," making his sentiments the subject of the story, not the thousands of families ripped apart—instead seeking to spin the order as a victory for both families and strong borders. While the episode dripped with hypocrisy, mendacity and even mindless cruelty, perhaps the most striking aspect is that the never-back-down president backed down in face of widespread revulsion. This most un-Trumpian response demonstrates in vivid Technicolor the spectacular failure of family separation policy.

After signing the executive order to sort out the self-inflicted family-separation mess, Trump managed to make the situation worse still by zigzagging wildly on what congressional Republicans should do. Having lit the touchpaper by canceling DACA, thrown oil onto the fire by separating children from their families, asked Congress to fix the mess, undermined all efforts to do so with a series of ill-informed and contradictory interventions, he then tweeted that "Republicans should stop wasting their time on immigration until after we elect more Senators and Congressmen/Women in November." When Trump finally threw his support behind a broad compromise bill designed to achieve consensus across conservative and moderate factions in the Republican House conference ($25 billion for the border wall, a reduction in legal immigration, allowing families to remain united in custody, while offering a path to citizenship for Dreamers), it was too late. With Democrats united in opposition and half of Republicans ignoring their president's call, it went down by 121–301 votes on June 27, 2018. The same day a federal judge critiqued the separation crisis as a "chaotic circumstance of the government's own making" and ruled that immigrant children must be reunited with their families.

Clearly, Trump pushed the implementation of immigration policy to the right, but much less so than is generally thought. The federal courts were key constraints, but Trump also faced considerable opposition within his own party. Moreover, while the Republican Party has become somewhat more conservative on immigration issues, these shifts preceded Trump and the party is still far from united. Trump placed himself assertively and vocally on one side of the division and sought to use executive power to back his rhetoric with short-term action, but was largely unsuccessful. He also failed to persuade his party to adopt radical reform in the policy area. But Trump has had some successes, especially on reducing refugee numbers and via behind-the-scenes efforts to restrict legal immigration by increasing administrative barriers to firms seeking to bring in skilled and unskilled temporary workers on H-1B and H-2B visas respectively as well as extending and complicating the citizenship process for permanent legal residents enlisted in the US armed forces (Jordan 2017). Nonetheless, these actions touch fewer lives and are substantively less important than Obama's executive action on Dreamers. Trump does not have his deportation force, his Muslim ban, or his wall, DACA and sanctuary cities continue to operate, and undocumented immigrants did not disappear from the United States in the first hour of his presidency as promised—"My first hour in office, those people are gone" (August 2016)—or any subsequent hour.

# 6    Trade and Infrastructure

Along with immigration, Trump's campaign for the presidency was built around opposition to what he called "unfair" and even "stupid" trade deals and the wider deleterious effects of global economic integration. Candidate Trump accused China of currency manipulation, dumping goods at low prices to destroy US industries, and intellectual property theft. He howled about the trade deficit—running at about $500 billion a year but frequently inflated by Trump—and painted it as a bottom-line "loss" for America. China, again, was fingered as a key culprit, accounting for roughly half the deficit. He promised to impose 45% tariffs on all Chinese imports. NAFTA was pronounced the worst trade deal of all time and the Trans-Pacific Partnership (TPP) almost as bad—"a horrible deal" which represented a "rape of our country."

Trump has maintained the anti-trade drumbeat in office and, in one view, matched it with some extraordinary actions. On day 3, he fulfilled his campaign promise and withdrew the United States from the twelve-nation TPP. Early in his term, he demanded renegotiations of NAFTA and the US-South Korea trade agreement. While these were significant changes, they were largely at the expense of US allies rather than the primary target of his invective, China. Indeed, leaving TPP even strengthened China's position in the Pacific. Trump refused to declare China a currency manipulator, arguing in a tweet, "Why would I call China a currency manipulator when they are working with us on the North Korean problem?" (Twitter, April 16, 2017).

Only as he entered his second year in office did Trump begin to act more directly on China. Some ground had been prepared by sharp increases in the number of investigations into unfair trade subsidies in smaller industries, but the first distinct move toward a feared trade war began on March 1 when Trump announced he would impose a 25% tariff on imported steel and 10% on aluminum for an unspecified "long period of time" and the next day tweeted to a bewildered world that "trade wars are good, and easy to win." Legal authority for Trump to impose tariffs without congressional approval rests in the 1962 Trade

Expansion Act (Section 232) subject to a finding by the Commerce Department that the relevant imports threaten national security. With the latter undefined, the president has considerable leeway to act.

Most presidents from Johnson to Obama have tried to use quotas or tariffs to protect the US steel industry against cheap foreign steel and generally without success. Steel prices rise and Americans pay more for goods incorporating steel, and counter-measures imposed by competitor nations curtail US exports. Trump was not much interested in this history of failure. China, the European Union (EU) and others predictably threatened retaliation. Trump then upped the ante by announcing a series of additional tariffs on Chinese goods worth $50 billion in addition to the tariffs on $3 billion worth of steel and aluminum imports. China matched Trump's $50 billion, which Trump claimed was "unfair retaliation" ("Rather than remedy its misconduct, China has chosen to harm our farmers and manufacturers," Trump tweeted). He counterpunched with another $100 billion, which China again matched, including carefully selected tariffs on products from farm-states which Trump won in 2016, including soybeans, sorghum, wheat, pigs and beef. The EU pondered increasing import duties on Harley Davidson motorcycles, made in Speaker Paul Ryan's district. Japan and Canada, close and loyal allies, wondered how their metal exports posed a threat to US national security. The most immediate and concerning consequence for Trump was that his announcements were met with a hail of criticism from well-organized business and farm interests and congressional Republicans.

Trump's efforts clearly represented a change in direction on trade policy and constitute a challenge to the Trump-is-ordinary argument. Nonetheless, many congressional Republicans representing economically exposed districts especially in the Rust Belt states are sympathetic to Trump's arguments, as are many in the Democratic Party and trade union movement. Moreover, his actions on trade have not come close to matching the grand scale of his campaign rhetoric. China has not been cited as a currency manipulator and while it faces considerable tariff barriers they fall far short of the 45% promised by Trump on the campaign trail. NAFTA lives on in a similar form, albeit with a different name. Trump's insistence that the US withdraw from the US-South

Korea trade deal (known as KORUS) was swerved by senior members of his own administration removing documents from his desk. Nor, more broadly, has Trump abandoned the pursuit of trade agreements, but prefers bilateral over multilateral ones. His challenges to China are hardly unprecedented. The Bush Jr. administration imposed tariffs on some steel products in 2002, like Trump, in an effort to try to tame the emerging giant, and Obama hit China with a tariff on tires.

Rather than characterizing Trump as anti-trade, his "fair trade" rhetoric captures a long-held sense on his part that free-trade agreements have disadvantaged the US and need to be revisited. His hardball tariff tactics are not designed to withdraw America behind a permanent or semi-permanent protective economic wall, but to create opportunities to renegotiate some trade deals on what he sees as fairer and better terms for the US. This is not to understate the very real risk of a trade war induced by Trump's protectionist moves, but a recognition that Trump's tariffs and fire and brimstone rhetoric are not as absolute as they first appear and are a means to the end of better trade deals:

> Tariffs have put the U.S. in a very strong bargaining position, with Billions of Dollars, and Jobs, flowing into our country.… If countries will not make fair deals with us, they will be 'Tariffed'. (Twitter, September 17, 2018)

On the issue of infrastructure, Trump's ambition also held the potential to contradict Republican orthodoxy given the tendency of Republicans to rely upon private markets, and not government spending, to deliver such projects. Trump highlighted the importance of the policy area in his 2018 State of the Union speech and released a proposal the next month. The key idea or hope was that $200 billion of government spending would leverage $1.5 trillion in investment from local government and the private sector. Parallel efforts would be made to speed up permitting processes. The proposal, however, triggered little legislative interest and a month later, Trump himself admitted that legislative action was unlikely until after the November midterms. Ironically, he chose an event designed to publicize and focus attention on the proposal to make this declaration. Again, Trump had challenged the orthodoxy and again, had little to show for it. Indeed, his promised program was a running joke. As Trump pledged action repeatedly during 2017, those pledges sounded increasingly hollow and became examples of Trump's willingness to speak off-the-cuff and with unrealistic expectations: "Nobody is so foolish as to believe that him saying, 'We're doing a big infrastructure bill,' means that the Trump administration is, in fact, doing a big infrastructure bill" (Yglesias 2017).

# 7    Conclusion

Trump was slow to act on many of his pledges that contradicted the Republican orthodoxy. He first resorted to executive action in most areas and although his State of the Union address proposed legislation on immigration and infrastructure and was followed by imposition of significant tariffs, he has not proved capable of securing major breaches with his party's ideological conventions in legislation. His executive actions did have major domestic and international repercussions, but Trump, like Obama before him, used executive action vulnerable to reversal by a successor. He was not constructing a long-term policy legacy. The existing order had not been overthrown, as Republicans did not accept the new Trump agenda and most of what he offered was either tempered by Congress or the courts, or he and his advisers adjusted to fit with established Republican positions. Instead, Trump looks like a rather ordinary Republican, both in terms of his agenda choices and his legislative achievements. His presidency, therefore, presents a contradiction to be explained. How did a president, apparently set upon tearing apart the establishment and bringing a revolutionary agenda to Washington, become a relatively standard Republican and win the supposed establishment's dedicated support in Congress? Trump's failure to overthrow the existing order requires a proper explanation. The next chapters seek to provide it.

# References

Bruni, Frank. 2018. "Ann Coulter to Donald Trump: Beware the Former Trumpers." *New York Times*, March 30.

Davis, Julie Hirschfield. 2018. "Trump Plans to Send National Guard to the Mexican Border." *New York Times*, April 3.

Dawsey, Josh. 2017. "Inside a $100,000-Per-Person Trump Fundraiser: Chicken, Asparagus and 20 Minutes of Talk." *Washington Post*, December 7.

Enten, Harry. 2017. "The GOP Tax Cuts Are Even More Unpopular Than Past Tax Hikes." *fivethirtyeight.com*, November 29. https://fivethirtyeight.com/features/the-gop-tax-cuts-are-even-more-unpopular-than-past-tax-hikes/.

Fahrenthold, David A., and Rosalind S. Helderman. 2016. "Trump Bragged That His Money Bought Off Politicians. Just Not This Time." *Washington Post*, September 7.

Fernandez, Manny. 2018. "National Guard Has Eyes on the Border. But They're Not Watching Mexico." *New York Times*, May 15.

Johnson, Jenna. 2018. "Drain What Swamp? Trump's Supporters Embrace Kavanaugh, Member of a Class They Once Rebuked." *Washington Post*, October 6.

Jordan, Miriam. 2017. "Without New Laws or Walls, Trump Presses the Brake on Legal Immigration." *New York Times*, December 20.

Jordan, Miriam. 2018. "U.S. Must Keep DACA and Accept New Applications, Federal Judge Rules." *New York Times*, April 24.

Kranish, Michael. 2018. "Trump's China Whisperer: How Billionaire Stephen Schwarzman Has Sought to Keep the President Close to Beijing." *Washington Post*, March 12.

Liptak, Adam. 2018. "Trump v. California: The Biggest Legal Clashes." *New York Times*, April 5.

Rein, Lisa, and Andrew Ba Tan. 2017. "How the Trump Era Is Changing the Federal Bureaucracy." *Washington Post*, December 30.

Resh, William G. 2015. *Rethinking the Administrative Presidency*. Baltimore, MD: Johns Hopkins University Press.

Sacchetti, Maria. 2018. "Federal Judge: Trump Administration Must Accept New DACA Applications." *Washington Post*, April 25.

Scherer, Michael, and Josh Dawsey. 2018. "Trump Cites as a Negotiating Tool His Policy of Separating Immigration Children from Their Parents." *Washington Post*, June 15.

Shear, Michael D., and Julie Hirschfield Davis. 2017a. "Stoking Fears, Trump Defied Bureaucracy to Advance Immigration Agenda." *New York Times*, December 23.

Shear, Michael D., and Julie Hirschfield Davis. 2017b. "Trump Moves to End DACA and Calls on Congress to Act." *New York Times*, September 5.

Thrush, Glenn. 2018. "Mulvaney, Watchdog Bureau's Leader, Advises Bankers on Ways to Curtail Agency." *New York Times*, April 24.

Watson, Kathryn. 2017. "'You All Just Got a Lot Richer,' Trump Tells Friends, Referencing Tax Overhaul." *CBSNews.com*, December 23. https://www.cbsnews.com/news/trump-mar-a-lago-christmas-trip/.

Woodward, Bob. 2018. *Fear: Trump in the White House*. London: Simon & Schuster.

Yglesias, Matthew. 2017. "Trump's Latest Big Interview Is Both Funny and Terrifying: POTUS Swings and Misses at the Softest Softballs." *Vox*, October 23. https://www.vox.com/policy-and-politics/2017/10/23/16522456/trump-bartiromo-transcript.

# 5

# Trump, the Media and the Public

## 1    Introduction

Trump promised a revolution. While that might sound like Trumpian exaggeration, the scale of his stated ambition is important. His campaign posed a challenge to the entire US political system, vowing to usurp those who held power in Washington and establishing an alternative establishment and agenda in their place. While most presidencies disrupt the existing order in one or more ways, Trump made spectacular, overarching promises that would have involved breaking down a series of structures, institutions, interests and ideas.

What followed however was sharply limited, both in terms of the volume of policy outputs and the degree of radical change, as the previous two chapters demonstrated. The ordinariness of Trump's presidency, however, stands in sharp contrast to the perceived extraordinariness of his promises and behavior. This discrepancy requires explanation, and that is the job of this and the next two chapters. The core argument is that at the heart of Trump's presidency is a grand strategic failure. It is, briefly stated, a failure of leadership. Trump's approach to leadership—what we have called his methodology—has

© The Author(s) 2019
J. Herbert et al., *The Ordinary Presidency of Donald J. Trump*,
Palgrave Studies in Political Leadership,
https://doi.org/10.1007/978-3-030-04943-0_5

seriously undermined his capacity to utilize the formal and informal powers of the presidency to effect the revolutionary change he promised. Most notably, his choice to cement his popularity among core supporters in the country at large via a highly partisan and culturally divisive communications strategy has driven away moderates and independents and reinforced the already determined opposition of Americans who identify with the Democratic Party.

Trump cultivates the idea that the American public love him and that he has an extraordinary appeal among voters. Conventional wisdom suggests that the support of his feverishly loyal "base" is what propelled him to office, that this was an extraordinary outcome, and that he is therefore spearheading a revolution in US politics that reflects deeper trends in the population toward the no-holds-barred, say-what-you-think, tear-down-what-you-cannot-abide politics that he seems to represent. Trump as the herald of the common people is certainly one of the elements of the president's self-image and one that observers argue is at the root of his extraordinary success. The analysis in Chapter 3, however, demonstrated that Trump's support in the presidential election of November 2016 was actually rather ordinary for a Republican candidate. What did not emerge was a significant shift either in the demographics of the voting blocs that secured the Electoral College for Trump, nor in the millions of voters across the nation who gave Hillary Clinton a larger share of the popular vote, if not the keys to the White House.

President Trump often argues in public, especially at the rallies that he holds for supporters, that the legitimacy of his presidency is based on his extraordinary appeal among the public and the high levels of support that he received to defeat Hillary Clinton. As a self-declared outsider president, Trump purports to be the authentic voice of the people in opposition to a corrupted Washington dominated by entrenched elites. Trump's basic strategy for governing relies to a large extent on public support, or at least his claims to have public support. His administration is founded on his desire to communicate with, and perhaps expand, his base. He believes that he can "go public" by winning popular support and so leading in Washington. In the longer term, building a Trump coalition is required for his reelection and to safeguard his long-term legacy. Trump needs the people. In order to win popularity, Trump has invested heavily in a communication strategy that allows him to reach out and speak directly to the American people, and in particular his base of core supporters.

Of course, "going public" is nothing new for presidents—indeed, it is usually one of the major advantages that presidents have over other US policy makers, since the president can ensure himself nationwide television airtime just by scheduling a major speech or an Address to the Nation in ways that members of the congressional leadership cannot. Trump's ability to use this method and build or draw on his perceived popularity is limited, however, by two major factors. First, large sections of the traditional media have emerged as a primary force criticizing and resisting the Trump presidency. This media opposition means that there is a difficult and complex relationship between the president and the "fourth estate". Second, the people themselves have given the Trump presidency a mixed reception. No matter how intensely the people at his rallies might profess their support for him, this has not necessarily spread to larger sections of the population. Republicans are more enthusiastic, but even they remain skeptical about many of Trump's less conventional policy ideas. As when they went to the polls, Republicans' support may be much more to do with their loyalty to their party rather than specific support for their president.

Trump has not been able to deliver the results he would have preferred. For all his experience as a television host and decades of engagement with the media, Trump's approach to communication has contributed greatly to his difficulties. The techniques he has used and the largely adversarial relationship that has developed with much of the media have done much to make the tasks of governing harder for Trump, costing him opportunities to lead the public and Washington. His communication, therefore, has done much to constrain his ability to win reforms and contributes substantially to the ordinary nature of his achievements. By examining Trump's media strategy and coverage and public responses to his presidency, the discussion below demonstrates that Trump's communications methodology has failed in its own terms. These very techniques render his presidency ordinary by constraining his opportunities for leadership and thus limiting his achievements. The chapter begins by exploring two presumptions that underpin Trump's extraordinary approach to communication: his base strategy and his philosophy and methods of communication.

## 2    The Base Strategy and Going Public

Every president has an interpretation of their ascent to office. It usually rests on a claim that their election victory was the most important in at least a generation and that it provides the basis for untrammelled authority and legitimacy in office and thus a mandate to enact the promises made while campaigning (Jones 1998, 2005). Trump is no exception, even though his grand claims to legitimacy are somewhat tenuous given the closeness of the election result (polling three million fewer votes than Hillary Clinton and winning the Electoral College by a relatively narrow 77-vote margin). While Chapter 3 demonstrated that Trump won office on a largely partisan vote, his own interpretation of his victory is deeply personalized. In his eyes, the victory was not a win for his party or its agenda, but a consequence of his personal appeal: Trump won, not the Republican Party. He is also clear, in his own mind, about who he appealed to. He believes that he triumphed by connecting with disillusioned and frustrated elements within the electorate, the so-called base or "my people" as Trump also refers to them. Imagined as culturally conservative, perhaps evangelical, white, lower- or middle-class Americans living in the non-coastal heartland, this group supported Trump even as the conventional wisdom claimed he could not be elected. Trump's sense of his legitimacy, therefore, is rooted in the lessons of his campaign to win the Republican nomination and then the presidency. It is also grounded in his struggle against what he perceives to be an out-of-touch and self-interested establishment elite—which includes elements of the Republican Party—and a subsequent belief that these elites should, as during the primaries, fall in line and join his revolution in the face of the widespread public support and particularly his base's overwhelming loyalty to him.

In Trump's view, he must retain the support of his base to maintain his legitimacy. He has thus carried his electoral strategy into office, deploying it as a governing strategy. This is quite unusual in that it dominates this president's approach to governing. He is far from the first elected official to recognize the utility of playing base politics, but most use it as an electoral strategy to fire up and turn out core supporters, which makes sense in a closely divided and polarized polity. Trump, in contrast, sees his appeal to his base as the foundation of his presidency. He has made little effort to take more moderate positions to win over independents and wavering middle-of-the-roaders. Much of his day-to-day activity as president is driven by his desire to maintain and enhance his relationship with the base. To do this, Trump relies heavily upon frequent direct communication. The president views politics as an activity lived out in the public sphere, particularly through the media. He believes that having mastered public communication in building the Trump brand and business he can pursue politics in a similar manner. Trump's personalized understanding of his 2016 victory, therefore, was accompanied by an unusually intense engagement with public politics by the president.

Trump's base strategy offers a twist on what political scientists call "going public." According to Kernell (1997, 2), this is

a strategy whereby a president promotes himself and his policies in Washington by appealing to the American public for support…forcing compliance from fellow Washingtonians by going over their heads to appeal to their constituents.

The rise of the electronic media and a series of developments in Washington, such as reforms to the internal workings of Congress in the 1970s, increased incidence of divided government and heightened polarization, have made presidential leadership a greater challenge. The number of people in Washington that need to be persuaded has increased and the people that the president needs to persuade are less easily persuaded. In this difficult environment presidents increasingly seek to utilize their popularity among the American public to leverage favorable outcomes in Washington. Going public "forces compliance" because the constituencies of Congress members overlap with the president's. If legislators vote against, or in some ways block, or even are not sufficiently enthusiastic about a popular presidential initiative, their constituents may punish them at the ballot box, kicking them out of office at the next opportunity.

Going public is by no means a uniquely modern phenomenon, but both the necessity and opportunity to go public have increased, according to Kernell (1997). But what does going public entail? It involves any activity in which presidents place themselves before the American people in an effort to promote themselves and their policy ideas. This could be done via a prominent set piece televised address to the nation, an interview on 60 Minutes, or a carefully scheduled series of public events built around a particular theme. The list is virtually endless—Trump favors tweeting and mega-rallies in deep red states—but the aim is always to increase support for the president and his policies among the American public in order to leverage the backing of politicians in Washington. Thus, in going public, Trump has adopted a strategy very familiar to observers of the presidency. But he does it with a number of unusual and important Trumpian twists, which collectively ensure its failure and help render his presidency ordinary. These ideas are developed below.

## 3    Trump: The New Great Communicator?

One of President Ronald Reagan's nicknames was "The Great Communicator." While he lacked a forensic command of the details of policies, even his own, Reagan was able to invoke a vision of what America should be that appealed across partisan boundaries. His language and grammar were uncomplicated and his manner folksy, and he was also able to connect to audiences on an emotional and visceral level, a skill perhaps innate and then honed through many years as a professional actor, sports commentator and aspiring presidential candidate.

Trump believes he, too, is a master of communication. From his early days as a property developer in New York City, Trump used the media to construct an image of himself as a hugely successful businessman and self-made billionaire. That he was able to do this despite being born into great privilege, despite his business being bankrolled by his rich father to the tune of over $400 million and evidence of large-scale tax avoidance, suggests Trump's belief in his powers of communication is not without merit (Barstow et al. 2018). The young and publicity-hungry Trump was able to insert himself into his city's imagination by constantly feeding intimate, and even sometimes true, stories about his business and private life to the tabloid press—in his own telling, he was a deal-making playboy who befriended, seduced and occasionally married some of the world's most beautiful women (Kranish and Fisher 2016). He megaphoned and fictitiously multiplied his wealth, badgering and duping *Forbes* journalists to over-inflate his ranking in the magazine's rich list. Trump also made much of his "ardent philanthropy," even if his giving was characteristically ostentatious, never private, done in pursuit of an image, and often falsely inflated to garner positive publicity (Fahrenthold 2016). Trump sought to build an image and brand through continually tracking, feeding and manipulating the media. He learnt which actions would win him attention in an intensely competitive media environment, and especially that being coy about one's achievements was not part of the plan. As he noted in *The Art of the Deal*:

A little hyperbole never hurts. People want to believe that something is the biggest and the greatest and the most spectacular. I call it truthful hyperbole. It's an innocent form of exaggeration—and a very effective form of promotion.

As Trump moved into politics, he translated these techniques to his new profession. Exaggeration and outrageous claims—such as the "birther" allegations that President Obama was either not born in the United States, was a secret Muslim, or both—won him widespread coverage. His 2016 primary and general election victories ratified this approach in his eyes. Manipulating the media seemed a successful means to conduct a political career and Trump therefore has continued to apply his winning formula by focusing his presidency on public communication, the media and his image. For Trump, they are his highest priorities. Indeed, they are his political reality and the political game is about dominating media coverage.

To do this, Trump spends considerable time and energy tracking his media coverage. He watches between four and eight hours of television a day, largely Fox. He rises early and tunes into "Fox and Friends" in his private White House living quarters—labeled "executive-time" by his close advisers—and rarely gets to work before 11 a.m. (Sargent 2018). Trump's viewing is complemented by a rolling crowd-sourcing process in which he reflects upon his coverage in conversations with associates and considers how it impacts his image. Katy Tur, who covered his 2016 campaign argues:

> Banter is part of his process. He's a person who crowd-sources. He likes to get everyone's take. He'll call anyone who will listen – friends, loved ones, business partners, lawyers, rivals, and, yes, even reporters. He was famous for it in the New York tabloids – calling to hear opinion, spread gossip, or just hype himself. (Tur 2017)

Trump continues this practice as president and has developed especially close relationships with Fox News and its hosts. Sean Hannity, Jeanine Pirro, Lou Dobbs and others have become informal but close advisers. Hannity often speaks with Trump after his weekday show and is even referred to as "shadow Chief-of-Staff" by some in the White House (Nuzzi 2018). Fox's worldview and Trump's understanding of his political appeal to his base are closely allied. Each touts a view of American values in peril and each blames Washington and its politicians—mainly but not only Democrats—for the problems. The lineage of this approach to news can be traced from the right-wing radio-talk populism of the 1990s. Trump lived in this world, appearing regularly on The Howard Stern Show and developing a sense of how communication works in these environments: always irreverent, sometimes misogynistic and unbound by elite conventions. Subsequently, Trump has transferred this style of communication from narrowcasting to the Washington mainstream, and Fox is his new talk radio. Watching Fox is a means for Trump to monitor how those with a similar worldview are interpreting events and how those events will be understood by the base. Most notably, of course, this includes monitoring how his own coverage is developing and, by extension, how the base receives his actions as president. But it also means that in this rather surreal presidency, the most powerful man in the world spends hours each day watching Fox News covering him.

One of Trump's guiding principles is to dominate media coverage in order to fire up his core supporters. Almost always, Trump's aspiration is to grab the headline in the current news cycle. After a career of image-building honed in the intensely competitive environment of the New York media, then mastered further in 14 seasons at the helm of his reality TV show The Apprentice, Trump regards himself as an expert in winning attention and grabbing headlines. He is right. This talent is now enhanced by social media, which gives the president the means to communicate with his base and the wider world instantly from the Oval Office or his White House bedroom. In his thinking, social media, specifically Twitter, allows him to bypass the ("fake") mainstream media and speak directly to the American people (Twitter, June 16, 2017). While Trump has exaggerated his number of followers by tens of millions, his basic claim that social media allows him to circumvent the traditional media has some validity. It is a powerful tool that previous presidents did not enjoy or, in Obama's case, did not fully grasp the possibilities of. Nonetheless, it would be a mistake to think that Twitter is Trump's only, or even main, method of communication. While he frequently berates what he calls the mainstream or fake news media, he knows full well the importance of it to his presidency. He thus consciously and frequently attempts to manipulate and win coverage from it. He provides material for headline-grabbing stories and utilizes his social media posts to leverage more coverage in the conventional press. Despite claiming to "go around them," his communication is designed to maximize the attention paid to his words by the establishment media that he professes to loathe. He recognizes the attention the conventional media will pay to his every public utterance if he makes those utterances interesting enough. Trumpian politics, therefore, is designed for mass media consumption as well as direct appeals to his base via social media.

Four key innovations in Trump's approach to communication are his personal control, responsiveness, need to dominate media coverage at all times and unconcern about being consistent. First, Trump's communication is deeply personalized. Equipped with his phone, Trump personally guides and often implements his administration's communications strategy. His hands-on approach reflects his belief that he is the best person to run what he regards as the most important part of his presidency. Undeniably, Trump has a sharp instinct for what will win media attention. He knows journalists need "copy" and headlines and offers them both in spades. He specializes in setting up confrontations—or "beefs"—with politicians and others that can run for days or months. Offering controversial presidential statements that challenge convention is another technique. Trump offers provocative opinions to draw attention and searches for the controversy that will launch a thousand online postings. Trump is not, though, all about picking fights. He is also very careful to pitch his messages in simple formats. Much of his communication, particularly in tweets but often on the stump too, is low-level sloganeering ("build the wall," "lock her up," "drain the swamp") with little explanation or underlying substance to what is said. The president's rhetorical style is distinctly original. Kathleen Hall Jamieson and Doron Taussig (2017) deconstructed Trump's "rhetorical signature" as "spontaneous and unpredictable... Manichean, evidence-flouting, accountability-dodging [and] institution disdaining" (2017, 23). Trump is also able to display his emotions and character traits—including anger, humor, confidence, arrogance and even ignorance—and thus present a more relatable, human side. In contrast, such emotions and traits are often deliberately suppressed by more conventional politicians. Both online and in person, Trump defies convention.

Second, responsiveness is also key. Trump's Twitter account (and continuing media attention to his use of it) has allowed the president to choose when in the news cycle he wants to intervene, although he is not slow to use public speech in a similar manner. Often this timing appears to be dictated by the emergence of stories unfavorable to the president. His tracking of what is being said about him often leads to immediate responses to any slight or negative headline, such as those around the investigation of Russian involvement in the 2016 election. He can respond quickly to any story that might compromise his image, using a counter-punching style that is uncompromising and direct and is itself likely to lead to more coverage. Trump may even insert himself directly into coverage by calling into Fox News. His interventions can be directly critical of a story, or a complete distraction, but Trump often wins attention for his statements, either changing the subject or delivering his message against the prevailing headlines. His intense sensitivity to the media's current headlines, and responsiveness, generates coverage and can make the president appear a master of distraction.

Third, Trump wants to dominate the media's political coverage and is keenly aware of the type and tone of political stories that will thrust him onto the newspapers' front pages and to the top of the evening news shows. Thus, his communication has often involved taking sides in culture war stories. With absolute positions expressed on both sides, and audiences easily outraged by positions opposed to their own, Trump recognizes media catnip when he sees it. Playing on people's fury, he delivers presidential communication much as right-wing talk radio and Fox News cover it, with strong, controversial opinions and loud, polarized and fiery debate, often tweeting in CAPITAL LETTERS to emphasize his rage and shout his points. The 140 and now 280 character format is perfect for his brand of short, sharp, pointed insults and proclamations. With his embrace of social media, Trump believes that he has a strong sense of how public politics is best practiced to draw public attention in the twenty-first century. And he is uncompromising and fearless. Populist messages are pitched according to the predicted response of his base audience, rather than the standards used by a Washington elite judging a presidency.

This is liberating, allowing Trump to experiment with unfamiliar techniques of presidential communication, and feeds into the fourth novel aspect of Trump's communication strategy. He feels unburdened by a need for factual accuracy or constancy in his communications. He is able to contradict himself and feels little obligation to maintain any ideological consistency. Where other political elites strive for consistency of message and precisely chamfer their statements in order to position themselves at a particular point on the ideological spectrum or to appeal to certain interests without offending others, Trump does not appear bound by any need to project a coherent ideological worldview. He has rejected elite standards of consistency, and with them, many of the concerns of intellectual conservatism. While other Republican elites are committed to principles such as free trade or small government, Trump ignores such constraints, instead taking contradictory positions and performing spectacular volte faces. He can, for example, eulogize about his tax cuts while simultaneously imposing taxes in the form of tariffs and $12 billion subsidy programs to compensate for the tariffs' impact. He is able to rage against the damage being done by cheap imports and unfettered immigration and globalization while simultaneously claiming the economy is booming and everything is rosy in Trump's America.

Most presidents occasionally use trial ballooning, the device of making an announcement (or leaking a proposal off the record) to judge its popularity before pushing forward with a course of action. Trump uses trial ballooning far more frequently and openly than his predecessors. It carries few risks because ideological consistency is not part of the Trump brand and he is unafraid to reverse his position in an instant. Indeed, Trump uses trial ballooning so frequently that his communication strategy can be viewed as persistent experimentation or "conditional positioning." He constantly tests the ground with announcements to see how media and base will respond and steps back when the response is too hostile. For example, Trump moved to end Obama's Dreamers' program that protected undocumented children from deportation but the very next week, perhaps sensing the negative responses to his action, tweeted that Dreamers were "good, educated and accomplished young people who have jobs, some serving in the military." Trump was playing both sides of the argument, seemingly without any serious concern about the apparent contradictions.

Relatedly and fortunately, Trump is tolerant of negative coverage— far more so than his predecessors—and sometimes even welcomes it. In *The Art of the Deal*, Trump (1987) suggested that the key quality is to be the center of attention, whether the coverage is good or bad. In Trump's political incarnation, Ezra Klein suggests his approach is similar:

Attention creates value, at least for [Trump]. Before Trump, every politician hewed to the same basic rule: You want as much positive coverage, and as little negative coverage, as possible. Trump upended that. (Klein 2018)

Trump's strongest desire is to dominate coverage, not least because that means his political opponents are not getting the coverage that they need or want. This calculation allows Trump to intervene with apparently less care as to what he is disrupting or how he is causing offense. But Trump also knows that causing offense can help his messaging. The controversy created by causing offense generates still more coverage, reinforces his message and ensures Trump is the story.

## 4    Trump's Message

Trump clearly has the tools to deliver a highly personalized communication strategy and thinks communication a high enough priority to warrant his focus. The nature of his communication is shaped by a set of unorthodox attributes designed to win media attention and promote himself. Trump does not care, and even celebrates, that his approach to communications breaks established rules of elite politics. But if his approach is unusual, what messages is Trump seeking to deliver to the American people generally and his base specifically? There are three core elements. Trump is a bold and decisive leader. Trump stands against the establishment. Trump puts America First.

It was noted above that Trump sees his election victory in personal terms. People voted for him and his leadership skills. In this view, then, Trump and his leadership is the story, rather than his policies or agenda. The purpose of presidential communication is thus self-promotion, reinforcing simple messages about his actions and leadership. The president is the brand. He writes and speaks frequently about his actions and his emotions, emphasizing his control and his decisions. The president's executive actions have a particularly prominent role to play in this image-building. His swathe of executive orders, from the high-profile

Muslim travel ban to largely symbolic proclamations, symbolize him as a man of action fulfilling his mandate for change (Mayer 1999). There is something deeply theatrical about the signing ceremonies in Oval Office as Trump's "stroke of the pen" appears to transform the political system. Moreover, these executive actions usually guarantee news coverage and can be released when Trump chooses, offering him another weapon in the battle for headlines.

The scorched-earth rejection of the established political order was central to Trump's campaign for office. But the move into the White House threatens Trump's narrative. He now faces a classic outsider's dilemma. He must work in Washington while remaining not of Washington. He risks becoming identified with the establishment he sought to repudiate (Skowronek 1997). While this dilemma cannot be resolved in practice, Trump has a rhetorical solution. His outsiderness is burnished by regular and dramatic expression of conflict with the establishment in which he is portrayed as the perpetual rebel. To maintain this narrative, Trump must find a range of ways to be seen as rejecting the establishment. He has very ably identified foils for his "Trump versus the World" approach, including significant figures in both political parties (especially congressional leaders), the courts, his own cabinet, the media, the FBI and even the Federal Reserve bank. For example, all presidents have disputes with other elites in their own party, but employ rhetoric to minimize or shroud the differences. Trump feels no such compulsion toward unity and instead attacks his fellow partisans publicly and with relish. This is not just a matter of temperament but a matter of "political calculation" (Dawsey 2017). His cries of "foul" merely serve to confirm the message that Trump stands alone as the disruptor of a rigged system, the only true representative of the American people.

Alongside his personal leadership and his anti-establishment messages, Trump advocates a series of signature issues rooted in his America First and ethnocentric nationalism to emphasize the difference between himself and the elite's established political order. Trump is willing to give profile to subjects that divide his own party, particularly when there is a gap between the opinions of the elite and his base. Immigration, trade policy and political correctness are key examples. Trump is particularly effective at using events to symbolize his positions. He drew much attention for his condemnation of American football player Colin Kaepernick and other US athletes who kneel in protest at racial injustice when the national anthem is played before sporting events, rather than standing hand on heart. Trump declared that sports franchise owners should fire the offending players, sparking further protests including some against his presidency. Even more controversially, following the murder of 32-year-old paralegal Heather Heyer during a protest against a white supremacist rally in Charlottesville, Virginia, in August 2017, Trump failed to directly condemn racist and Nazi protestors. The president appeared instead to condone their actions by pointing to "hatred, bigotry and violence on many sides," thus dominating the political agenda, giving oxygen and legitimacy to the so-called alt-right, and playing to the racial and cultural biases of many of his base. In each case, Trump placed himself against "political correctness" and by implication with white Americans less tolerant of the high profile given to racial issues in US politics. Trump also used the testimony of Christine Blasey Ford during Brett Kavanaugh's confirmation hearings to suggest that American men—and implicitly himself—are facing a torrent of unfounded allegations of sexual assault. "It's a very scary time for young men in America," said Trump. These controversial and provocative arguments and actions allow Trump to present himself as fulfilling his populist mandate by clashing with elites, kicking out at alleged political correctness, and representing the concerns of his base, but without any direct action on policy. Trump plays symbolic politics frequently and brutally.

In sum, Trump's communication strategy is unorthodox in both process and message. But unorthodox does not necessarily mean ineffective. After all, it won him the presidency of the United States. The key question, however, is whether it can help him win as president and make his presidency a successful one. Has Trump's communication strategy built support for himself and his policies that he can in turn leverage to get wins in Washington?

# 5     Trump and the "Fake" Fourth Estate

Trump's communication techniques were intended to place himself front and center in the nation's political life, even more so than presidents usually are. There is substantial evidence that his efforts have been hugely successful in this regard. The Shorenstein Center's analysis of his first one hundred days showed Trump receiving three times the coverage of other presidents at a similar point in their presidency (Shorenstein 2017). His constant appeals for attention have led to an extraordinary period for presidential media coverage. Trump's techniques, perhaps helped by events, have created a presidential story moving from subject to subject at unprecedented speed.

At the center of this story has been Trump's strange and ambivalent relationship with the media industry. Trump has not held back with his negative views of traditional print and television media, encapsulating in a tweet on February 17, 2017, the abusive attitude he had repeated over and over in his stump speeches while campaigning and just as frequently once he became president:

> The FAKE NEWS media (failing @nytimes, @NBCNews, @ABC, @CBS, @CNN) is not my enemy, it is the enemy of the American People!

He does not respect the role that a free press plays in democratic societies—which is to hold power to account as the so-called fourth estate—or recognize that it enjoys constitutional protection. He instead seeks to delegitimize the media by repeatedly labeling it "fake news" and disparaging journalists as "horrible, horrendous people" suffering from "Trump Derangement Syndrome" who are "unpatriotic" for scrutinizing the government's decision-making process. His tirades portray a vast network of media organizations conspiring to destroy his presidency, which in part explains why his attacks on it are more vehement and confrontational than any president before him, including Nixon. He tends to exclude Fox News of course, which is generally a booster for the Republican president, even though at times it too is critical of him or the positions he takes. As noted above, though, while the media are an excellent foil for a president who wishes to demonstrate his rejection of the establishment, Trump knows that he must work with the mainstream media in order to deliver his message to the American people. After all, the vast majority of Americans do not follow their president on Twitter or watch Fox News' coverage of him.

Trump may be winning coverage, but much of it is profoundly negative. For all of Trump's professed expertise in and commitment to communication, coverage of his presidency is overwhelmingly negative both in absolute terms and relative to previous incumbents. Some outlets appear to have established themselves as key nodes of resistance against Trump's presidency, many of whom Trump name-checked in his enemy-of-the-people tweet above. A content analysis by the Pew Research Center of over three thousand news stories published by 24 separate media outlets (newspapers, TV, radio and websites) during Trump's first 100 days—the honeymoon period when new presidents can usually expect sympathetic coverage—found that his coverage was overwhelmingly negative. Overall, 44% of the stories analyzed by Pew were negative compared to 11% positive, a ratio of 4 to 1 against Trump, while 45% were neutral. The coverage was also skewed 3 to 1 toward issues of leadership and character rather than policy issues (Mitchell et al. 2017).

In comparison with previous presidents' media coverage, Trump fares very poorly. Pew found that during the first 60 days their presidencies, Bill Clinton had 27% positive media coverage, George W. Bush had 22%, and Barack Obama an extraordinary 42% positive. Just 5% of Trump's coverage was positive. In terms of negative coverage, Trump's figure was even more extraordinary compared with his three predecessors. Clinton and Bush both had 28% negative, Obama had just 20% negative, but Trump's coverage in the same 60-day period was 62% negative. And compared with these other presidents, more of the stories about Trump were not focused on substantive policy issues but rather on questions of character and leadership (Mitchell et al. 2017). Pew's findings are broadly backed up by another study of Trump's first 100 days by Harvard political scientist Thomas E. Patterson. Excluding neutral content, Patterson (2017) found 80% of Trump's coverage was negative and just 20% positive, a 4 to 1 ratio that precisely replicates Pew's assessment.

Moreover, across all outlets studied, there was no single issue on which Trump enjoyed positive coverage. Even on the economy, 54% of all (non-neutral) news stories were negative. On the question of his fitness for office, 81% of stories were negative, and on immigration the negativity rating rose to 96%—even Fox's immigration coverage was 81% negative (Patterson 2017).

While Trump is sometimes portrayed, and likes to portray himself, as a master manipulator of the media through his distraction and confrontation techniques, he has clearly been no more successful in controlling what journalists write or say about him than his predecessors. All presidents suffer this democratic curse; Nixon warned his associates that "the press is your enemy…because they're trying to stick the knife right into our groin." Journalists in the US are trained to chase the story, to question authority. It is a complicated relationship, but at least since the unraveling of the Vietnam War and the Watergate scandal there has been a generally adversarial position between the media and the White House. Trump should hardly be surprised that media outlets allocate so many headlines to allegations of collusion between his 2016 campaign and the Russian state or the episodic failures of his healthcare initiatives.

The negative coverage has inflicted direct costs upon Trump. His exposure to the usual scrutiny of the media has not just led to public criticism, but to a torrent of investigations. The fourth estate has become a key node of resistance against the Trump presidency. While one can quantify the number of stories based on investigative journalism—one in five of all stories about him, according to Pew—it is difficult to judge their effect especially in the short term. But America's journalists have distinguished themselves in their efforts to uncover nepotism, collusion, corruption, incompetence, ignorance and deep discord at the heart of the administration. In turn, some of the investigative reporting that exposes the administration's wrongdoings and weaknesses has triggered legal challenges. Trump himself has acknowledged the extent to which these multiple cases drain his time and mental capacity. These investigations have come unusually early in Trump's presidency compared with other presidents such as Nixon, Reagan and Clinton whose presidencies were dogged by scandals that only came to light or intensified later in their presidencies. These direct costs are only part of the damage incurred by Trump's approach to the media. He has gambled that his media tactics and consequent negative mainstream coverage will not harm his presidency. While he is proving effective at grabbing headlines, he does so at the cost of focusing the political agenda. Furthermore, Trump has created a direct competition over how the administration should be understood. Trump tells one story, the mass media largely another. Trump's going public strategy, and potentially his reelection and legacy, rely to a great extent on the outcome of the contest.

# 6    Focusing the Agenda

Presidents who want to achieve major reforms must command the Washington agenda. If they manage to do so then they can focus the political system, including the media and potentially the public, on the work the president wants done. That focus must be achieved in the face of much competition for agenda space. Focusing the system on the president's agenda is, therefore, a crucial presidential task. Yet Trump seems unaware of, or unconcerned about, this task. In sharp contrast to the idea of focusing on key issues and proposals, Trump's communication tactics offer an ever-changing and fractured agenda. In pursuing coverage as an end in itself or sometimes to firm up his base, the president moves from subject to subject quickly and unpredictably, and often without consultation with the rest of the White House, let alone potential allies on Capitol Hill or in the media. This approach limits his capacity to govern.

The subjects of Trump's communication, and the techniques he uses, distract attention from his policy priorities. Trump is very interested in being seen to perform leadership personally, rather than promoting his policy agenda. His attacks on the media as "fake news," on Democrats as "nasty," and on some members of his own party as "unelectable" may be effective demonstrations that Trump is disruptive and confronts elites, but they do not help build support for his key agenda items. His focus on controversies surrounding his personal legitimacy has the same effect. From the first moment of his presidency when he sent out Press

Secretary Sean Spicer to claim his inauguration crowd was the largest in history through his claims about being one of the most successful presidents ever, Trump has maintained a self-aggrandizing but easily ridiculed posture. Moreover, a substantial proportion of his communication is occupied with vitriolic attacks on those investigating administration scandals. He also appears susceptible to fits of personal pique and indulges in petty squabbles frequently. For example, the decision in the Trump University case triggered messages from Trump personally condemning Judge Gonzalo Curiel. His tweeted interventions simply drew more attention to the case and Trump's failed business venture. The president struggles to compartmentalize his personal and public lives, and much presidential communication is actually focused on the former rather than the latter. Another large chunk is devoted to image-building and the Trump brand.

Even when Trump communicates about matters that are more general than his personal legitimacy and brand, it is often on controversial subjects that have little direct connection to policies that the federal government might change and even less to the policies his administration is, at that time, trying to advocate. Trump tweets and speaks about events that he either has no intention or even capacity to do anything about, or appears to deliberately stoke controversy about events that might warrant a more measured presidential response. He does so either because the political posture appeals to his base or distracts attention from other stories. Posturing as a combatant on the right wing of the culture wars is a primary example. His symbolic politics, as exemplified by the Kaepernick and Charlottesville furores, may command column inches and retweets, but it shifts focus away from his policy priorities and so fails to make Washington pay attention to his programs. All-in-all, @realDonaldTrump involves a great deal of communication that has very little to do with policy.

Winning attention should be easy for a president. It is not unusual for presidents to set the news agenda by saying or doing something. They do so quite naturally by dint of their centrality to US politics, their global significance, and the fact that to a large extent the media relies on official sources to signal what is going to happen, what is important and how to interpret events. Presidents and their advisers do so as a matter of routine in a more manipulative way—deliberately leaking information or a perspective on an issue, manufacturing a news event through a scheduled speech or summit meeting, making an international visit or hosting a significant person or event or any number of other examples of spin control. This media management has been a staple of White House tactics for at least 40 years, coming into its own during the Reagan administration and developing levels of sophistication since. Trump's specific tactics and the extreme levels to which he is willing to go to grab the headline might well be unique, but seeking to manage the 24-hour news cycle is actually a very standard goal of all modern presidencies.

But much of what Trump does is negative agenda control, often firefighting some intended controversy or unintended gaff by the president and seeking to displace it from the headlines with yet another controversy. Achieving negative agenda control, though, should not be mistaken as an achievement. Effective leadership demands positive agenda control: The process of establishing what the news is about, not what it ignores. It is one thing to dominate any given 24-hour news cycle, but quite another to manage the agenda to focus on the president's policy priorities. The latter is a resource to generate, maintain and use for advantage in dealing with legislators and interests in the policymaking process. Trump's disruptive approach to politics, lived out through a hyper-responsiveness to today's media headlines, has a cost: a fragmented, scattershot narrative for his presidency. Trump's responsiveness to media concerns and desire to distract creates inconsistent communication. In turn, this contributes to a public face of the presidency that is a convoluted saga of insults, personal feuds, position reversals and controversies. That has been useful to the administration amid a rolling series of scandals, but means that Trump does not control the message or meaning of his presidency. He perceives no problem with that approach, but it is an exercise in self-sabotage and a major contributor to his lack of policy success. Trump fails to concentrate Washington's attention on the subjects he needs to pursue to achieve genuine change. As he drags the agenda hither and thither and flips and flops positions on key issues, it becomes unclear what the president wants and where he stands. Trump layers distracting concerns over his core messages and often creates stories through his self-contradiction. In a system where plenty of players wish to take the agenda in other directions, Trump's inconsistency helps his opponents; rather than having to face voters, activists, funders or interest groups fired up by consistent presidential attention to an issue, those opponents can simply wait, safe in the knowledge that Trump will soon move the agenda onto the next distraction and relieve the pressure. Trump fails to use the opportunity the office provides to exert political pressure.

Trump's negative control of the agenda, achieved through distraction and disruption, does maintain the media spectacle, but it costs him positive agenda control and undermines his capacity to achieve presidential leadership. He squanders presidential resources, undermines allies keen to support him and enables opponents to block his initiatives. Trump dominates media coverage, receiving unusual levels of attention even for a president, yet is not able to dominate the agendas within other political institutions, most notably Congress.

Nowhere has this been clearer than in the administration's communication around the issue of infrastructure. This key campaign promise to rebuild America's infrastructure has been repeatedly undermined by distractions, mainly from the president himself. The White House prepared meticulously for an "infrastructure week" in June 2017, for example, but Trump damaged the message by fighting on Twitter and in the media with London Mayor Sadiq Khan and blaming his own Department of Justice for watering down the Muslim travel ban (Zanona 2017). The "forthcoming infrastructure reform" became a running joke in coverage of Trump's first year as the president's communication undermined his administration's own carefully laid plans (Casselman et al. 2017). Similarly, his administration's efforts to coordinate a media blitz to celebrate the allegedly most successful first 500 days of any presidency were eclipsed on the same day by Trump's startling tweet that he had the right to pardon himself.

The infrastructure example also points to a further problem of Trump's communication strategy. Focusing the agenda is only one part of the process; administrations must also develop effective messaging around each policy proposal. The narrative around each item on the agenda must be controlled in a manner that increases the probability of presidential success. The president who wishes to sell his agenda needs a coherent messaging operation; any substantial reform is likely to trigger opposition from those who will disseminate criticisms and often misrepresent the president's proposals. The presidency must prepare and distribute an elaborate but precise series of messages, with variants pitched to the needs and sensitivities of different interested communities, to meet this opposition. White Houses often develop complex rollout plans that map out public and congressional strategies for the revealing and selling of a new proposal, with the intention of maximizing support. The machinery of the White House is potentially a formidable tool for propagating messages which, with careful timing and coordination, can encourage support for presidential initiatives. Such efforts demand coordination of the White House. There is clear evidence that Trump's communications team recognize the importance of such work; they identify clearly stated priorities as their themes of the week and prepare events to highlight the president's concerns and cast his initiatives in a positive light.

However, if that machinery is unaware of the president's priorities and the timing of announcements, it is less effective. Trump's approach to communication undercuts his communications team and prevents the effective deployment of these valuable resources. His White House cannot plan to sell his policies effectively because they are unclear what his priorities will be or how they might change on any given day, let alone week or month. Trump's tendency to release, or reverse, policy in an instant and in public has left staffers shocked by policy announcements and, importantly, poorly placed to support the new policy. For example, Trump signed a joint communiqué with other G7 members at the end of their summit in June 2017, but then changed his mind within hours and decided not to endorse it, publicly blaming Canadian Prime Minister Justin Trudeau in a pair of blunt tweets, calling him "very dishonest & weak." Trump's scant communication about policy detail produces incomplete and often incoherent messaging and sabotages attempts to coordinate the extensive resources of the presidency. Where an administration would hope to issue a series of carefully tailored messages for different audiences, staffers and surrogates have not been provided with relevant talking points, so questions about potential flaws in, and opposition to, policy proposals go unanswered. Potential allies are confronted with half-developed policies (a process reinforced by Trump's disrespect for the policy process) and little guidance on how to defend them. While White House staff scramble to provide scaffolding around presidential policy announcements, Trump moves on to the next issue, further sabotaging any attempt to achieve coherence (Green 2017; Nelson 2018; Wolff 2018; Woodward 2018). Timing and coordinating policy rollouts is impossible when the president may change positions or make and announce policy decisions without explanation or notice. The communication resources of the presidency cannot be coordinated. Rather than proving a master of the media's agenda, Trump's efforts further distract from his policy priorities. Trump's deeply personalized communication tactics squander the resources of the presidency and constrain his capacity to achieve a focused agenda and coherent messaging.

## 7 Trump and the Public

Presidents design their communication efforts to rally people behind their policy agenda and increase or at least cement their own popularity. Judging Trump's success therefore requires consideration of the president's approval levels and the popularity of the policies he advocates.

Compared to his predecessors, Trump's approval ratings have been relatively low, suggesting that his strategy of focusing on communication has not been a success. Indeed, on entering office Trump set new records; no new president had ever been so unpopular. Where presidents have often been afforded a "honeymoon" period of relatively high approval ratings in their early months in office, Trump had no such luck. His first quarter average approval rating was 41%, way below the presidential norm according to Gallup's polls (Jones 2018). Notably, Trump also achieved record disapproval ratings: a month after taking office his overall disapproval rate was 53%. This majority disapproval endured through to the end of his second summer in office, barely wavering (Brenan 2018a). Nor did his approval ratings recover, settling immediately into the 36–42% range that would characterize his first six quarters in office (Jones 2018).

Over time, by stabilizing in the 36–42% range, Trump's approval ratings have become more normal relative to his predecessors. Presidents usually experience a decline in their ratings after their honeymoon period. While those ratings do not normally sink as low as Trump's (only Carter had a lower average rating in the sixth quarter of his presidency), recent presidents such as Reagan, Clinton and Obama all endured job approval ratings of less than 50% at an equivalent point in their first terms. After a difficult start, Trump was not in an exceptionally bad position. Notably, though, he did not have to contend with poor economic conditions as his low-rated predecessors had done. His unpopularity was achieved despite a thriving economy.

The explanation of Trump's return to a relatively normal pattern of ratings as his term progressed lies in partisanship and an important Trump success. High presidential approval ratings early in a president's term are normally a function of support from independents and those identifying with the opposing party. These supporters tend to drift from supporting a president who does not share their party label, and the president's approval ratings hit a normal base level founded largely on their own partisan support. Trump, in contrast, never enjoyed their support in the first place. He bypassed this honeymoon phase and quickly established a low but solid level of support based on the allegiance of core partisans. Democrats were predictably resolute in their opposition. About 8 in 10 Democrats do not just disapprove but strongly disapprove of the job the president is doing. Independents are skeptical as well: Gallup's polling shows that consistently about one third approve of the job Trump is doing. And even in the first week of his presidency, only four in ten approved.

Nevertheless, in a notable achievement, Trump retains very high approval among Americans who identify with the Republican Party. In August 2018, Gallup found 85% of Republicans approved of his performance in office, a number that has been relatively stable during his presidency to date (Brenan 2018a). This level is equivalent to those achieved by recent presidents among supporters of their own party.

After some hesitation during 2017, the president's party does appear to have embraced his leadership (Dunn 2018). Despite some continuing suspicions expressed at the elite level, the mass Republican Party has rallied behind Trump. This impression is not quite the whole of the story, however. While 85% support is impressive, polls reveal some consistent patterns among those within the party who do not support Trump. Moderate Republicans and Republican-leaning independents were reluctant to back "their" president as they were alienated by the president's attacks on Muslims, African-American NFL players, immigrants from what Trump called "shithole countries," his support for disruptive tariffs and his penchant for dictators over long-standing allies. While the vast majority of Republican identifiers continue to back him—notably Tea Partiers and evangelicals—GOP moderates, Catholics and non-religious conservatives are less enthusiastic. When considered alongside the gradually shrinking levels of identification with the Republican Party as some disenchanted identifiers melt away, there is a serious question of whether Trump is driving moderate Republicans out of the party, a point easily missed given his impressive approval ratings from within the party (Greenberg 2018).

While Trump has had mixed results in trying to win personal popularity, he has had significant problems in trying to win support for his less conventional policy positions. For example, Trump has repeatedly communicated with the public about immigration policy. The impact seems to have been exactly the opposite of that intended as Trump has driven voters of both parties further away from his chosen position. Democratic voters are now on average more resolutely pro-immigration, perhaps because Trump is against it. According to Pew's 2017 survey data (Pew 2017), 84% of self-identified Democrats and those leaning toward the Democratic Party agreed with the statement that immigrants strengthen the country with their hard work and talents. Notably, 42% of Republicans agreed with them. The pro-immigration trend for both groups has been liberalizing since 2010, but it has accelerated under Trump. Overall, 65% of Americans believe immigrants strengthen the country and only 26% disagree, the most pro-immigration response for more than a generation. More recent Gallup data confirm Pew's earlier findings. Polled in early June 2018, just before the family separation crisis shook the country, 75% of Americans viewed immigration as good for the country, up four points in a year (Democrats at 85 and Republicans at 65%). Conversely, the proportion saying immigration should be reduced fell from 35 to 29% over the year, while those saying it should be increased rose four points from 24 to 28%. A combined 67% were content with the current level or said it should be increased, including 55% of Republicans, also the most pro-immigration response in a generation (Brenan 2018b).

The same Gallup poll showed majorities opposed to Trump on the wall, Dreamers, and ending family reunification. Fully 83% of Americans (and 75% of Republicans) want Dreamers to have a path to citizenship, 57% do not support significantly expanding the construction of walls along the border with Mexico and 52% oppose stopping legal immigrants sponsoring family members to enter the United States. Only on sanctuary cities do a bare majority of Americans stand close to Trump, with a tight 50 to 46% in favor of banning them (Newport 2018). On the wall, 53% expressed support in 2010, including 60% of Republicans, 46% of Democrats, and 52% of independents, according to a Fox poll. But by 2018, overall support was pegged at just 38% in a CBS poll using very similar wording. Although 78% of Republicans expressed support, just 13% of Democrats and 34% of independents did so (Hohmann 2018). In politicizing the issue, Trump has solidified support among his base, but lost nearly everyone else in the process.

Perhaps most notable of all is that Trump has managed to turn immigration into an issue that benefits the Democrats. Pew regularly asks Americans which party does a better job dealing with specific issues such as the economy, trade, healthcare and so on. Before Trump's swearing-in as president, the two parties were essentially tied over which one could do a better job on immigration, but by early June 2018 the Democrats opened up a 16-point advantage (48 to 32%) over the Republicans, even before the family-separation story hit the headlines (Pew 2018). Trump adviser Stephen Miller has consistently argued that the administration wins whenever people are focused on immigration, but his claim is not backed up by the data.

Trump's strategy of appealing to the base by going public has won neither himself nor his policies public support. Democrats are unified in opposition. A large majority of independents—about two thirds—do not approve of the job he's doing. And some moderates in the Republican Party have been reluctant to support him. Still, the vast majority of Republican identifiers approve of their president's performance, even if they are less convinced by his specific policies. Trump has reinforced the partisan divide.

# 8    Conclusion

Trump's overall understanding of how he should lead from the Oval Office is fairly simple. His strategy consists of concentrating presidential communication on his electoral base, with faith that this strategy will indirectly influence Washington to follow the president. His personal conduct of this strategy is unusual. Trump deploys convention-busting communication tactics, even if in service of the fairly standard presidential strategy of going public. In terms of his approach, as we argued in the Introduction to this book, President Trump *is* extraordinary. What is important for our argument, however, is the extent to which this extraordinary approach is bringing about ordinary outcomes for his presidency.

In that respect, the outcomes for his presidency have been less than impressive. Trump may win a great deal of coverage because he follows rules honed by decades of vying for attention from the New York media, but like most modern presidents practicing spin control, Trump has found that he doesn't get the results he wants. He has won headlines, but also profoundly negative coverage from the media. Trump has focused all his efforts on keeping his base on side. And in this he has been very successful. But the problem is that his base constitutes a minority of American voters. Even with approval ratings of 85–90% among Republicans, consistently less than half of Americans think he is doing a good job and a good proportion of these are implacably opposed to his presidency. In shoring up his base, Trump has driven away moderates and been unable to extend a hand to Democrats. In going public with a divisive base-focused communications strategy, Trump has not been able to build the broad and deep support that would have enhanced his leverage in Washington.

Going public seems not to have worked. Worse, Trump's techniques for winning coverage have undermined his capacity to lead. Going public is normally considered as a means to focus media, public and Washington attention on the president's agenda which in turn allows him to lead and win policy changes. Yet Trump's domination of the agenda has been achieved at the very expense of this focus. His chosen techniques diminish the power of the presidency to lead, and so play an important role in generating the ordinary outcomes of his presidency because Trump is less able to bend the rest of the political system to his will. As the next chapter but one details, Trump's personal conduct of his communication strategy has not only failed in the president's own terms, but it has also created him further significant problems in his attempts to pass his agenda through Congress. Before that, however, the next chapter highlights the dysfunction right at the heart of the Trump presidency—in his own White House—and explains how this has also undermined his efforts to achieve major legislative wins.

# References

Barstow, David, Susanne Craig, and Russ Buettner. 2018. "Trump Engaged in Suspect Tax Schemes as He Reaped Riches from His Father." *New York Times*, October 2.

Brenan, Megan. 2018a. "Snapshot: 4 in 10 Still Strongly Disapprove of Trump." *Gallup.com*, August 29. https://news.gallup.com/poll/241787/snapshot-strongly-disapprove-trump.aspx.

Brenan, Megan. 2018b. "Record-High 75% of Americans Say Immigration Is Good Thing." *Gallup.com*, June 21. https://news.gallup.com/poll/235793/record-high-americans-say-immigration-good-thing.aspx.

Casselman, Ben, Maggie Koerth-Baker, and Anna Maria Barry-Jester. 2017. "Trump Keeps Derailing His Own Agenda." *fivethirtyeight.com*, August 18. https://fivethirtyeight.com/features/trump-keeps-derailing-his-own-agenda/.

Dawsey, Josh. 2017. "Fallout Grows as Trump Continues Attacks on Fellow GOP Members." *Politico*, August 25. https://www.politico.com/story/2017/08/25/trump-gop-attacks-fallout-grows-242051.

Dunn, Amina. 2018. "Trump's Approval Ratings so Far Are Unusually Stable—And Deeply Partisan." *Pew Research Center*, August 1. http://www.pewresearch.org/fact-tank/2018/08/01/trumps-approval-ratings-so-far-are-unusually-stable-and-deeply-partisan/.

Fahrenthold, David A. 2016. "Trump Boasts About His Philanthropy. But His Giving Falls Short of His Words." *Washington Post*, October 29.

Green, Joshua. 2017. *Devil's Bargain: Steve Bannon, Donald Trump, and the Storming of the Presidency*. New York: Penguin Press.

Greenberg, Stanley B. 2018. "Riling Up the Base May Backfire on Trump." *New York Times*, June 18.

Hohmann, James. 2018. "Under Trump, Americans Are Becoming More Supportive of Immigration." *Washington Post*, June 22.

Jamieson, Kathleen Hall, and Doron Taussig. 2017. "Disruption, Demonization, Deliverance, and Norm Destruction: The Rhetorical Signature of Donald J. Trump." *Political Science Quarterly* 132 (4): 619–650.

Jones, Charles O. 1998. *Passages to the Presidency: From Campaigning to Governing*. Washington, DC: Brookings Institution Press.

Jones, Charles O. 2005. *The Presidency in a Separated System*. 2nd ed. Washington, DC: Brookings Institution Press

Jones, Jeffrey M. 2018. "Trump's Sixth Quarter His Best; Remains Weak Historically." *Gallup.com*, July 24. https://news.gallup.com/poll/237878/trump-sixth-quarter-best-remains-weak-historically.aspx.

Kernell, Samuel. 1997. *Going Public: New Strategies of Presidential Leadership*. Washington, DC: CQ Press.

Klein, Ezra. 2018. "Trump Is Winning." *Vox*, January 29. https://www.vox.com/policy-and-politics/2018/1/29/16900646/trump-administration-tweets-media-polarization.

Kranish, Michael, and Marc Fisher. 2016. *Trump Revealed: The Definitive Biography of the 45th President*. London: Simon & Schuster.

Mayer, Kenneth R. 1999. "Executive Orders and Presidential Power." *Journal of Politics* 61 (2): 445–466

Mitchell, Amy, Jeffrey Gottfried, Katerina Eva Matsa, and Elizabeth Grieco. 2017. "Covering President Trump in a Polarized Media Environment." *Pew Research Center*, October 2. http://assets.pewresearch.org/wp-content/uploads/sites/13/2017/10/10164210/PJ_2017.10.02_Trump-First-100-Days_FINAL.pdf.

Nelson, Michael. 2018. *Trump's First Year*. Charlottesville: University of Virginia Press.

Newport, Frank. 2018. "Americans Oppose Border Walls, Favor Dealing with DACA." *Gallup.com*, June 20. https://news.gallup.com/poll/235775/americans-oppose-border-walls-favor-dealing-daca.aspx.

Nuzzi, Olivia. 2018. "Donald Trump and Sean Hannity Like to Talk Before Bedtime." *New York Magazine*, May 14.

Patterson, Thomas E. 2017. "News Coverage of Donald Trump's First 100 Days." Harvard Kennedy School Shorenstein Center on Media, Politics and Public Policy, May 18.

Pew. 2017. "The Partisan Divide and Political Values Grown Even Wider." *Pew Research Center*, October 5. http://assets.pewresearch.org/wp-content/uploads/sites/5/2017/10/05162647/10-05-2017-Political-landscape-release.pdf.

Pew. 2018. "Voters More Focused on Control of Congress—And the President—Than in Past Midterms." *Pew Research Center*, June 20. http://assets.pewresearch.org/wp-content/uploads/sites/5/2018/06/22114930/06-20-2018-Political-release.pdf.

Sargent, Greg. 2018. "Alarming New Revelations About Trump's Addiction to Fox News." *Washington Post*, May 14.

Skowronek, Stephen. 1997. *The Politics Presidents Make: Leadership from John Adams to Bill Clinton*. Cambridge, MA: Belknap Press.

Trump, Donald J. 1987. *Trump: The Art of the Deal*. New York: Random House.

Tur, Katy. 2017. "'Come Here, Katy': How Donald Trump Turned Me Into a Target." *The Guardian*, October 11.

Wolff, Michael. 2018. *Fire and Fury: Inside the Trump White House*. London: Little, Brown.

Woodward, Bob. 2018. *Fear: Trump in the White House*. London: Simon & Schuster.

Zanona, Melanie. 2017. "Trump's 'Infrastructure Week' Goes off the Rails." *The Hill*, June 9.

# 6

# Trump in the White House

Trump arrived in Washington promising to overthrow the establishment. Few people assumed, however, that established powerholders would simply step aside and hand the reins of power to Trump. Instead, he would face an extraordinary challenge, even with the support of Republican Party identifiers among the public. Astute leadership would be required to plan a radical agenda and then work out how to steer it through the political system. But Trump has not proved capable of such leadership. He lacks the managerial skill to command and corral the resources the White House offers to help presidents lead.

Rather than operating as leader of the executive branch, Trump has personalized his presidency to serve his strategy of communicating with the base. This modus operandi centralizes power with Trump personally. That might sound like a reasonable thing for an elected president to do, but it misses a fundamental point about presidential power. The president heads the Executive Office of the President (EOP), a remarkably useful institution—constituted of hundreds of able people and formidable resources within the White House and the neighboring Old Executive Building—designed to support the elected leader of the United States. By seeing himself as sitting apart from that institution,

© The Author(s) 2019
J. Herbert et al., *The Ordinary Presidency of Donald J. Trump*,
Palgrave Studies in Political Leadership,
https://doi.org/10.1007/978-3-030-04943-0_6

Trump has failed to commit the time and effort to making sure that its processes run effectively, including policy planning, liaising with interest groups and Congress, and running an effective communications strategy. These are the means to get things done in Washington. With careful management, the president can use the EOP and the broader executive branch to help in his pursuit of influence. The EOP includes within it some of the levers of power that successful presidents need to grasp in order to effect change, but Trump tends to ignore them. Instead, he tweets a flow of poorly considered comments and interventions from the Oval Office, damages his capacity to lead by constantly shifting both the agenda and his position on individual agenda items, and actively sabotages his White House's efforts to provide coherence and direction to the policy process. Further, Trump has failed to properly manage the appointments process which would, if done properly, have allowed him to install around him a team of intelligent, knowledgeable and dedicated people who knew how to get things done in Washington. Trump has largely failed in this vital managerial task in part because of his personalized approach. Instead, he has installed a toxic mixture of Trump loyalists shy on expertise and Washington smarts alongside more traditional conservatives plucked from the higher echelons of the Republican Party, at least some of whom see it as their role to "resist" the president and protect the country from his most dangerous impulses and policy prescriptions. A chaotic and self-destructive fight has erupted literally in the president's own house over the very nature and meaning of his presidency. In sum, Trump's unusual conduct and approach to being president means that he is less able to exert influence and lead Washington and is, therefore, seriously undermining his own presidency.

# 1    The Challenge of a Trump Agenda

Trump won the 2016 election but lacked a coherent, detailed and ranked policy agenda. Candidate Trump had articulated some broad nationalist principles to underpin his future policies. His core ideas could be thought of as constituting a worldview, but not an internally consistent one, and certainly not one accompanied by an extensive series of policy proposals (Laderman and Simms 2017). Symbolic, high-profile pledges such as building the wall on the Mexican border and threatening to withdraw from the North American Free Trade Agreement (NAFTA) were useful campaign slogans that represented Trump's broad concerns in clear terms, but neither symbolism nor Twitter fury demand the same level of policy detail and precise language as congressional bills or even executive orders.

While Candidate Trump dealt in the currencies of symbolism and fury, there was little evidence that the team around him were busy thinking through how his pledges could be enacted if he actually made it to the White House, let alone a sense that Trump engaged with any such operation. The Trump agenda was, in effect, hollow. Trump's unrealistic promises on the stump only sharpened the challenges. How would he get Mexico to pay for the wall? How would he make healthcare both better and cheaper? How would middle-class wages be increased or the massive infrastructure plan be financed? Trump's bold and angry rhetoric did not convert easily into policymaking blueprints. Detailed legislative and budgetary proposals and plans for executive action would be required to move from pledges to action, but none existed. Nor were Trump's priorities clear. What problems would he address first? No one knew. Trump wanted to overthrow the establishment but had no plan.

Even if Candidate Trump and the small team around him did not pay much attention to, and were not generally interested in, the nitty gritty of policy development, winning candidates usually draw on the ideas and policy blueprints of ideological sympathizers in Washington's plethora of think tanks and research shops (Polsby 1984; Sundquist 1968). Trump's presidency, though, simply lacked the connections to adopt this intellectual heritage. All the big brand conservative think tanks opposed him during the Republican primaries and most carried their opposition into the general election. His disparate and controversial ideas had not motivated much policy planning or development of intellectual capital to support a Trumpist movement. Notably, a group of academics convened at the American Greatness website and the *American Affairs* journal in recognition of this shortcoming and aimed to give the new Trump presidency some "intellectual heft" once his presidency had already begun, but in the short term this effort merely served to emphasize the problem (Johnson and Dawsey 2017). Trump's own efforts to explain his policies did not help. He was remarkably ill-informed and others were not able to fill in the gaps because his ideas were not rooted in a coherent movement with foundations in established ideological trends. Trump perhaps held the potential to become a point of crystallization for a new movement, but there was no legislative agenda waiting in the wings to be enacted.

It is a substantial undertaking to transition from campaigning to governing, and to mobilize the full power of the office of the presidency behind a coherent and politically viable agenda. Trump did not have such an agenda, but he was further disabled by his approach to leadership and particularly his inability to organize the White House. It is to this problem we now turn.

## 2    Trump's Personalized Presidency

As we saw in the previous chapter, Trump's primary concern is communicating with his base. To do this, he has created a bubble in which he tracks media coverage and runs his communications strategy. In the bubble, Trump has his own political reality in which he is the master political puppeteer, pulling the strings, running the show.

The bubble is sustained by Trump's firm belief in the superiority of his own judgment and a corresponding distrust of and discomfort with the advice of others. He has a preternatural belief in his own brilliance—he believes himself to be not just "like, very smart" but nothing less than "a very stable genius." This confidence in his extraordinary ability underpins a decision-making style that is deeply personalized rather than evidence-based, technocratic or even ideological. Instead, as he puts it, "historically, I like following my instincts." For example, he presents his North Korea policy as being founded on instinct:

> I know when somebody wants to deal, and I know when somebody doesn't. A lot of politicians don't. That's not their thing, but it is my

thing... But I know for a—I just feel very strongly—my instinct, my ability, or talent—they [North Korea] want to make a deal.

In addition to instinct, the president's emotions also play an unusually prominent role. Emotional decisions (such as bombing a Syrian government airbase in response to a chemical weapons attack) and emotional reactions (personal pique lived out through Twitter fury) are legitimate in his eyes. This belief in his gut instinct encourages Trump to resist advice, especially if delivered by alleged experts. He has always been resistant to expertise, expressing his skepticism of it in *The Art of the Deal*, but this rejection is also integral to his rebellious image (Trump 1987, 51–52). To take expert advice would be a concession to the establishment and contradict Trump's self-image as a disruptor. Trump's confidence in his own decision-making leaves him vulnerable, however. It makes him dependent upon his own very limited knowledge and narrow information sources and helps undermine his presidency.

First, Trump is spectacularly ignorant of the details on most aspects of public policy, including his own. This is demonstrated most notably in his inability to discuss policy questions coherently in any number of interviews. He claims to be an expert on tax policy, nuclear weapons, monetary policy or nearly any other issue imaginable (Schmidt and Shear 2017), but answers policy questions with rambling, incoherent discussions that reveal only fragments of relevant information. Videos of Trump overseeing policy debates display a president unfamiliar with the basics of policies and their political implications, even on central campaign issues such as immigration and healthcare. Perhaps nothing captures his ignorance better than his famed comment during the healthcare fight of 2017: "Nobody knew that healthcare could be so complicated." Yet anyone who paid the slightest attention to the subject *did* know.

Nor has Trump demonstrated a willingness to learn about policy. Even on the life-or-death issue of national security, Trump is by many accounts unable or unwilling to assimilate new information, especially if it clashes with his established views of how the world does and should work. Ezra Klein's analysis is particularly scathing:

Over the course of reporting on the Trump White House, I have spoken to people who brief Trump and people who have been briefed by him. I've talked to policy experts who have sat in the Oval Office explaining their ideas to the president and to members of Congress who have listened to the president sell his ideas to them. I've talked to both Democrats and Republicans who have occupied these roles. In all cases, their judgment of Trump is identical: He is not just notably uninformed but also notably difficult to inform — his attention span is thin, he hears what he wants to hear, he wanders off topic, he has trouble following complex arguments. Trump has trouble following his briefings or even correctly repeating what he has heard. (Klein 2018)

Trump's lack of expertise and inattention to policy is not completely unprecedented among presidents although it is probably at the more extreme end of the spectrum. George W. Bush, Reagan and Nixon were all disengaged from policy detail. Presidents, even successful ones, do not have to be and indeed cannot be the most informed person in the room on every subject. They will be overwhelmed if they try to be so. But that is why presidents have such an extensive staff that they rely on to support them and help them take the best decisions possible. But in Trump's personalized presidency where the principal is driven by instinct and emotion and a firm belief in his own extraordinary attributes and brilliance, the White House staff play a limited role in helping the president deliver the most successful presidency possible.

Second, Trump's choices of information sources are problematic. His understanding of the world is greatly influenced by the conversations he has in his crowd-sourcing process and his tracking of Fox News. Fox's fierce ideological angle, its lack of factual fidelity, its sympathy for conspiracy theories and the style in which it covers news and politics combine with Trump's reluctance to absorb expert advice, meaning the president does not receive a balanced assessment of the issues, or even a clear sense of which issues matter (Cassino 2016). His ability to understand events is hampered, and his existing prejudices are sometimes reinforced. For example, he regards the Mueller probe as a personal attack upon him rather than a methodical and forensic legal investigation and describes the investigation as a Deep State conspiracy and witch hunt by Democrats, as per Fox News and Sean Hannity. Trump risks both information and opinion bias in his decision-making.

These vulnerabilities are compounded by Trump's dedication to his communications strategy and his desire to control it. Communications are primary and impose themselves on most other processes of governing and in turn demand that Trump can bend those processes to serve his communication needs. Sustaining the president's communications becomes the defining consideration in areas as diverse as appointments and policy planning. Trump, confident in his instincts and with at least one eye on the television screen, interferes in executive branch processes at will, despite his lack of expertise and sometimes limited understanding. He shows no sense that formal decision-making processes matter. He reaches decisions by instinct or driven by emotions, responding to media coverage instantly, perhaps announcing a dramatic new position or just stirring things up publicly via a tweet (Woodward 2018, 231–232). Trump, therefore, not only runs his own communication strategy, but is when he chooses his own policy shop, congressional liaison, personnel officer, interpreter of the Constitution, Ambassador to Taiwan, and so on. The list is extensive. The responsiveness imposed by the need to impose himself on the media agenda means that Trump often takes his decisions when only partially briefed or simply on the basis of what he is watching on television at that moment.

Effectively, Trump has personalized the presidency, centralizing power at his "Resolute" desk in the Oval Office by taking instant decisions driven by communication needs in service of his base strategy. These are the acts of an extraordinary *president*. But it is ineffective as a means of governing and at the core of why Trump struggles to provide leadership. Indeed, it empowers more conventional Republicans to assert their agenda because the chaos in the White House opens up a policy space and gives them the opportunity to fill it. The communication required to command headlines and service the base is not the same type of communication required for a policy revolution. On the contrary, Trump's methodology has constrained, not enabled, his presidency in two main ways.

First, on entering the White House, Trump did not organize a proper system for supporting his decision-making, either through appointments or day-to-day management of White House processes. Even when conceding that such a system needed to exist and allowing its creation, Trump has refused to be bound by it or to oversee it properly, negating its purpose. Trump's poor management of others and reluctance to allow others to manage him have damaged the design and promotion of his policy agenda. Furthermore, it has empowered conventional Republicans, sacrificing control of his own policymaking processes and allowing his revolution to be undermined from within. He has created a battle-zone in his White House, with some actively blocking or undercutting his initiatives (Anonymous 2018; Woodward 2018). Unsurprisingly in this environment, Trump has not been able to plan a clear agenda, nor properly organize his team to sell it. His personalization of decision-making sabotages the machinery intended to help him as president; he denies himself opportunities to lead, takes ill-informed decisions and fails to recognize dangers to his presidency. Second, he is also undermined by specific features of his communication strategy. The qualities required to command attention in the media interfere with other governing tasks which might have allowed him to pursue more substantive goals effectively. Both Trump's shallow engagement with policy and the inconstancy imposed by his responsiveness to the media agenda sabotage White House planning.

Trump's business experience suggested that he might be a good chief executive of the federal government, managing one of the most unwieldy organizations in the world. However, Trump's management is characterized primarily by his systematic resistance to process. Perhaps considering the presidency his personal fiefdom, he interferes in any process, imposing his own personal and often communication-driven concerns in ways that make it very hard for those processes to run and achieve results, even though they only exist to serve the president himself. The following analysis considers Trump's approach to appointments, his partial engagement with decision-making processes and his sabotage of his White House staff's best efforts to help him. Trump's management style leaves him hosting an empowered "resistance" within his own White House and reduces his opportunities to lead.

# 3     Appointments

The president's inattention to and apparent lack of interest in making careful appointments to the White House and wider executive branch have been particularly telling. As a president wishing to overthrow the establishment, Trump would need fellow revolutionaries to support his efforts. To deliver the president's goals, staff usually have to subscribe to the president's ideology and priorities. Some balance must be struck, though, between ideological loyalty and expertise. Ideally, administration members should share the president's views, have a detailed knowledge of the relevant positions and know how to implement them (Pfiffner 1996; Weko 1995).

Trump, however, has not offered the ideological clarity required to give his views appropriate weight in the appointments process. Nor does he value expertise. Instead, he overemphasizes the importance of personal loyalty. James Comey described the president's obsession with loyalty as "Mafia-like" (Comey 2018). Trump does not countenance employing anyone associated with the "Dump Trump" resistance to his candidacy during 2016 and is also deeply suspicious of those associated with the Bush presidencies. Instead, Trump has surrounded himself with a small group of loyalists from his 2016 campaign, rather than established Republican experts and Washington insiders, even after a disorganized operation run by an ever-changing cast of players (Lewandowski and Bossie 2018). Steve Bannon, Michael Flynn, Reince Priebus, Kellyanne Conway and Hope Hicks all graduated from the campaign to White House posts, but brought little experience of governing with them. Appointing his daughter Ivanka and her husband Jared Kushner as senior staffers offered Trump a greater chance of loyalty, but neither knew much about getting things done in Washington. Kushner in particular emerged as poster boy for the ill-equipped nature of the staff as his portfolio of responsibilities expanded exponentially across policy areas in which he had little or no experience.

Personal loyalty is not Trump's only criterion for assessing job candidates, however. With his emphasis on public communication, the president is drawn to candidates who project the desired image, particularly on television, and rejects those who do not. Trump thought Jeff Sessions too short to be Vice President, and John Bolton was initially sidelined as National Security Advisor because the president apparently did not like his moustache. Conversely, Trump is impressed by Generals and their uniforms, referring to these cabinet picks as being from "central casting." His appointment of NBC television commentator Larry Kudlow as his chief economic adviser caused particular consternation and earned the president the label "casting agent-in-chief" (Grynbaum 2018).

Trump's deeply personalized appointments process emphasized personal loyalty and a media-friendly demeanor over expertise and ideology, but the bypassing of expertise created some intractable problems for his presidency. Many staff in the White House were, just like Trump, on a sharp learning curve as they took office. They knew little of Washington or even the areas they were tasked with giving advice on, so Trump reduced his chances of receiving good guidance. The administration also struggled to recruit and retain the best talent. Normally, a senior administration appointment might be regarded as a plum job to burnish a CV and open lucrative career opportunities post-service, but many potential recruits fear how future employers might view their Trump association. Moreover, the loyalty test is so strict and the available talent pool so shallow that the White House ran job shops to persuade suitably conservative and possibly qualified talent to consider working for Trump (Karni 2018).

Even with talent proving hard to attract, Trump compounds the problem by treating staff badly. Nearly every significant figure in Trump's circle, bar immediate family, has been humiliated or at least undermined by the president. His trolling of Attorney General Jeff Sessions proved the most egregious and public but even son-in-law Kushner has been mocked privately. Trump's early tenure witnessed record-breaking turnover at cabinet level. Kathryn Dunn Tenpas and colleagues at the Brookings Institution (Tenpas et al. 2018) estimated that the turnover rate in Trump's A-Team—that is, the 65 top positions among White House staff and the Executive Office of the Presidency, such as Chief of Staff, National Security Advisor, Press Secretary, but excluding cabinet secretaries—was 34% in the first year, compared to 9 and 6% for Trump's two immediate predecessors. Nearly every account of life in the White House, except Trump's own, speaks of low morale and a dysfunctional environment, dominated by the whims, feuds and appetites of the man in the Oval Office.

It is easy to cast these problems as uniquely Trump's. Yet some of them are structured into the outsider's governing situation. Trump took office with limited experience and short of the one thing he could have called on to compensate: a network of people from established political and policy realms. The revolution lacked a vanguard class. The new president had connections with political operatives from his 2016 campaign, and he appointed them. Beyond this group, he lacked people he could trust or consider as understanding his approach to policy and being president. The contrast with a candidate with established party links and a strong sense of its ideological agenda is very clear; Trump faced an extraordinary challenge. Instead, Trump was forced to turn to his party. Beginning with Reince Priebus as his first Chief of Staff and proceeding through many cabinet appointments, Trump selected many party insiders for key roles despite his anti-establishment stance.

The problem of Trump's absent revolutionary army extends to the broader federal government. Just as the newcomer lacked the extensive network of informed and ideologically committed supporters needed to appoint a senior staff, he could not meet the challenge set by the Plum Book, which contains an estimated 4100 political federal positions to be filled by an incoming administration (Sullivan in Rein 2016). Trump lacked the roster to fill these second and third order positions; he simply did not know enough people, or even know people who knew enough people. Without an alternative source of experienced political operatives to call upon, Trump again had to turn to his party for these lower level but still crucial posts. Thus, many Trump appointees to federal agencies have extensive Republican Party backgrounds.

Asking whether Trump was "draining the swamp," Anne Joseph O'Connell used the indicator of nominees' official residencies to understand how many Trump nominees were from inside the "swamp" of Washington, DC. Over a quarter of Trump's nominees (26.3%) in his first year came from the DC area, a score roughly parallel with those of Clinton (23.2%) and George W. Bush (29.9%) (O'Connell 2018). Not every appointee brings conventional Republican approaches to office, but Trump has not been able to bypass the Republican establishment. Given the importance of lower tier appointments in managing agencies' operations each day, those choices represent a significant delegation of power. In the absence of concerted leadership, the bureaucracy largely gets on with what it was doing; Trump does not or cannot control the appointment process closely enough to make sure that it is properly overseen. The Trump administration's casual attitude to staffing makes it difficult to outwit the stallers and guide reforms through to their conclusion. Despite high-profile promises to "deconstruct the administrative state," the president has appointed a series of Republicans to head that administrative state, empowering the establishment that Trump appeared, in 2016, to challenge.

In sum, Trump struggled to appoint and maintain a senior team both sympathetic to his agenda and expert in policy. He has presided, therefore, with a rolling cast of people who have been learning on the job, just like him, while undertaking such fundamental tasks as designing a policy agenda and running foreign policy. An inexpert president made appointments that further insulated him from expertise and so limited his capacity to lead. Worse, by failing to use ideology as a criterion for appointment, Trump appointed people to the most senior levels who were not necessarily sympathetic to his agenda. Trump institutionalized the contest between establishment Republicanism and his challenge to them in his own senior management team. He created a system by which his alternative agenda confronts the buzzsaw of established order representatives.

## 4    A Divided White House

Unsurprisingly, Trump's management and staffing problems generated conflicts over policy. Deep White House rifts became a staple of the administration's coverage in the media. For example, the first half of 2018 featured noisy, public disputes between Trump officials over trade. The "globalists"—fully intended as a term of abuse when used by Bannon, Miller and Trump—such as economic adviser Gary Cohn and members of Trump's own family, argued with protectionists—later labeled "patriots"—such as Assistant to the President Peter Navarro and US Trade Representative Robert Lighthizer. The fight over the very nature of the Trump presidency is lived out in the White House.

Contests over policy in the White House are neither unusual nor necessarily damaging. However, they require careful management because they must be resolved before they become destructive by causing public embarrassment and preventing proper planning. Presidents rely on their staff to manage responsibilities where they lack expertise. With skilled delegation and careful oversight, a president can guide the policy planning process with limited direct involvement while ensuring that decisions are taken by informed allies. A system for "staffing out" decisions to guarantee thorough briefings and expert advice is usually developed, allowing administrations to identify options and think through potential repercussions. This process protects presidents from making ill-informed decisions. Trump, though, did not construct a methodical and thorough decision-making process on taking office. Instead, following his desire for a personalized presidency, he wanted advice and to take decisions as and when he wished on the basis of his instincts. As his own de facto chief of staff and head of policy, Trump created chaos.

The president, by surrounding himself with competing advisers and creating competition for his attention, triggered extraordinary political infighting. With no functioning or formal policy process, anyone wishing to shape the administration's direction had to influence Trump (Lewis et al. 2018). To the extent that there was any sort of process earlier in the Trump presidency, participants did not trust or adhere to it, and thus sought to bypass it. Accounts of competing White House staff members trying to get Trump to sign-off on particular policy decisions reveal a staff that adjusted to a president liable to persuasion by the last person in the room. Each adviser sought to complete an "end run," by which a staffer persuades the president to act while bypassing others (Wolff 2018). For example, during the early months of Trump's presidency, Steve Bannon was widely recognized as the lead "Trump whisperer" convincing the president to issue executive actions quickly with few in the administration involved in, or even aware of, presidential decisions until they were announced. The notorious Muslim travel ban is a prime example. During the 2018 battles over trade policy, stories emerged of Navarro and Commerce Secretary Wilbur Ross attempting to appeal directly to Trump, circumventing the series of weekly trade meetings designed to develop considered policy (Colvin 2018).

Trump, moreover, rarely provided the clear statement of priorities or policy decisions needed to curtail debate. The administration already faced the lack of clarity associated with an outsider presidency as all involved try to understand the president's priorities. Bold, consistent ideological statements might have helped even if specific policy instructions were not forthcoming from the Oval Office, but Trump's willingness to change policy positions, suggesting that his commitments were not deeply held, encouraged further debate. Indeed, there were few clear points of closure; with Trump willing to reverse some of his own decisions, he created the potential to act as an infinite court of appeal, with interested parties looking for ways to challenge decisions they did not favor long after the issue had been allegedly resolved.

Even when General John Kelly arrived in the White House as Trump's second Chief of Staff and established a full formal process, Trump refused to be bound by it. Kelly managed the process below Trump in a traditional form, organizing schedules for policy planning, managing the appropriate range of personnel into meetings, preparing briefing papers and assessing each policy option and its repercussions carefully. Yet, the president maintains his own partially separated and parallel process that still allows him to stake out new positions in an instant via Twitter, thus sabotaging the planning schedule. Trump interferes in the formal policy process instantly and often decisively, wrecking efforts to plan policy carefully and systematically. Administration members find out about some changes after the decision has been issued, without being consulted (Harris et al. 2018). Chris Liddell, Deputy Chief of Staff and overseer of Trump's policy shop, expressed this very effectively. Observing his charting of the policy process on his office whiteboard, he claimed: "I have a high degree of tolerance for ambiguity. I could come in tomorrow and rub that board out because it's going to change… The reality [is] that everything is fluid based on daily developments" (Restuccia and Cook 2018).

After Trump's interventions, the formal process tries to catch up with its president, reworking its plan to fit with the new commitment. The extraordinary image created is of a policy staff hanging on their president's next tweet to see where the administration will head next. While Kelly could "manage down," creating a policy process to coordinate efforts of many beneath him, his primary problem was "managing up," that is, convincing the president to operate within the White House structure (Bernstein 2018). The White House's formal process still regularly confronts sabotage by its own principal. With a president willing to operate outside any process and announcing his decisions immediately often via Twitter or an off-hand remark to the media, policymaking is only slightly less than a free-for-all, as demonstrated during the trade disputes of 2018.

All-in-all, Trump's management style is chaotic and in turn breeds chaos among his team. His appointments process did not create a White House focused on his agenda, but one divided between Trump revolutionaries and more conventional Republicans. Rather than managing this division via clear guidance, processes and timely interventions, Trump's personalized approach to decision-making incapacitates the White House's efforts to support him. His White House is divided with little way to resolve the divisions. The consequences of this mismanagement are serious. Trump's personalized approach to decision-making has led to a series of ill-advised choices that have damaged his administration and his capacity to lead the system in his chosen direction.

## 5 The Consequences of Mismanagement

First, Trump's personalized decision-making leaves him vulnerable to making poor decisions. He lacks access to appropriate expertise because decisions are not staffed out. Instead, Trump shoots from the hip, sabotaging the formal policy process that might otherwise protect him and instead allowing instincts rooted in information and opinion bias to drive his presidency. The result is that Trump makes poorly evidenced decisions on some issues. Certainly, media coverage suggests that there have been many "you can't do that, Mr. President" conversations after one or other of Trump's policy interventions. Sometimes his staff have only had the opportunity to explain the consequences of his policy pronouncements and negotiating positions after he has staked them out. In turn, this has led to public reversals by the president and denials that initial statements were even made, contributing to his image of inconstancy. Some policies that have been issued were very poorly planned, leaving them vulnerable to challenge in Washington. The multiple iterations of the ban on immigration from certain Muslim nations are a good example. The original drafting, largely undertaken by presidential adviser Stephen Miller who had little knowledge of executive action, produced a deeply flawed order that invited a range of legal challenges, as we saw in Chapter 4. Simply writing the executive order to align more closely with existing law would have produced fewer and less credible challenges to Trump's executive action. By accessing expertise in the relevant area, Trump could have implemented his goals more effectively, but he chose not to.

Second, Trump's appointments facilitated a "resistance" within his own administration, limiting his capacity to focus the White House on pursuing his chosen agenda. The impacts are greater than simply creating a divided and quarrelsome White House. When the *New York Times* published an anonymous editorial explaining the efforts of "senior officials" in the administration working to "frustrate parts of [Trump's] agenda and his worst inclinations," it confirmed many existing impressions (Anonymous 2018). Indeed, it echoes revelations in Bob Woodward's account of the administration, *Fear*, which detailed top officials taking documents from the president's desk to prevent them being signed (Woodward 2018). Enabled by Trump's mismanaged appointments process, his lack of attention to policy and his half-hearted oversight of process, these officials have worked to contain the president.

The "Anonymous" senior staffer of the *New York Times* Op-Ed justifies his or her action on the basis of Trump's decision-making, suggesting that the president's "half-baked, ill-informed and occasionally reckless decisions …have to be walked back" because "the president continues to act in a manner that is detrimental to the health of our republic" (Anonymous 2018). In one obvious example, the myriad of agencies involved in protecting national security have refused to toe the Trump line that Russia did not meddle in the 2016 elections. After the president meekly accepted Putin's assurance that Russia was not involved, the intelligence agencies held firm and Trump was publicly and humiliatingly forced to back their judgment. In fact, much administration foreign policy is characterized by this dual track approach. The president says one thing, his staff do another. Trump says Russia is not meddling in the 2018 midterms; top officials including Secretary of Homeland Security Kirstjen Nielsen and Director of National Intelligence Dan Coats immediately hold a public briefing setting out clear evidence of interference and what they will do to combat it. "Our democracy itself is in the cross hairs," says Nielsen. Trump says he will meet Iranian leaders anytime and without preconditions; Secretary of State Mike Pompeo promptly sets out unmatchable preconditions including a nuclear non-proliferation agreement. Trump maintains he has solved the Korean nuclear problem while tweeting childish platitudes to Kim Jong-Un— "Thank you for your nice letter—I look forward to seeing you soon"; his intelligence staff release evidence demonstrating that nuclear missile production continues. Trump trash-talks NATO; key administration officials leap to its defense. The virtues of resisting Trump's sometimes bizarre understandings and initiatives are not the central point here; it is that his presidency is being shaped by those who block him, enabled by his own appointments and inattention.

Third, as chaos developed in the White House, the administration has found it very hard to generate any kind of an agenda, or even coherent responses to events in Congress. Early in the administration, there seemed very little prospect of the administration developing a series of coherent reform proposals. Instead, the result was familiar, to presidential observers at least. As the incoming administration cast around for a policy agenda, entrepreneurial advisers rushed in to fill the void, some of whom were more qualified than others. Just as previous administrations had searched for detailed policy solutions to fulfill their broad campaign pledges, Trump turned to those who promised that they could deliver his agenda. Inside the White House, Stephen Bannon presented himself as having a plan for Trump's use of executive power that could enable him to pursue his radical, nationalist agenda, despite

Bannon's own inexperience of such operations. Sometimes working with Stephen Miller, Bannon produced an early swathe of executive orders to communicate the president's priorities, even if many of them were simply symbolic proclamations. Executive power held substantial potential in policy areas most important to Trump such as trade and immigration. For example, Obama's Deferred Action on Childhood Arrivals executive memorandum had created a framework Trump could, it seemed, dismantle. Their confidence was misplaced, however. The failure to consult, and so access expertise, produced poorly considered executive actions which met a storm of legal opposition. DACA remains in place and Dreamers continue to enjoy authorized residency in the USA. Trump's dependency on others, created by his lack of an agenda and misplaced attempts to address it with inexperienced staff, has undermined his capacity to impose his policies on Washington.

Trump also found himself incapable of delivering the key campaign pledges he had offered. For example, he made repeated claims that he would shortly deliver a plan for infrastructure reform throughout 2017, but the administration seemed incapable of presenting such a bill after months of pantomime promises. Even more significantly, the administration was barely capable of engaging with the process of developing and debating healthcare reform, leaving much of the planning to Republicans in Congress and failing to use the power of the White House to draw together a coalition behind a common plan the party could support. The administration could not offer clear policy positions, and Trump did not make the statements required to even attempt to rally support behind a detailed proposal (Pfiffner 2018). The disorganization of Trump's White House played a key role in the healthcare reform's humiliating defeat (Cook 2017; Noonan 2017).

Trump's mismanagement generates poor decisions and poor planning. The administration created a series of initiatives that were easier to resist than they needed to be. Also, Trump's improvised and instant decision-making damages White House planning so badly that they amount to a surrender of power to other players in the political system.

# 6    Conclusion

Trump's personal attributes and extraordinary approach to the job undermine his opportunities to lead by sacrificing his power to influence Washington. As the outsider promising to vanquish the establishment, he applies a style of leadership that is more of an obstacle to his agenda's progress than an asset. His refusal to manage the White House closely has led to division and chaos. His personalization of the presidency, through instinctive decisions and instant communication, undermines his administration's capacity to plan policies and their paths to passage. He does not recognize that he is part of an institution and that, through mismanagement, he denies himself the advantages offered by the presidency and so the means to influence other players in the system. The result, despite all his claims to the contrary, is a rather ordinary presidency.

Trump has also enabled Republicans to resist aspects of his radical agenda. His appointments process did much to further the conventional Republican cause by installing large numbers of mainstream Republicans at the heart of his presidency. In doing so, he guaranteed extensive clashes within his administration, but his management style also undermined his capacity to resolve them, leaving a White House debilitated by conflict and uncertainty over its direction. Again, the costs to Trump are control and influence over the direction of his presidency. As explained in the next chapter, his decisions on his initial legislative agenda represented a further substantial delegation of power.

# References

Anonymous. 2018. "Opinion: I Am Part of the Resistance Inside the Trump Administration." *New York Times*, September 5.

Bernstein, Jonathan. 2018. "John Kelly's Problems Go Well Beyond Porter Mess." *Bloomberg.com*, February 14. https://www.bloomberg.com/view/articles/2018-02-14/john-kelly-s-problems-go-well-beyond-porter-mess.

Cassino, Dan. 2016. *Fox News and American Politics: How One Channel Shapes American Politics and Society*. New York: Routledge.

Colvin, Jill. 2018. "Trump Shuffle: Suddenly Trade Guru Navarro Takes Spotlight." *US News and World Report*, March 7.

Comey, James. 2018. *A Higher Loyalty: Truth, Lies, and Leadership*. New York: Macmillan.

Cook, Nancy. 2017. "Trump Finds Success on Taxes Doing What He Knows Best—Selling." *Politico*, December 18. https://www.politico.com/story/2017/12/18/trump-taxes-sales-congress-302241.

Grynbaum, Michael M. 2018. "Trump, the Television President, Expands His Cast." *New York Times*, March 16.

Harris, Shane, Felicia Somnez, and John Wagner. 2018. "'That's Going to Be Special': Tensions Rise as Trump Invites Putin to Washington." *The Washington Post*, July 19.

Johnson, Eliana, and Josh Dawsey. 2017. "GOP Despairs at Inability to Deliver." *Politico*, July 23. https://www.politico.com/story/2017/07/23/republicans-trump-despair-deliver-240868.

Karni, Annie. 2018. "Trump White House Recruits at a Hill Job Fair Amid Staff Exodus." *Politico*, June 13. https://www.politico.com/story/2018/06/13/white-house-hill-job-fair-645592.

Klein, Ezra. 2018. "Trump Is Winning." *Vox*, January 29. https://www.vox.com/policy-and-politics/2018/1/29/16900646/trump-administration-tweets-media-polarization.

Laderman, Charlie, and Brendan Simms. 2017. *Donald Trump: The Making of a World View*. London: I.B. Tauris.

Lewandowski, Corey R., and David N. Bossie. 2018. *Let Trump Be Trump: The Inside Story of His Rise to the Presidency*. New York: Center Street.

Lewis, David E., Patrick Bernhard, and Emily You. 2018. "President Trump as Manager: Reflections on the First Year." *Presidential Studies Quarterly* 48 (3): 480–501.

Noonan, Peggy. 2017. "Trump, ObamaCare and the Art of the Fail: What Happens When We Elect a President Who Prefers to Freelance Rather Than to Lead." *Wall Street Journal*, July 20.

O'Connell, Anne Joseph. 2018. "After One Year in Office, Trump's Behind on Staffing but Making Steady Progress." *Brookings Institution*, January 23. https://www.brookings.edu/research/after-one-year-in-office-trumps-behind-on-staffing-but-making-steady-progress/.

Pfiffner, James P. 1996. *The Strategic Presidency: Hitting the Ground Running*, 2nd ed. Lawrence, KS: University Press of Kansas.

Pfiffner, James P. 2018. "The Contemporary Presidency: Organizing the Trump Presidency." *Presidential Studies Quarterly* 48 (1): 153–167.

Polsby, Nelson, 1984. *Political Innovation in America: The Politics of Policy Initiation*. New Haven, CT: Yale University Press.

Rein, Lisa. 2016. "The Plum Book Is Here for Those Angling for Jobs in Trump's Washington." *Washington Post*, December 4.

Restuccia, Andrew, and Nancy Cook. 2018. "This New Zealander Is Trying to Tame Trump's Chaotic Policy Shop." *Politico*, July 3. https://www.politico.com/story/2018/07/03/trump-foreign-policy-chris-liddell-692613.

Schmidt, Michael S., and Michael D. Shear. 2017. "Trump Says Russia Inquiry Makes U.S. 'Look Very Bad'." *New York Times*, December 28.

Sundquist, James L. 1968. *Politics and Policy: The Eisenhower, Kennedy, and Johnson Years*. Washington, DC: Brookings Institution.

Tenpas, Kathryn Dunn, Elaine Kamarck, and Nicholas W. Zeppos. 2018. "Tracking Turnover in the Trump Administration." *Brookings Institution*, March 16.

Trump, Donald J. 1987. *Trump: The Art of the Deal*. New York: Random House.

Weko, Thomas J. 1995. *The Politicizing Presidency: The White House Personnel Office, 1948–1994*. Lawrence, KS: University Press of Kansas.

Wolff, Michael. 2018. *Fire and Fury: Inside the Trump White House*. London: Little, Brown.

Woodward, Bob. 2018. *Fear: Trump in the White House*. London: Simon & Schuster.

Yglesias, Matthew. 2017. "Trump's Latest Big Interview Is Both Funny and Terrifying: POTUS Swings and Misses at the Softest Softballs." *Vox*, October 23. https://www.vox.com/policy-and-politics/2017/10/23/16522456/trump-bartiromo-transcript.

# 7

# Trump and Congress

In pursuit of success and a lasting legacy, presidents try to shape the nation's laws. Unfortunately, from their perspective, the primary responsibility for passing laws lies not in the White House, but with Congress. A president's capacity to influence Congress is, therefore, a crucial element of his leadership. As noted in the previous two chapters, much about Trump's approach to being president, including his style of communication and mismanaged White House, damages his capacity to lead. He has not seized the reins of power effectively and so has failed to maximize his influence over the rest of the political system.

Chapter 4 recorded Trump's meager and rather conventional Republican achievements. While this is a normal return for most modern presidents, in Trump's case the mismatch with his revolutionary aspirations is particularly notable. Trump's radical, nationalist agenda has foundered. To some degree, the failings are personal: Trump's divisive and bombastic style has not proved very effective in influencing legislators. More than that, however, his failings have been strategic. Trump began his term in office by letting congressional Republicans take control of the legislative agenda rather than pushing his own

© The Author(s) 2019
J. Herbert et al., *The Ordinary Presidency of Donald J. Trump*,
Palgrave Studies in Political Leadership,
https://doi.org/10.1007/978-3-030-04943-0_7

radical populist priorities. Additionally, his strategy of appealing directly to his base using divisive communications has translated poorly from campaigning to governing. His base strategy may have won him support among most Republicans in the country and Congress, but it has not enabled Trump to win mass support for his radical policy positions or his presidency beyond his own party. He has not even sold all of his party on his radical vision. Instead, Trump's combative and divisive style and his contentious values and policy positions have actively alienated moderates, both among the public and in Congress.

In consequence, Trump's governing strategy has failed to deliver him influence in Washington. He can call on much of his congressional party's support, but in a finely balanced 115th Congress where Republicans held only narrow majorities, it was not enough to pass most reforms. Trump needed to win over moderates for Congress to fully embrace his agenda, but failed to do so. As the few relatively centrist legislators looked for cues as to the president's ideology and his popularity among the wider electorate, they were not persuaded that they should or must follow him. The inability of a disorganized White House to exert systematic pressure upon centrists to support the president also gave them extra leeway to resist. Hence, moderates have used their position as pivotal voters in Congress to prevent the passage of most Trump policies that challenge the Republican orthodoxy. They have greatly constrained his legislative achievements and so are perhaps the most important cause of his ordinariness. While some observers suggest he has taken over the Republican Party, his achievements are in fact only those that congressional Republicans have been willing to tolerate because they fit largely with the party's core principles.

The delegation of agenda control and thus power to the Republican Party in Congress is a major but often overlooked feature of Trump's presidency. The first part of this chapter examines this "great delegation," exploring its form and why it happened. Subsequent sections analyze the difficult congressional math that Trump faced as well as the ineffectiveness of his legislative strategy and inability to persuade key members of Congress to support his policy positions.

# 1    The Great Delegation

As he prepared for office, Trump faced a crucial problem. He wanted to overthrow the Washington orthodoxy (possibly including the legislators who would need to help him do it) but had no clear policy proposals or much idea about how to effect change. The promises of a free-wheeling campaign had not been translated into the substance of draft legislation during the transition period between winning election in November and becoming president in January. Trump was a president in need of a legislative agenda.

As the post-election transition developed, however, cooperation between Trump and Republican legislators looked possible in certain policy areas. His campaign had supported abolishing Obamacare, passing tax cuts, deregulation and the appointment of social conservatives to the judiciary, all of which were mainstream Republican goals. This was not the radical anti-establishment agenda that Trump believed had propelled him to office, but it was not without substance. The president-elect was presented with a plan by House Speaker Paul Ryan. Ryan, recognizing the difficulties of achieving reforms with a very narrow Republican majority in the Senate—rather than the supermajority needed to pass most legislation—presented Trump with a strategy that dealt first with Obamacare. Cutting federal expenditure on healthcare would open up an opportunity for larger tax cuts under reconciliation procedures that only required simple majorities in both houses to pass.

Even though Trump had pledged to repeal and replace Obamacare, his heart was not in it. He even suggested at times that the federal government's intervention in the healthcare market should be expanded. But he was very keen to achieve tax reform and, anyway, abolishing Obamacare would count as a win: Ryan's plan promised big legislative victories on Trump's campaign pledges. He would look like a man of action even though he had delegated control over the congressional agenda to fellow Republicans on Capitol Hill. Allowing Congress to pursue shared goals promised achievement without painful conflicts. In a neat division of labor, Trump could cooperate with Republicans to achieve legislative reforms where there was shared agreement on outcomes and, in areas where consensus might be difficult to achieve, he could operate untrammeled through executive power. Within days of his inauguration, Trump's legislative agenda—which was in reality Ryan's legislative agenda—was announced at a GOP Policy Retreat. The new president and the Republican-led Congress declared that they would achieve healthcare and tax reforms within the first 200 days of the administration (Snell and DeBonis 2017).

So, rather than "draining the swamp," the new insurgent populist president delegated agenda control to the mainstream Republican congressional leadership. He had agreed to two standard Republican policy priorities to head his agenda, laying aside his more radical ideas and his rejection of the Washington establishment. He gave control to those he had promised to usurp. Extraordinary influence fell to Ryan as the person who offered the means to fill the void that was the Trump agenda.

## 2    Trump Tries to Deal

Trump's presidency began, then, with a conventional Republican congressional agenda. However, even with this mainstream agenda, Ryan still needed Trump to lead the charge and sell healthcare reform and tax cuts both on the Hill and to the country. It was unclear whether Trump could do that. There was also uncertainty over what form repeal and replacement of Obamacare should take, and tax reform also required extensive bargaining between entrenched interests and different positions in Congress. Furthermore, Trump would need to steer budgets and judicial appointments through Congress and he would have to persuade Congress to accept or at least turn a blind eye to his executive actions on more controversial issues. Trump needed to exercise leadership, much like all modern presidents, if his presidency was to succeed.

To achieve reforms, Trump had a difficult situation to overcome in Congress. The Republicans had unified control of government, but barely. The math in the Senate was particularly perilous at 52 votes to 48, well below the 60 votes needed to overcome a filibuster. The filibuster, as a device the minority can use to prevent votes, meant that major reforms would either require some Democratic support or procedural manipulations to pass with a simple majority (with corresponding limitations on what could or could not be done). Even ordinary business, such as passing budgets, would be harder without a little Democratic support. With the Senate balanced precariously, passing major reforms seemed likely to demand compromise with forces in the political center and even possibly the left.

Meanwhile, the apparent advantage of a larger Republican majority in the House of Representatives (241 vs 194) was compromised by the party's internal divisions. Even before Trump's emergence, the congressional Republican Party was divided. A large section of the congressional party were part of the mainstream and long-established pro-business, free trade but socially conservative group aligning themselves with the Republican Study Committee (RSC). A smaller, emergent and more doctrinaire group, associated with the Tea Party movement, coalesced into the House Freedom Caucus. More moderate elements of the party are represented by the Tuesday Group and the Republican Main Street Partnership caucus. The RSC and Freedom Caucus share some basic ideological sympathies, but often differ on emphasis and strategy. Tea Partiers were more strident in their rhetoric and more aggressive in their desire to cut back government. They were more inclined to stand their ground in any conflict and to focus on maintaining ideological purity, labelling their opponents as Republican In Name Only (RINOs). More pragmatic, if still ideological, conservatives focused on victory at the ballot box and getting the policy gains available at the time. Tensions between the groups had played out during the Obama administration and it remained to be seen whether the groups could act in concert with a president of their own party.

The division was not just at the congressional level. The rise of the Tea Party had created a series of active groups in the country at large who wished not only to elect fervently anti-government ideologues, but to hold those elected officials to account once in office (Skocpol and Williamson 2016). Within the Republican Party, principled opposition on ideological grounds became a touchstone, at the expense of the compromise required to govern within a separated system of distributed powers. Trump inherited a party divided over its approach to governing and in the habit of opposing the presidency and the party's own congressional leadership. If Trump had to rely on his own party alone in the House, he would need to keep the vast majority of members happy and respond to concerns of the cohort of between 30 and 40 House Freedom Caucus members on the right (Huetteman 2017). In combination then, the Senate and House provided Trump with a particularly awkward situation, needing to find ways to win some Democratic support in the Senate and to win Freedom Caucus support in the House, with each chamber needing to pass the same reforms to become law.

Trump brought his allegedly unparalleled negotiating skills to this difficult context. However, much Trump saw himself as leading a people's rebellion, his campaign had still traded on his ability to get a better deal for Americans. Most obviously, he would have to persuade Congress to support the mainstream reforms of the Republican leadership while tolerating his potentially divisive and radical executive actions. His efforts to act as a Washington insider and dealmaker, however, revealed a flawed negotiating style.

A president attempting to muster support from other Washington power brokers depends on building a reputation for good and successful judgments (Neustadt 1990). When bargaining with others, the president's position is stronger if he can persuade them that he is taking actions that they would pursue for themselves. Moreover, they must be able to rely on the president to advocate the right course of action and to honor agreements in an extended sequence of decisions. The president who can do this successfully builds a good reputation that can be traded upon in later negotiations. Reputation becomes, therefore, a crucial resource for a president to nurture as an integral part of coalition building (Neustadt 1990; Bowles 2005).

Trump has struggled to build a strong reputation with Republican legislators. His approach to negotiations, despite his claims to being the "great deal maker," has weakened his reputation and made it harder for him to bargain effectively. His character, his ignorance of policy and politics, his negotiating techniques, his lack of respect for legislators and his demand for unreciprocated loyalty all compromise his capacity to win colleagues' respect, undermine his powers of persuasion and so contribute to his limited legislative record.

Whether Trump really has the ability to make personal connections with fellow power brokers is a matter of great contention. On one side of the debate, Trump is portrayed as deeply flawed. He can be bombastic, charmless, sullen, petty, graceless and prone to picking unnecessary fights. On the other, Trump can deliver a torrent of flattery and deploy a charismatic presence. Examples abound of each side of Trump and claiming that one or the other tells the whole story would be a mistake. There are, though, certain aspects of Trump's character and approach to congressional liaison that clearly reduce his capacity to succeed in negotiations.

First, Trump's ignorance of both policy and politics is a major contributor to his lack of success. As he discusses putative reforms with other participants in the process, he is not in a position to appreciate the repercussions of his statements for allies and enemies alike. His discussions and commitments made in them undermine the bargaining process as he contradicts his own previous positions. In January 2018, a televised White House meeting on immigration with legislators of both parties exemplified the problem. As legislators asked Trump what he would be willing to sign in a reform, Trump appeared to move between a series of different positions. At the beginning of the meeting, he appeared to advocate a comprehensive solution taking in border security, an end to "chain migration" and abolition of the lottery program. During the meeting, he volunteered to sign whatever legislators could agree, then demanded funding for a wall as a condition for progress, accepted the need to lead with a "clean" bill to resolve the DACA issue alone, but then asked for a combination of DACA and border security. Throwing in spectacular digressions to the issue of infrastructure, and vagueness on how many miles of wall might be required for an agreement, Trump left legislators utterly confused as to his priorities. This performance revealed the president simply did not understand the issues and that the contradictions in his statements would have negative repercussions (Trump 2018). Reports abound of similar Trump misadventures. Whether taking public positions on Twitter or dealing with legislators in person, Trump looks out of his depth. Most notably, in the healthcare debate, Trump's interventions regularly sabotaged or reset ongoing negotiations (Bade et al. 2017). Trump lacks the expertise to engage with policy negotiations. The allocation of a simpler sales role to him during the subsequent tax reform effort spoke to this shortcoming being recognized by White House and congressional leaders alike (Woodward 2018, 294–296). Trump's ignorance is just one element contributing to his broader inconstancy, a quality that poses enormous problems as he tries to deal with Washington.

A second problem is that Trump does not seem to know where he stands on most issues, even those apparently important to him, or at least fails to project a consistent and committed stance in his statements, meetings and tweets. The outstanding question that hamstrings the administration's internal policy processes, "what does the president want?", also hinders negotiations with other players. Trump's perpetual wildcard performances, by which his policy positions are inconsistent and unpredictable, generate instability in negotiations. For Trump, presentation of a moving target is a virtue: Volatility is part of his much-touted negotiating style (Trump 1987). His negotiations in business were often noted for dramatic changes of position to unsettle those he was pushing for a deal. However, this behavior does a great deal to undermine congressional negotiations.

Trump, whose positions and priorities are poorly understood due to his outsider status, reinforces the problem by not allowing the positions he takes to be considered definitive. This problem prevents political allies and enemies alike from understanding which positions are worth fighting for and which are not. Allies cannot provide unequivocal support for his positions without a risk of having to reverse themselves, while adversaries are encouraged to prolong resistance. The idea that senior figures in Congress cannot leave the room after a meeting with Trump sure in the knowledge that whatever has been agreed with the president will still apply tomorrow is deeply problematic. After an agreement is reached, these power brokers have to persuade others—allies, special interests, constituents—to support the president's position; they invest time, effort and most significantly credibility in their persuasion of others. The consequences of being undercut by the president at a later stage are anything but trivial. Each of Trump's dramatic shifts cuts through a web of commitments in finely honed policy negotiations, disrupting a myriad of interrelated calculations for the players involved.

Trump executed sharp reversals in his policy commitments, most notably during the party's torturous attempts to reform, repeal or replace Obamacare (Graham 2017). His contradictory declarations of support for different proposals at different points in the process may have begged questions about the White House planning process and Trump's credibility, but they also undermined the efforts of potential allies in Congress. For legislators staking their public reputations on particular options, presidential support and its withdrawal are important. They bemoaned the administration's disorganization as the healthcare debate developed, confused and appalled by the inconsistent cues coming from different players in the White House. Even Senate Leader McConnell publicly demanded guidance on what Trump might or might not sign, hoping for clarity (Newmyer et al. 2017). Trump's willingness to declare support and then let down his co-partisans, apparently without compunction, was not well received and encourages a hesitation to trust Trump in future dealings.

Third, Trump doesn't just burn bridges during the intricacies of legislative negotiations, but in the name of public image-building, or perhaps just temper, is oddly happy to attack and abuse publicly those whose support he may need now or in the future. The president regularly demonstrates his anti-establishment credentials by articulating his lack of respect for other institutions of US government and their constitutional roles. He criticizes his own party, including its leaders and many of his senatorial colleagues, which carries a high cost in Washington. The combination of Trump's ignorance of detail and his impulsiveness means that he is not always aware of, or fails to care about, the repercussions of his actions. His Twitter thumbs allow action instantly, without consultation or constraint, and can create serious political problems for him. He often picks his fights without an eye to future repercussions, driving potential allies away. His attacks hold obvious potential for him to sour any personal dealings with the potential allies he has criticized. He creates confrontation and unnecessary barriers to cooperation, reducing his opportunity to persuade others to support his reforms and build coalitions. Trump depends upon the cooperation and votes in the legislature of those he has attacked, but his tweetstorms have alienated legislators personally and so made persuasion more difficult (Cillizza 2017; Costa 2017). One indicator of this problem is the hope of those around him in the White House, and many of his supporters in Congress, that they could persuade Trump to give up tweeting. They hoped he might constrain his self-destructive behavior. Trump has resisted all attempts by his advisers to wrestle control of his phone from him and all entreaties to curb his Twitter habit (Haberman et al. 2017; Karni 2017). He robustly defended the rationale to his staff for his Twitter usage, even though his Director of Strategic Communication told him directly: "You can't just be a loose cannon on Twitter. You're getting killed by a lot of this stuff. You're shooting yourself in the foot. You're making big mistakes." Trump, however, was unrepentant:

> This is my megaphone. This is the way that I speak directly to the people without any filter. Cut through the noise. Cut through the fake news. That's the only way I have to communicate. I have tens of millions of followers. This is bigger than cable news. I go out and I give a speech and it's covered by CNN and nobody's watching, nobody cares. I tweet something and it's my megaphone to the world. (Woodward 2018, 205–206)

To relinquish his access to social media would be to relinquish his control of his communication, at least in his eyes. Trump believes Twitter played a key role in winning him the election and that it will similarly win him the governance, but the worries of his advisers are well founded. How he uses Twitter is extraordinary, but it helps render his presidency ordinary by limiting his effectiveness.

Amid the abuse, Trump also expects Republicans to be personally loyal to him (while offering little reciprocal loyalty in return). This loyalty should be expressed through regular declarations of fealty and legislators voting his policy positions. He appears to regard the tone of his first, notorious cabinet meeting, which amounted to a festival of supplication, as an appropriate model and expects the same of all Republicans. Legislators are expected to vote Trump's position whatever it is today and may be expected to vote the opposite way tomorrow if that serves the needs of Trump's communications. In its most dramatic form, this attitude negates any need, in Trump's mind, to negotiate with legislators; more usually, it seems to produce a resentment and reluctance on Trump's part when he is called on to deal with influential, sometimes pivotal legislators.

Fourth, just as Trump has sabotaged the communications and policy planning operations in the White House through his personalized decision-making, he has undercut his legislative liaison operation. It has been extremely difficult for Trump's White House to generate coherent congressional strategy. Most presidents depend upon their legislative staff to guide reforms through Congress. These staff use their expertise to plan a reform's intricate path to passage. They establish the head count, calculating how to find a suitable majority to pass the bill. Pivotal voters must be wooed. Messaging, timing, committee pathways and, importantly, bargaining on the details of legislation are all needed to navigate a bill through choppy political waters to passage. A strategy is planned to achieve the president's policy objective, allowing the White House staff to organize themselves and the presidency's resources behind the bill. Public communication and private negotiations can be coordinated to maximize the chances of passage; negotiating details of the bill to bring diverse supporters behind it or applying presidential pressure to the right people at the right time to win passage. EOP staff coordinate their efforts to magnify the impact of the presidency, acting as the president's representative and protecting the president's time.

For Trump's congressional liaison staff, such planning is near impossible. Using White House staff to build a congressional coalition to support legislation is undermined when the president is liable to change positions on legislative proposals at little or no notice and without briefing his own people. Strategies can be rendered moot with a single tweet. Legislators bemused by a dramatic Trump communication approach the administration to clarify the president's position, only to find that Trump's own staff, too, are adjusting to the new message. Outsiders wishing to work with the administration confront a baffled presidential staff unable to provide a trustworthy statement of his priorities. Washington, including his own staff, must monitor the president's Twitter feed to see what he is thinking or feeling at any given moment. Trump's individualistic style wrecks the opportunity for negotiations with Congress to be planned and coordinated effectively.

These character traits and approaches to the job limit Trump's effectiveness as a negotiator with other power brokers, despite his confidence in his extraordinary deal-making capacity. He has particularly struggled to secure the party allies whose support he needed in Congress to pass healthcare, immigration or infrastructure reform. His personal conduct is clearly a central consideration, doing much to engender distrust. As proven in a series of reversals, Trump's word cannot be considered his bond, reducing his capacity to use promises of future favors as a negotiating tool. In sum, Trump has failed to build himself a strong presidential reputation. One analysis seven months into his presidency argued that "It remains unclear whether he's capable of [governing and legislating] – the give-something-to-get-something, the slow build of capital that then can be cashed in, not flimsy, news-cycle-feeding insta-alliances but the long-game cultivation of critical relationships" (Kruse 2017). Little about his second year in office suggested that Trump held the overarching vision of his political situation needed to build a reputation for integrity and good judgment.

# 3    Failing to Sell the Trump Vision

For all his personal limitations, broader forces constrain Trump's capacity for extraordinary achievement. The talent or limitations of the presidential salesman are only part of the story. What Trump is trying to sell is at the center of legislators' calculations. The president must be selling a credible product if he is to persuade a legislator to do business. The interests and calculations of the legislator are key. Could the president offer a vision of shared political interests to persuade his party's legislators to follow his lead?

Trump's challenge to the existing system of conservative, Republican politics in Congress was effectively a request to his party allies to move from their political moorings. He wanted them to support him and his policies but with limited evidence to suggest that voters and funders would support the change that was, in many cases, in direct contradiction to some of their ideological beliefs. For a legislator, moving from an established position has costs. Which commitments is the legislator willing to risk stretching, or even breaking, to follow the president in a new direction? These binds are stretched at the potential expense of reelection and achieving ideological goals. Trump's desire to disrupt the Republican Party system would involve reorganizing around the president as a new lodestar.

Such a change is inherently risky, as legislators are sharply aware. Trump might re-arrange Republican politics successfully around new principles and new electoral appeals, or he might drive the party into a ditch, damaging Republicans' electoral appeal, restricting their capacity to pursue their ideological principles and wrecking the party that acts as the vehicle to pursue those goals. Legislators have much at stake and look carefully for cues to steer their decision-making on how far to support the president's agenda. They could support or distance themselves from Trump in response. He has to offer a compelling vision of where the party should go which would win legislators their reelection and allow them to achieve ideological goals. Legislators, therefore, scour the political environment gathering evidence on which to base their decisions. They need to know the nature of Trump's ideology, to establish whether his electoral appeals would work for them and to assess his stewardship of the party. Trump's record in each of these areas has been distinctly mixed, which has led to similarly mixed results in his efforts to lead the party.

Legislators considering Trump's electoral record, and the potential to deploy his style for their own future success, have reasons to doubt Trump's leadership. The 2016 election was traumatic for the Republican Party, even allowing for the presidential victory. Trump's message—confused, but often nationalist, misogynist and ethnocentric—posed some serious problems for elected Republican officials as they faced questions on whether they supported the unconventional statements and positions of their candidate (Liu and Jacobson 2018). Particularly, Trump's capacity to alienate groups of potentially important voters, especially racial and ethnic minorities, made Republicans fear for the long-term well-being of the party at a time of changes in demography that made these groups increasingly important. Some of these concerns would have been allayed by a decisive set of results in the 2016 elections. Trump, though, was on shaky ground in claiming to be an electoral asset and that he had a mandate to lead. The narrow victory in the 2016 Electoral College and loss of the popular vote did not send a clear message to partisan allies that Trump's message was the party's future. Trump had faced a very unpopular opponent, had high disapproval ratings himself, and largely mobilized the party base and drew on Republican Party loyalty among moderates to scrape a victory. His personal unpopularity was record-breaking. The 2016 election had not provided a resounding vote of confidence in Donald Trump or changed the electoral calculus. Nor, given the fantastic policy promises and apparent incoherence of Trump's pledges, was there necessarily a policy agenda that had been given greater credence through an election victory. Rather, as we observed in Chapter 3, as an anti-partisan and anti-Democrat, Trump had merely managed to muster a standard Republican coalition.

Nor had Trump articulated a message that swept many other Republicans into office on the back of his popularity. As Trump was measuring for new curtains at 1600 Pennsylvania Avenue, a net of six Republican representatives and two senators were bubble-wrapping family photos after being dumped by their voters. Coattails matter for presidential leadership because the president's newly elected co-partisans in Congress are inclined to rationalize that their electoral success is due in some part to the new president. Very few congressional Republicans credited Trump for their victories, and in some cases, he may have jeopardized their success. The appeal of Trump's message and the degree to which it could be transferred to individual legislators was open to debate. Legislators would need more evidence to suggest that Trump's approach could motivate the activists, donors, interest groups and voters needed to further their goals. That evidence was not forthcoming as the party experienced a series of discouraging results during Trump's early presidency. Most notably, a humiliating Senate defeat in Alabama, a supposedly safe seat, in December 2017 suggested Trump was on the wrong track, quite apart from the result inflicting further damage on Trump's capacity to lead in the Senate. The defeats of some candidates following in Trump's divisive tracks reduced the credibility of the president's offer (Costa 2018).

Trump's approval ratings are also problematic. His failure to command majority public support suggests that his message might not even be working for the president himself. However, those with a keen eye on the polls are also aware of a very significant Trump success. His expectation that legislators should show loyalty to him is not entirely based on an assumption that the presidency was due such deference or that he is the best negotiator. He expects legislators' support because he won his party's nomination and demonstrated his popularity with Republican voters. Republican legislators should follow him not because he won them over personally, but because the costs of resisting him, by defying their own voters, would be too high. As noted in Chapter 5, his impressive approval numbers among Republicans support the president's claim, suggesting that Republicans in Washington have to acknowledge that Trump is, indeed, a Republican because loyal partisans among the public have decided so. Judging by those numbers at least, Trump has begun to move the party network in support of him by leading the public. Legislators looking nervously at their chances of being renominated by their party have a strong reason to support Trump. The president's going public strategy with its base twist reaped a key reward to assist Trump in his leadership of Washington.

Equally, Washington Republicans have to consider how great a challenge Trump poses to their ideological and policy commitments. His campaign statements challenged core Republican positions. As Republicans monitored the development of Trump's policy and ideology, they feared that Trump would see through this betrayal of their long-set commitments. Trump's skittishness magnified the uncertainty; defining his vision is, to say the least, difficult during his communication-driven presidency. However, his choice of first-year agenda for Congress offered Republicans much comfort. His decision to follow Ryan's plan, pursuing healthcare reform and tax cuts encouraged Republican legislators on two fronts. First, the policies advocated fitted the Republican orthodoxy. Second, Trump would not be asking his fellow partisans to cross their own orthodoxy in congressional votes. In fact, Trump showed only a limited inclination to fight in Congress for the less conventional policy positions that he campaigned on. For example, although Trump still persists in demanding the border wall be built, he was strangely circumspect in pursuing funding for it during budgetary negotiations in 2017. His own statements in support of Dreamers also challenged his apparently devout anti-immigration position. As Trump appeared to come to an agreement on Dreamers with Democratic congressional leaders in September 2017, and as he declared his willingness to negotiate a settlement to normalize their status in January 2018, the minority of dedicatedly anti-immigrant Republicans expressed fury at his betrayal.

This combination of supporting orthodox proposals and failing to advocate his alternative agenda consistently offered Republicans an opportunity to support "their" president without crossing their ideological commitments. Trump did not ask the party to move from its ideological moorings and left the party network relatively intact and optimistic. They were asked to tolerate Trump's controversial executive actions, but these could, largely, be considered the president's responsibility and could be disowned at a later date if necessary and might even be overturned by a future Republican president with more moderate sentiments. Only in early 2018 did Trump change tack and ask for more challenging legislation, by which time his dissipated mandate and looming congressional elections meant that his agenda would only receive limited legislative attention.

Trump's leadership of the Republican Party is another key test for those considering whether to support him. Presidents can play a key role as party builders. Given Trump's outsider status, history of supporting Democrats, anti-establishment position and lacerating attacks on party leaders, there were reasons to doubt the president's loyalty to the party cause as he took office. Might Trump actually try to purge those who opposed him within his own party, threatening incumbents with nomination contests? His inexperience also raised doubts about his capacity for party leadership. Much of Trump's leadership of the party seemed amateurish and directionless. His involvement in the Alabama contest, especially, where he could not seem to find a clear position or commit to it, suggested that he knew neither where he wanted to take the party nor how to take it there. Coupled with his continuing vindictive, potentially harmful, attacks on those who dared to oppose him, legislators lacked compelling evidence of the need to support the Trump product. These weaknesses reduced Trump's capacity to persuade Republicans in Washington to support him. Early in 2018, however, Trump poured balm onto this particular wound by withdrawing any threat to purge his party. Having previously shown support for insurgent candidates and attacking "establishment" incumbent Republicans, Trump engineered a spectacular normalization as the party prepared itself for the 2018 midterms. Behaving much more like a conventional Republican president, Trump declared that he would not oppose incumbent Republicans and promised a series of fundraisers and public engagements to support his party's candidates. By the middle of the year, the president appeared alongside Republican Party candidates and offered strongly partisan rhetoric in support:

> So we need more Republicans. We've got to get out there in the midterm. We've got to get more Republicans. Got to get more Republicans. A vote for a Democrat for Congress is really a vote for Nancy Pelosi and her radical agenda. (June 20, 2018)

The president endorsed or helped clear the path for nearly every incumbent Republican senator, including those who had previously attracted his ire (such as Dean Heller in Nevada), and he swung behind establishment candidates in open primaries, even those with whom he had traded insults in the past (including Mitt Romney in Utah). Disruptive, anti-Washington, anti-establishment candidates suddenly became less seductive from the perspective of the Oval Office. Trump declined to support some candidates in his own image (like Chris McDaniel in Mississippi and Don Blankenship in West Virginia). The rebel was emphatically toeing the party line and fulfilling the traditional presidential role as party "cheerleader" for the midterm elections. The Twitter abuse directed at some Republicans did not stop entirely, but Trump's willingness to campaign for Republican candidates and avoid civil war in the party alleviated many partisan concerns.

Nonetheless, Trump still posed a problem for some incumbent Republicans. When casting a vote in Congress, legislators had to consider the electoral risks of supporting Trump's message, his commitment to their conservative principles, and whether his new party-building efforts were genuine. They were confronted by a mixed set of cues and how they chose to interpret them depended very much on their individual situation. Some clearly decided not to vote with Trump on occasion, which cost him dearly. Trump was more likely to win legislative successes when the vote was tied to the party's existing ideological orthodoxy. The Republican Party certainly did not reject his leadership outright—as long as he led them where they wanted to go. However, Trump was rebuffed when he posed a genuine legislative challenge to traditional Republican positions. On scathing funding cuts to federal departments, the wall, immigration reform and infrastructure, the party refused to support Trump. Many of these proposals did not even come to a final vote that would have embarrassed the president.

Trump is not without leverage in his party, however. For most Republicans in safe seats, the high personal support the president commands from rank-and-file Republicans among the public is important. They fear a primary challenge from a Trump loyalist in their district more than they fear defeat in the following general election. This popular support was instrumental, for example, in winning over the congressional Freedom Caucus. After initial skepticism and a high-profile spat over Trump's healthcare initiative, caucus leader Representative Mark Meadows recalled the irritation of conservative voters toward him back home: "It was not a fun time in the district" (Meadows quoted in Bacon 2018). Trump's popularity among Republican identifiers pushed the Freedom Caucus to find areas of shared interest with Trump.

While Trump has made peace with many in the congressional party— or at least signed an armistice—and can win most of the party most of the time, crucially this support is not sufficient to push legislation through precariously balanced Congresses. With congressional Democrats lined up in lockstep against Trump during the 115th Congress, it took only a very small number of Republicans to prevent Trump's initiatives from becoming law. Even on issues which potentially unite the party, such as healthcare reform, the necessary votes have been elusive. An examination of support that Trump's proposals have won from individual legislators make the problem clear (FiveThirtyEight 2018). While the Freedom Caucus initially resisted Trump but have now been won over, the key group of Republicans that Trump has failed to persuade to his cause are largely moderates representing marginal districts.

Trump's popularity may have encouraged most Republicans to support him, but moderates have been more reluctant. Senators such as Jeff Flake, John McCain and Ben Sasse attacked Trump, emphasizing his breach with traditional party values and the dangers he threatened. Even former President George W. Bush joined in. While these objections were principled, they also had an electoral dimension. In the long term, party elders fear for the party's future. Trump's lack of ethnic inclusiveness sets a worrying direction for the party that seems likely to face a white-minority electorate by mid-century. In the short term, polls suggest the president may be driving moderates in the electorate away from the Republican Party, although the evidence is not yet conclusive. Nor do the polls suggest that Trump's policies command widespread support. For legislators in competitive districts worried about moderate swing voters, Trump's disappointing overall approval numbers and divisive approach to politics are at least as important as his support from within the party. They fear an electoral challenge from a moderate Democrat, knowing that they must win independents and potentially even centrist Democratic support to be reelected. Trump may be driving these middle-of-the-road voters away, and thus, some Republican members of Congress see little benefit in being loyal to him.

These ideological and electoral concerns generated Republican resistance to Trump in Congress. In the highest profile individual case, Senator John McCain cast the decisive vote to torpedo the Trump-backed proposal for healthcare reform. McCain's action symbolizes a broader moderate skepticism among Republican legislators vulnerable to Democratic attacks in their districts (FiveThirtyEight 2018). Here, Trump's divisive base strategy reinforced by vigorous and persistent public communication backfires badly by driving away moderates.

The result is that Trump cannot win all of his party to support the reforms he offers. He commands high levels of support within his party, but not high enough to pass his more controversial reforms. His base strategy was a success with most Republicans but has not sold moderates the agenda he offers, despite the need for their support to navigate a Congress where small margins matter. His base strategy has been a stunning strategic failure in Washington. Trump's campaign for public support undercuts his own ability to achieve a Trump Revolution. This phenomenon is best demonstrated by an examination of what we call "hostage politics". Here, Trump's base strategy, "going public" and alleged bargaining skills combine to render his levels of achievement very ordinary indeed.

# 4     Hostage Politics

Presidents can try to structure political battles in ways that advantage them. Their office gives them an opportunity to take the initiative, a first-mover advantage, by choosing the initial terms of engagement over an issue. Trump, with his keen eye for the dramatic and newsworthy gesture, has established a means of doing this that combines action to win popularity from his base and gaining leverage over potential negotiating partners in what can be characterized as "hostage politics". It is a simple two-step process. First, the president takes a policy hostage to excite his base. With bold and often controversial rhetoric and action, the president takes a distinct stand, offering "red meat" to his supporters. Second, he tries to use the hostage as leverage to gain his preferred outcome in negotiations with Congress or with other political actors domestically or internationally. It rarely works, though, and can sometimes make a bad situation worse. In appealing to what Trump calls "my people" and "my base" in this way, he alienates both the wider American public and the policy makers he is trying to persuade, thus further hindering his prospects of success. This is not a new strategy for Trump; it is one he utilized, sometimes to good albeit short-term effect, in his business career.

The clearest example of Trump playing hostage politics is on behalf of his key campaign promise to build a wall along the US-Mexico border. The wall stands almost zero chance of winning congressional approval as a standalone measure, even when he had Republican majorities in both chambers of Congress. He is also certainly not going to get Mexico to pay for it, even though he has asserted that is what is going to happen. Perhaps the only way to get it funded is to package it up with a series of other immigration measures that collectively could win congressional approval. But the president does not have the temperament, eye for detail or ability to stay on message that are required to sculpt and champion a comprehensive package of immigration reforms that could keep enough cultural conservatives onboard while winning the support of a critical number of moderate Democrats. Trump said in his 2018 State of the Union address that he would accept a "fair compromise where no one gets everything they want," but compromise is not part of his modus operandi. And so he plays base politics with a hostage twist. For example, Trump took Obama's DACA program—which offered regularized legal status and protection from deportation to Dreamers who had entered the US illegally as children—hostage on September 5, 2017. He signed an executive "death warrant" for the policy but delayed its execution until March 5, 2018, to give Congress six months to come up with the ransom: funding for the wall. On the one hand, Trump thought the DACA death warrant would play well with his conservative political base hungry for red meat on the immigration issue. On the other, he calculated that he could trade his hostage for congressional funding for the wall. It appears a neat and profitable deal on paper: the first step reinforces the base, the second step gets a congressional win, fulfils the key campaign promise, and further solidifies the base.

Unfortunately for Trump, the plan did not deliver his wall. It failed in part because of its inherent flaws and in part because he overplayed a relatively weak hand. Trump's own team in Congress is divided and a critical number are unwilling to trade a wall for a path to citizenship for Dreamers or in their thinking an amnesty for lawbreakers. Worse, even if every Republican Senator supported the legislation, Trump would have been nine votes away from the 60 required to overcome a filibuster. Trump needs Democratic votes in both chambers, but his red meat hostage politics almost guarantees that he will not get them. For one thing, opponents who trade with Trump—paying a ransom (in the form of a wall) to get the hostage released (DACA)—are likely to be viewed as weak and supine by their own supporters. Trump's antics incentivize his opponents to stay strong and refuse to trade except on the most favorable terms. Anything less and they lose face. For another, Trump is so undisciplined that he cannot hold the line in tough negotiations, despite all his claims that he is the greatest negotiator there is. At one point leading up to the March 5 deadline, it appeared that Trump had reached a deal with Nancy Pelosi and Chuck Schumer for more border funding and a DACA replacement—a "bill of love" claimed a straight-faced Trump—but at the last moment White House senior policy adviser Stephen Miller persuaded the president to push for a reduction in legal immigration in addition to wall funding. The administration miscalculated how much the DACA hostage was worth, and the Democrats walked away, leaving the president with a hostage and no payday. Worse for Trump, the hostage was well liked by the American public and even some members of his own party in Congress who preferred an unconditional release.

A shrewd, tactically sophisticated leader may at this point have paused and reflected on the efficacy of their particular approach, and changed approach if it was not working. Trump characteristically doubled-down, following the same game plan but this time with even higher stakes. In the second iteration of his effort to force Congress to fund his border wall, hostage politics shifted from metaphor to reality. The failure of the DACA hostage plan had coincided with a rise in the number of undocumented migrants entering the United States. With no wall to placate his base and in a bid to drive numbers down, Attorney General Jeff Sessions announced a new crackdown at the border: The criminal prosecution of all adults crossing illegally, including those accompanied by children. Bush and Obama before Trump had been far from soft on illegal border crossers, and Obama even went so far as to hold parents and children together in secure facilities. However, after a federal court ruled that children could not be confined for more than twenty days, the Obama administration changed position and began releasing families into the community while they awaited their day in court. But so-called catch and release would end under the zero-tolerance policy of Sessions. The criminal prosecution of adults who crossed with children required those children to be removed from their parents or guardians. The subsequent images and audio of separated children, including toddlers, being held in metal cages horrified America and the world. The Trump administration in its effort to deter undocumented migrants and leverage Congress into passing an immigration bill appeared to be literally, rather than politically, holding children hostage. After weeks of protests and in the face of blanket criticism around the world, from the Pope to every living First Lady including the president's own wife Melania, Trump capitulated and signed an executive order on June 20, 2018, to end family separation and signal another failure for hostage politics.

Creating and utilizing leverage seems to be the prerequisite of Trump's strategic approach across a wide range of policy areas. In *The Art of the Deal*, Trump emphasized the importance of negotiating from a position of strength, using it to leverage the best outcome possible: "The best thing you can do is deal from strength, and leverage is the biggest strength you have. Leverage is having something the other guy wants. Or better yet, needs. Or best of all, simply can't do without" (Trump 1987). But while it is his go-to negotiating tactic across a wide range of areas including, as we'll see in the next chapter, in the administration's approach to foreign policy, mostly it has not worked domestically because Trump has not been in a position of strength and has had little leverage, even when he has taken a policy hostage.

Not only do hostage politics and the base strategy not work in obtaining the desired policy goals in the short term, but they are actually destructive to the president's wider agenda in the longer term. One key problem is that they engender and harden opposition and tend to make public opinion less favorable. Before Trump's primary campaign and later promotion to the White House, for example, immigration was the most important concern of a small but determined subset of Republican activists. Similarly on the Democratic side, the issue preoccupied a relatively narrow coterie of immigrant-rights groups and community activists. In expanding attention to the issue, Trump expanded the circle of interested parties and mobilized opinion both for and against his policy proposals. Progressive groups such as MoveOn.org and Indivisible have subsequently placed immigration front and center in their mobilizing efforts, and they and immigrants-rights groups are forging closer links with organizations such as Black Lives Matter and the NAACP who represent other marginalized communities that have been subject to Trump's racial outbursts. Congressional roll calls on immigration are being scrutinized more carefully and the issue is increasingly becoming a political litmus test—like abortion—on which there is only one acceptable position. Those voting the wrong way—such as Chicago Representative Dan Lipinski—are increasingly likely to find themselves facing a heavily financed primary challenge (Holland 2018). Before Trump, some congressional Democrats had opposed awarding Dreamers legal residency, but the president's antics united them against his position. In a closely tied legislature, making enemies is inadvisable, but Trump provided a master class on how to do it. Just ten years before Trump won the presidency, a young senator called Barack Obama voted for the Secure Fence Act that established a 14-mile fence along the border between San Diego and Tijuana, an almost inconceivable position for an ambitious Democrat today.

# 5    Conclusion

There are those who argue that Trump has taken over the Republican Party. The president's capacity to command partisan support in Congress speaks to the idea that the party is now Trump's. His major victories in achieving tax reform and establishing a new wave of conservative appointments to the courts are both substantive achievements. Congressional Republicans seem reluctant to speak out against Trump—to "poke the bear" in the words of Senator Bob Corker—or to hold him to account. Proponents of the "Trump Takeover" thesis point to the subservience of congressional leaders McConnell and Ryan, the reluctance of free-trade Republicans to stand up to him on tariffs, widespread support for detente with North Korea and the decision of his most prominent critics, notably Senators Jeff Flake and Bob Corker, not to seek reelection. Perhaps most significantly, some Republicans adopted his campaigning style during the 2018 midterms, and whether a potential candidate has supported or criticized Trump became a litmus test of potential Republican candidates in some primary contests. The risk of opposing him has certainly increased, as suggested by Trump's role on the one occasion that he targeted a Republican incumbent, in the primary defeat of South Carolina Representative and persistent Trump critic Mark Sanford. "Look what happened to Sanford," think worried Republicans on the Hill. Trump has made it difficult to oppose him, largely because of his support among Republican voters. The president's "base strategy" would seem to have had an impact.

This interpretation of Trump's leadership is mistaken. He has not managed to dominate Washington. He has not engineered an ideological transformation. On the contrary, Trump's extraordinary approach to being president—what we have called his methodology—has seriously undermined his capacity to utilize the powers of the presidency to effect the revolutionary change he promised. His personal style is flawed; his White House staff are hamstrung by his continual disruption and efforts to coerce opponents are not well coordinated. Most notably, his choice to cement his support among core supporters via a highly partisan and culturally divisive communication strategy has driven away moderates and independents and reinforced the already determined opposition of Democrats. Key players in Washington, whose support Trump needs to enact his radical reforms, are unimpressed by the president's public prestige and see little danger in opposing him. Trump, the alleged master of leverage, has little leverage where it matters, among the moderates of congressional politics who make the difference between achieving majorities to pass legislation or not. Sometimes even with Trump's agreement, congressional Republicans have been allowed to dominate the legislative agenda and deliver conventional Republican priorities while being able to reject Trump's more radical proposals. Trump may overshadow his party, like most presidents do, but he has simply installed himself at the top, not remolded it.

# References

Bacon, Perry, Jr. 2018. "How the Freedom Caucus Learned to Love Trump." *fivethirtyeight.com*, July 31. https://fivethirtyeight.com/features/how-the-freedom-caucus-learned-to-love-trump/.

Bade, Rachael, Burgess Everett, and Josh Dawsey. 2017. "Trump Sides with Democrats in Debt Limit, Funding, Harvey Deal." *Politico*, September 6. https://www.politico.com/story/2017/09/06/schumer-and-pelosi-offer-support-for-harvey-aid-and-debt-limit-boost-242376.

Bowles, Nigel. 2005. *Nixon's Business*. College Station: Texas A&M University Press.

Cillizza, Chris. 2017. "Burning Every Bridge." *Washington Post*, August 24.

Costa, Robert. 2017. "Pressure Cooker." *Washington Post*, October 9.

Costa, Robert. 2018. "Pennsylvania Vote Shows That Trumpism Has Its Limits—Even in Trump Country." *Washington Post*, March 13.

FiveThirtyEight. 2018. "Tracking Congress in the Age of Trump." *fivethirtyeight.com*. https://projects.fivethirtyeight.com/congress-trump-score/. Accessed October 21, 2018.

Graham, David A. 2017. "'As I Have Always Said': Trump's Ever-Changing Positions on Health Care." *The Atlantic*, July 28.

Haberman, Maggie, Glenn Thrush, and Peter Baker. 2017. "Trump's Way: Inside Trump's Hour-by-Hour Battle for Self-Preservation." *New York Times*, December 9.

Holland, Joshua. 2018. "In the Long Run, Trump Could Be a Huge Setback for the Anti-immigration Movement." *The Nation*, April 5.

Huetteman, Emmarie. 2017. "On Health Law, G.O.P. Faces a Formidable Policy Foe: House Republicans." *New York Times*, March 20.

Karni, Annie. 2017. "John Kelly's Losing Battle with Trump's Twitter Feed." *Politico*, November 29. https://www.politico.com/story/2017/11/29/trump-twitter-fringe-websites-270490.

Kruse, Michael. 2017. "The Loneliest President." *Politico*, September 15. https://www.politico.com/magazine/story/2017/09/15/donald-trump-isolated-alone-trumpology-white-house-215604.

Liu, Huchen, and Gary C. Jacobson. 2018. "Republican Candidates' Positions on Donald Trump in the 2016 Congressional Elections: Strategies and Consequences." *Presidential Studies Quarterly* 48 (1): 49–71.

Neustadt, Richard. 1990. *Presidential Power and the Modern Presidents: The Politics of Leadership from Roosevelt to Reagan*. New York: The Free Press.

Newmyer, Tory, Juliet Eilperin, and Sean Sullivan. 2017. "McConnell Says Trump Needs to Provide Clarity on Health Care." *Washington Post*, October 22.

Skocpol, Theda, and Vanessa Williamson. 2016. *The Tea Party and the Remaking of Republican Conservatism*. Oxford: Oxford University Press.

Snell, Kelsey, and Mike DeBonis. 2017. "Republicans Set Aggressive Agenda on Health Care, Regulations and Tax Reform." *Washington Post*, January 25.

Trump, Donald J. 1987. *Trump: The Art of the Deal.* New York: Random House.

Trump, Donald J. 2018. "Remarks in a Meeting with Members of Congress on Immigration Reform and an Exchange with Reporters." January 9. http://www.presidency.ucsb.edu/ws/?pid=128934.

Woodward, Bob. 2018. *Fear: Trump in the White House.* London: Simon & Schuster.

# 8

# Trump's Ordinary Foreign Policy

The front page of the June 9–15, 2018, *Economist* magazine carries a cartoon image that neatly sums up conventional wisdom on the nature of Donald Trump's approach to foreign policymaking. Under the simple banner headline, "America's foreign policy", is an illustrated image of Trump astride a dark globe, head thrust back with hair and tie flowing, dangling from a chain in a parody of pop singer Miley Cyrus in the video for her 2013 hit song "Wrecking Ball." The implication is obvious: Trump is a reckless disruptor, smashing his way through the niceties of international diplomacy, dismissing statesmanship as irrelevant, tearing up international agreements and wildly destroying the architecture of the global political system.

This chapter examines the extent to which Trump has departed from previous US approaches to foreign policy. It looks at the question of Trump's style and the underlying logic of his foreign policy strategy. It argues that the Trump administration has rooted its foreign and security

© The Author(s) 2019
J. Herbert et al., *The Ordinary Presidency of Donald J. Trump*,
Palgrave Studies in Political Leadership,
https://doi.org/10.1007/978-3-030-04943-0_8

policy in the idea of "peace through strength," adopting a strategy that lies very much within conservative Republican foreign policy traditions. Historically, this approach has been controversial with allies and increased tensions with adversaries, but while disruptive and risk-laden it is not a novel approach. The degree to which Trump and his advisors have followed this approach, what it has meant practically in terms of policy and action, how it has been received by allies and the effects it has had on adversaries will be explored. The chapter will show how the administration has emphasized the projection of power and resolve to demonstrate the credibility of US strength in what it perceives as an environment hostile to American interests and damaged by Trump's predecessor's apparent inadequacies and weaknesses.

It will argue that Trump's foreign policy inexperience coupled with a foreign policy team that lacks internal unity are not unusual characteristics, particularly for first-term US presidencies. It will consider how Trump's leadership style and personal idiosyncrasies add layers of complication for the administration's efforts internationally and suggest why it seems the president is more comfortable working with adversarial dictators rather than his democratic allies. Although his lack of careful engagement frustrates seasoned members of the foreign policy elite and academic and media observers, the underlying logic and approach is not such a radical redirection and there is a useful and important distinction to be made between the rather orthodox and ordinary approach and objectives of the Trump administration, as laid out in a series of official strategy documents, and the often extraordinary rhetorical performance of President Trump. The chapter will conclude that there has been significant continuity in US foreign and security policy despite the disruptive personality of the US president. US foreign policy has hardly been characterized by unbridled success in the twenty-first century prior to Trump taking over the Oval Office. The limitations on the ability of the United States to secure its interests and achieve its objectives have been apparent to critics for many decades. Provided he does not accidentally or intentionally precipitate a major conflict of global proportions, he is likely to preside over a rather ordinary foreign policy despite his forthright attitude and lack of diplomatic tact.

# 1    The "Revolutionary"?

Like most new presidents, Trump was determined to distinguish himself from his immediate predecessor in foreign policy. This imperative was perhaps even stronger for Trump since as we have seen he had built his presidential campaign on a rejection of politics as usual in Washington, promising to Make America Great Again by putting America First and discarding the more multilateral approach of the Obama administration to global affairs. Following Trump's inauguration speech, conservative columnist Charles Krauthammer summed up the conventional wisdom of many pundits when he stated with some alarm that the new president's foreign policy stance was nothing short of "revolutionary" (Krauthammer 2017). Compared with Barack Obama, Trump's attitude and approach to foreign policy did appear extremely different.

Obama recognized and acknowledged the complexities and inter-relating difficulties of international affairs and seemed to accept that there are significant limits to what the US can achieve globally regardless of its immense military, economic, political and cultural power. While Obama's critics lambasted him for his apparently naïve idealism and alleged weakness, a realist streak could be discerned in his thinking. Acknowledging and understanding the limits of US power were regarded within the administration as a point of strength from which the US could realistically pursue its international goals and objectives to prosper more effectively in matters of security and economic stability. The administration of George W. Bush had blithely disregarded these limits in ways that ultimately placed the US in a range of vulnerable positions as they overstretched militarily in Afghanistan, Iraq and elsewhere while fostering an economic environment in which a disastrous financial crisis emerged. By attempting to work within the recognized limits of US power, the Obama administration sought to re-establish military and economic security with an emphasis on multilateralism. Finding comprehensive solutions to complex international problems of an interdependent nature necessitated partnering with allies and engaging with adversaries. Working collaboratively, though still with the US as the primary partner, was Obama's preferred approach to most issues.

While Trump may have had no experience and little knowledge of foreign affairs, he was convinced that not only Obama but also a host of previous American presidents had got things completely wrong and that he was the man to fix it. Those views had been long in the making. Since at least the 1980s, Trump's mantra in his books, media interviews, speeches and even full-page advertisements he paid for in newspapers had been that America's leaders were "foolish," that they were constantly letting down the United States and failing to promote its interests effectively, whether they were Democrats or Republicans. As he put it in a full-page advertisement in the *New York Times*, *Washington Post* and *Boston Globe* on September 2, 1987: "The world is laughing at America's politicians." In a follow-up interview the same day on *Larry King Live* on CNN, he reiterated that he believed Washington's allies "laugh at us because of our own stupidity and [that of our] leaders" (Laderman and Simms 2017, 32–34).

Long before seriously contemplating a presidential run, Trump also promoted the view that he was uniquely placed personally to deliver better solutions to the world's problems than the policy makers that had represented the United States in recent decades. In a 2000 interview with the *Observer* newspaper, he claimed in relation to the Middle East that "Everything can be solved if you have the talent," implying that as the great "dealmaker," he was the man to do it. Ten years later on CNN, he made quite clear that he believed he had the credentials necessary to resolve the world's problems, since all that was needed was "somebody that knew something about the art of the deal." By 2011, Trump was highly critical of President Obama, reiterating to the Conservative Political Action Committee Conference the same complaint he had made about the Reagan administration in 1987: "America today is missing quality leadership and foreign countries have quickly realized this. It is the reason that the United States is becoming the laughing stock of the world" (Laderman and Simms 2017, 70–75).

Despite Trump's self-confident view of his own ability to succeed in international affairs where he believes his predecessors have failed, there is much in his extraordinary style and personal approach to international affairs so far that is criticized for being ill-conceived, counterproductive and even dangerously contrary to the best interests, prosperity and security of the United States as well as to international stability. Obama made careful attempts to construct a sophisticated and reflective approach to foreign policy that acknowledged and attempted to work across the complex connections between policy areas in what he regarded as an increasingly interdependent globe. By contrast, Donald Trump seems allergic to complexity, prefers to compartmentalize issues into simple boxes and regards international affairs in an extremely orthodox, states based, interest and power driven, ethnocentric manner.

Obama's preferred approach was collaborative, seeking a full range of policy advice from inside and outside the administration, deliberating often for long periods of time, before reaching a decision that was usually careful and considered. Trump is again quite the opposite. He impatiently, sometimes angrily, and often publicly, ignores or dismisses the counsel of his national security team and others in the administration. On the campaign trail in particular, but also since taking office, he has largely turned his back on the foreign policy elite in his party. He has also been more than willing to publicly disagree with, criticize or embarrass the leaders of even the closest traditional allies of the US. Obama was sometimes criticized for being too deliberative in his foreign policy approach, not least by his opponents who viewed his measured approach to decision-making as prevarication or indecision. Trump again is in complete contrast, making what seem impetuous, rash decisions and often reducing the complexity of foreign and security policy to a series of 140 or now 280 character rants on Twitter. Trump's brash assertiveness and wanton disregard for diplomatic etiquette is what leads his critics to label him a disruptor, determined to shake up world politics just as keenly as he desires to "drain the swamp" in Washington. The conclusion reached by these observers is that Trump is very likely to have damaging and destabilizing effects upon long-term alliances and delicate regional security apparatus, as well as deepening domestic political divisions over the purposes and objectives of US foreign policy. His attempts at disruption at home may well have been tempered by the traditional checks and balances within the political system, by the demands of Republican Party politics, and by a mass media determined to hold him to account for his more extreme behavior. In foreign affairs, however, it is argued by many analysts that he has extraordinary potential to cause chaos and ignite conflict, not least because presidents usually enjoy greater levels of autonomy in priority setting and action beyond the water's edge.

Trump has characteristically thrown aside the diplomatic handbook during his first two years in office, often treating leaders and high representatives of other countries with the same kind of contempt that he would dispense with contestants on his reality TV show *The Apprentice*. It has not only been adversaries and enemies, such as North Korean premier Kim Jong Un who he labeled "little rocket man" in 2017, who have faced Trump's disdain, but also his allies. Canadian Prime Minister Justin Trudeau was condemned by Trump as "dishonest and weak" after the G7 summit in Quebec in June 2018. The next month, Trump embarrassed British Prime Minister Theresa May during his first trip to the UK. In an interview with *The Sun* newspaper, published as the two leaders met for talks designed to reinforce the transatlantic relationship, he strongly criticized his host's approach to the "Brexit" negotiations with the European Union and said her political rival Boris Johnson, who had just resigned from cabinet, would make a "great prime minister." Trump's actions in diplomatic settings have also been criticized for being disrespectful and offensive, particularly when they project his apparent lack of interest in certain regions of the world such as the African continent. During his first year in office, for example, Trump removed his translation headphones as the president of Niger began to speak at a May G7 meeting, walked out of a session on African migration and health issues at the G20 in July leaving his daughter and adviser Ivanka Trump to represent him and repeatedly mispronounced Namibia as "Nambia" while also confusing Nigeria with Liberia when addressing the aftermath of the Ebola crisis at a lunch with African leaders at the UN in September.

It is not only Trump's negative comments about world leaders, however, that have courted controversy. His refusal to be publicly critical of the Russian President Vladimir Putin, for whom he aired great admiration while running for president, has been a conspicuous exception to his often damning attitude toward other political leaders. The context for this "bromance" makes it all the more surprising and contentious. The allegations that Russia made extensive and sophisticated attempts to influence the outcome of voting in favor of Donald Trump's candidacy in the 2016 US presidential election have cast a long shadow over the president's efforts at refreshing the relationship with Moscow and making a personal connection with Putin. US intelligence agencies, including the CIA, FBI and the Office of the Director of National Intelligence, have undertaken detailed investigations and concluded that Russia was responsible for an extensive cyber espionage campaign designed to harm Hillary Clinton's campaign for the presidency. The Democratic Party National Committee computer systems were hacked, documents were stolen, damaging leaks to the public were orchestrated, and fabricated or misleading advertisements and other anti-Clinton material were distributed on Facebook and Twitter using thousands of imposter accounts.

The allegations go further with suspicions, vehemently denied by President Trump, that there was direct collusion between the Trump campaign and the Russian government. Meetings between campaign officials and Russian citizens are alleged to have taken place to attain information that could damage the Clinton campaign. Less than four weeks after he became Trump's first National Security Advisor, Michael Flynn resigned when it was revealed that prior to taking up his post he had held conversations with the Russian Ambassador to the US and then tried to cover up the contact. The controversy over whether Trump or his administration was seeking to obstruct the investigations, particularly after he fired FBI Director James Comey, led to the appointment of Special Counsel Robert Mueller by the Justice Department to fully explore the claims of Russian interference and possible collusion. The Mueller investigation began to yield arrests and convictions of former Trump campaign officials in late 2017, including his former campaign manager Paul Manafort, with Flynn also facing conviction in late 2018. The common perception in the US that Russia is testing the West's resolve, not only with the election interference but also with aggressive actions such as the annexation of Crimea and its intervention in Syria, also deepened in 2018, not least due to the alleged Russian sanctioned poisoning of former Soviet double agent Sergei Skripal and his daughter in Salisbury, England.

In this context of controversy and assertive Russian foreign policy actions, criticism of Trump's positive attitude toward Putin and the nature of their relationship came to a head at the press conference following the Helsinki Summit between the two leaders in July 2018. Although he backtracked in the days afterward and claimed to have misspoken, in his direct answers to questions from journalists, Trump pointedly refused to confront Putin over the alleged Russian election meddling, saying he believed the Russian leader's denials of involvement while appearing happy to criticize his own intelligence services. Trump's comments drew great opprobrium from not only his domestic opponents but also members of his own Republican Party and further energized the Mueller investigation. Former CIA Director John O. Brennan was perhaps strongest in his condemnation, tweeting that Trump's performance in Helsinki was "nothing short of treasonous." A host of Republican lawmakers, however, also condemned Trump with similar levels of surprise and scorn, with Senator John McCain stating: "No prior president has ever abased himself more abjectly before a tyrant." The disjuncture between Trump's apparent friendliness toward Putin compared with his adversarial attitude toward Washington's allies appeared even starker when contrasted with the hostile positions he had taken the previous week with leaders at the NATO summit and his seemingly lukewarm, even two-faced, support for the British prime minister.

Trump's personal approach during the first months of his presidency, then, was brazen and often aggressive in its rhetoric, seeming to jar not only with the approach of his immediate predecessor but also other previous administrations led by members of his own party. Much of the foreign policy elite in the Republican Party had strongly opposed Trump's candidacy, with 50 former Republican national security officials writing an open letter to the *New York Times* (August 8, 2016) claiming Trump was "not qualified to be President and Commander-in-Chief" and warning that he would make a "dangerous" national leader who would "put at risk our country's national security and well-being." Trump's response was completely dismissive, claiming that he did not need the support of experienced officials. Indeed, in an interview on MSNBC's *Morning Joe* in March 2016, he made clear that he believed the best counsel he could seek on foreign policy was his own:

I'm speaking with myself, number one, because I have a very good brain and I've said a lot of things. I know what I'm doing and I listen to a lot of people, I talk to a lot of people and at the appropriate time I'll tell you who the people are. But my primary consultant is myself and I have a good instinct for this stuff.

Yet despite this public rejection of the Republican Party foreign policy elite coupled with his open hostility toward many members of the Republican leadership in Congress, once he became president Trump nonetheless rooted the underlying logic of his foreign policy approach in the long-held conservative Republican Party principle of "peace through strength."

## 2  "Peace Through Strength" and the Republican Party Tradition

In his Inaugural Address, Trump declared that the idea of America First would be the fundamental core of his foreign policy. That same day the administration refreshed the White House Web site, completely replacing the Obama administration's content and adding a range of short summary pages of its own main policy positions. The "America First Foreign Policy" page stated that "Peace through strength will be at the center of that foreign policy." It argued that: "This principle will make possible a stable, more peaceful world with less conflict and more common ground" (White House Website 2017). When the website was refreshed again in 2018, the statement became even clearer in its projection of the significance of the idea as the guiding principle of the Trump administration, emphasizing the perceived need to increase US military capabilities: "Rebuilding US deterrence to preserve peace through strength must be our nation's top priority" (White House Website 2018). This maxim of "peace through strength" is hardly a new approach, however. It has been a foundational idea of conservative Republican Party foreign policy thinking since at least Ronald Reagan's presidency in the 1980s, with deeper roots in the failed presidential campaign of Barry Goldwater in 1964, and places the stated strategic approach of the Trump administration squarely within long established traditions.

The basic assumption of the "peace through strength" approach is that its allies and adversaries must perceive the United States as being in a position of strength internationally if its ultimate goals of global peace and stability are to be achieved. There are usually three main elements to an administration's initial approach to foreign policy if it adheres to the "peace through strength" idea, emphasizing the "strength" side of the equation on coming to office: a condemnation of the previous administration's apparent weakness and ill-conceived policies that have allegedly placed the US in a vulnerable position internationally; the projection of US power and resolve through assertive, uncompromising and often nationalistic rhetoric; and also a buildup of military resources coupled with a demonstrable willingness to both threaten and use force. Once an administration is convinced that its strength has been sufficiently projected and demonstrated, and its resolve and credibility are established, then it can move to the negotiation and conciliation phase that "peace through strength" implies.

It is an approach, however, that brings with it substantial levels of risk, especially if the efforts to project strength are overplayed or if they are misinterpreted abroad. Allies might be offended by US attitudes and actions, causing them to cease to be cooperative in endeavors that require collaboration. Rather than being convinced to either qualify their behavior or seek negotiation with Washington, adversaries may become so antagonized that they deepen their resolve to oppose or resist US goals and objectives. Most dangerous of all, a "peace through strength" strategy might lead to the destabilization of conflict situations with either the US or its perceived enemies determining that they must use force to defend or protect their interests, or act in other counterproductive ways that escalate into crisis and result in damage to US interests.

Whatever the risks, the idea of "peace through strength" has deep roots in conservative Republican Party thinking on foreign and security policy. Perhaps its most influential early exposition is in Barry Goldwater's 1960 manifesto, *The Conscience of a Conservative*. Goldwater argued that "peace" is a "proper goal for American policy" but that it cannot be achieved except from a position of US strength. Goldwater laid out the core principles of the approach:

> Our national posture must reflect strength and confidence and purpose, as well as good will. We need not be bellicose, but neither should we encourage others to believe that American rights can be violated with impunity. We must protect American nationals and American property and American honor—everywhere. We may not make foreign peoples love us—no nation has ever succeeded in that—but we can make *them* *respect us*. And *respect* is the stuff of which enduring friendships and firm alliances are made. (Goldwater 2007, 116)

Goldwater is often characterized by the left as a Dr. Strangelove-style character, ready to unleash nuclear destruction upon the so-called Daisy Girl in President Lyndon Johnson's highly effective election campaign television advertisement in 1964. Renowned conservative commentator George F. Will has claimed, however, that despite his crushing defeat in the presidential election, Goldwater's nomination as the Republican candidate sealed "the ascendency of conservatism within the party." In foreign policy specifically, Will credits Goldwater with creating what he calls the conservative propensity for a "muscular foreign policy backing unapologetic nationalism" (Will 2004).

The greatest proponent of the "peace through strength" approach to US foreign policy was Republican President Ronald Reagan during his two terms in office from 1981–1989. Reagan believed in the approach with great conviction: "The reality is that we must find peace through strength" (Reagan 1983). He argued that his strong anti-Soviet rhetoric, his willingness to threaten and use force either directly in places like Grenada and Libya, or indirectly using proxies in Afghanistan and Central America, his forward deployment of nuclear cruise missiles in Europe, and the development of the Strategic Defense Initiative (SDI) were essential steps in projecting US strength and resolve in order to then negotiate for credible peace. The approach could be credited with eventually contributing to the conditions that enabled deeper nuclear arms reduction agreements with the Soviet Union. It was an extremely high-risk strategy, however, that destabilized international relations and greatly re-intensified the Cold War, deepened tensions in Europe, the Middle East, and the Americas, and almost resulted in the outbreak of nuclear war in November 1983 when Moscow misinterpreted NATO military exercises codenamed Able Archer as preparation for an actual attack and almost launched a preemptive strike against the US (Jones and Blanton 2016; Browning 2018).

Donald Trump's statements on foreign policy and America's role in the world dating back several decades reveal that he has been attitudinally predisposed toward the idea of "peace through strength" since long before his presidency began. In a 1980 interview with Rona Barrett on NBC television, for example, Trump emphasized the importance of gaining "respect" from other countries, a belief he would reiterate in many interviews over the years where he castigated US leaders for allowing the country to be "kicked around" not only by adversaries but also by its supposed allies: "Respect can lead to other things. When you get the respect of other countries, then the other countries tend to do a little bit as you do, and you can create the right attitudes" (Laderman and Simms 2017, 27). Trump believed the US had lost this respect due to the "foolishness" and lack of "toughness" among its leaders. The fundamental nature of this view is clear in the frequency and consistency with which he aired it. In a 1990 interview in *Playboy*, Trump spoke about these ideas extensively and advocated "the power of strength," not only in business deals but also in international relations. He again chastised US leaders for being too "weak":

> Some of our Presidents have been incredible jerk-offs. …We need to be tough. Tough is being mentally capable of winning battles against an opponent and doing it with a smile. Tough is winning systematically. … I think if we had people from the business community…negotiating some of our foreign policy, we'd have respect around the world. (Plaskin 1990)

Although he denied an interest in running for political office at that time, he did speculate on how a President Trump would approach foreign policy to overcome the perceived weakness of the US: "He would believe very strongly in extreme military strength. He wouldn't trust anyone.…he'd have a huge military arsenal, perfect it, understand it"

(Plaskin 1990). The peace through strength approach to foreign policy also sits perfectly with the assumptions that Trump articulated about his approach to business negotiation in his 1987 book *The Art of the Deal*. As noted in the previous chapter, Trump argued: "The best thing you can do is deal from strength, and leverage is the biggest strength you have" (Trump 1987).

Although Trump's historical criticisms of US presidents took in both Republicans and Democrats, his expressed attitudes about respect and strength in foreign affairs sat firmly within the Republican tradition of "peace through strength" so it was perhaps not surprising that the new administration tapped this vein of thinking on taking office. The concept has been core to its rhetoric and actions toward North Korea, Iran, Afghanistan and Syria, as well as NATO, and has been codified in the security and defense strategy documents that the administration has issued. Most significantly, the 2017 National Security Strategy (NSS 2017) has "Preserve Peace Through Strength" as one of its four "pillars" that underpin the "strategic vision" of the administration, alongside protecting the US and its people, promoting American prosperity, and advancing "American influence." The document states that the "peace through strength" strategy will entail "rebuilding our military so that it remains pre-eminent, deters our adversaries, and if necessary, is able to fight and win." The NSS lays out the logic of this thinking and why the administration believes that establishing the credibility of US strength, especially in the perception of adversaries, but also in the eyes of allies, is essential to achieve the ultimate goal of greater peace and stability:

Experience suggests that the willingness of rivals to abandon or forgo aggression depends on their perception of U.S. strength and the vitality of our alliances. The United States will seek areas of cooperation with competitors from a position of strength, foremost by ensuring our military power is second to none and fully integrated with our allies and all of our instruments of power. A strong military ensures that our diplomats are able to operate from a position of strength. In this way we can, together with our allies and partners, deter and if necessary, defeat aggression against U.S. interests and increase the likelihood of managing competitions without violent conflict and preserving peace. (National Security Strategy 2017, 26)

The Trump administration has given greater attention to the "strength" side of this equation in its rhetoric and actions so far, with little of the subsequent conciliation that the approach implies. Trump and his advisers have condemned Obama administration policies and agreements as weak and lacking resolve, not least in their rhetorical assault on and then withdrawal from the "worst deal ever" as Trump characterizes the so-called Iran Nuclear Deal or Joint Comprehensive Plan of Action (JCPoA). At the center of its military refresh and signaled buildup has been a new Nuclear Posture Review (NPR) that seeks to broaden US options by extending deterrence to non-nuclear strategic threats and suggesting a lower threshold for limited nuclear use, as well as increasing the diversity and flexibility of its forces with new low-yield non-strategic nuclear weapons. The administration has also sought to demonstrate its willingness to not only threaten but also use military force and to do so compellingly and without hesitation.

Just under two months into his presidency in April 2017, the administration signaled the degree of this willingness with Tomahawk missile strikes against the Syrian government air base at Shayrat in response to an alleged use of chemical weapons from the base on the rebel-held town of Khan Sheikhoun. The airstrike was significant as it was not only the first time since US forces intervened in the Syrian civil war that they had deliberately targeted Assad's government forces, but also because Russian forces used the base in their efforts directed against Islamic State and anti-government groups. The attack signaled to Moscow that although their main priority might be propping up Assad that the US would hold the Syrian regime to account if it resorted again to chemical weapons, despite the risks of direct confrontation with American and Russian forces operating in such close proximity and with somewhat competing agendas. Less than a week later, however, the Trump administration chose Afghanistan as the location for its most dramatic show of force, using the largest non-nuclear bomb in the US arsenal, the GBU-43/B Massive Ordnance Air Blast (MOAB) bomb. Nicknamed the "Mother Of All Bombs," it was deployed against Islamic State targets in the Achin district of Nangarhar province to devastating effect, allegedly killing 92 militants and destroying a network of bunkers and tunnels. The bombing had even greater symbolic value for the Trump administration, however, as a highly publicized flexing of US military capabilities designed as much to signal to other potential adversaries that the new president and his advisors not only possess the most advanced and deadly weapons but that they are more than ready and willing to actually use them. As a Pentagon report into the MOAB's effectiveness as a weapon had concluded: "It is expected that the weapon will have a substantial psychological effect on those who witness its use" (Wright 2017).

The Trump administration's adherence to the "peace through strength" strategy has been demonstrated most clearly in its approach to North Korea. Since the 1990s, the most fundamental point of contention in the uneasy peace between the increasingly isolated North Korea and US-supported South Korea has been Pyongyang's ambitions to develop nuclear weapons. Consecutive US administrations have opposed the policy as being highly destabilizing for the region and contrary to the provisions of the Nuclear Non-Proliferation Treaty (NPT), which North Korea had joined in 1985 but withdrew from in 2003. North Korean "Supreme Leader" Kim Jong Un decided to test the new US president's resolve early in 2017 with a resumption of ballistic missile and nuclear testing. Trump responded with unequivocal and highly provocative rhetoric in a series of speeches and tweets, threatening to strike North Korea "with fire and fury like the world has never seen" and proclaiming that if the US was "forced to defend itself or its allies, we will have no choice but to totally destroy North Korea." Trump's long-held views on nuclear proliferation and specifically North Korea suggested that his resolve to use force to combat Kim's nuclear ambitions should be believed. In 2000, he had stated: "I advocate a surgical strike against these outlaws before they pose a real threat." Furthermore, he appeared to understand such action in the context of the "peace through strength" concept, adding that such a response would have the additional benefit of sending "a message around the world that the United States is going to eliminate any serious threat to its security, and do so without apology" (Michaels and Williams 2017, 60–61).

The escalating war of words with North Korea was accompanied by increased security levels and an expansion of military preparedness in the region, extensive military exercises with South Korea and Japan, and diplomatic pressure on China and other states to impose and enforce stronger sanctions against Kim Jong Un's government. The policy was "peace through strength" in action: rapidly upping the ante with the intention of clearly signaling US strength and resolve. The approach was extremely risky, however, as rising tensions and tit-for-tat insults made ever more likely that provocation or misperception could lead to direct conflict. Allies became nervous, particularly in the region itself, that rather than halting or reversing Kim's nuclear ambitions, the "peace through strength" approach would spiral out of control and lead to a conflict that could escalate and draw in other major powers such as China and Russia. The Pentagon warned of catastrophic levels of destruction and casualties on all sides, as well as great potential for regional escalation, should war break out between the Koreas.

Trump appeared unmoved, however, until an offer of direct talks was made by Kim through South Korean intermediaries in March 2018. For over a year, the emphasis in policy toward North Korea had been almost exclusively on the "strength" side of the equation, but now Trump seemed to move to the "peace" side more rapidly than most commentators believed prudent. In June 2018, Trump held a summit with Kim in Singapore, the first ever between a US president and a North Korean leader, and declared confidently that denuclearization would now be achieved. Although he had secured no formal treaty and few concrete items in the summit agreement, Trump announced that there was "no longer a nuclear threat from North Korea." In the president's view, the relationship with North Korea had been transformed, and it had been so as a direct result of his adoption of the "peace through strength" approach. Negotiations were possible because Trump's uncompromising rhetoric and threat of force had convinced North Korea that the US was a credible adversary, that its resolve was firm, and that its strength as a world power could no longer be questioned. No matter how far from a comprehensive settlement of North Korea's nuclear question the two sides might be, Trump claimed it was a victory that vindicated his strong arm tactics and suggested "peace through strength" was a route to success for the administration.

The approach can be observed in other aspects of the administration's foreign policy. Another of Trump's long-standing views from before he sought political office is the strong belief that US allies are free riders which receive great support and generosity from Washington but give nothing in return and are not living up to their burden sharing responsibilities. As he put it in an interview for ABC News in 2011: "They wouldn't be there if it weren't for us. We protect them. We keep those countries going and we get nothing for it" (Laderman and Simms 2017, 83). In office, Trump has not tempered his thoughts, chastising many members of NATO for failing to commit the agreed proportion of their budgets on defense spending. Prior to the annual NATO summit in July 2018, for example, Trump sent pointedly critical letters to nine NATO leaders, including Angela Merkel of Germany, expressing the "growing frustration in the United States that some allies have not stepped up as promised" and implying that the US may not feel able to fulfill its collective security responsibilities if members do not pay their way: "It will…become increasingly difficult to justify to American citizens why some countries do not share NATO's collective security burden while American soldiers continue to sacrifice their lives overseas or come home gravely wounded."

Trump's belief is clearly that if he signals a strong position and makes threats, that allies will take him seriously, admire his resolve and adhere to US demands for increased defense spending within NATO. While the level of his rhetoric and the extent of the threats he is making may be more extreme, his calls for NATO spending are actually not unusual for a US president. Indeed, both Trump's predecessors also used NATO summits to put pressure on their alliance partners to increase their defense spending in line with agreed commitments. In Bucharest in 2008, George W. Bush said: "At this summit, I will encourage our European partners to increase their defense investments to support both NATO and EU operations. America believes if Europeans invest in their own defense, they will also be stronger and more capable when we deploy together." Similarly, Barack Obama stated in 2016: "If we've got collective defense, it means that everybody's got to chip in, and I have had some concerns about a diminished level of defense spending among some of our partners in NATO. Not all, but many." Issues over burden sharing among allies have been commonplace concerns for US presidents and NATO states, under pressure from Washington, began addressing their spending commitments before Trump became president.

In trade relations also, the same maxim of "peace through strength" can be discerned in policies that have rejected US participation in multilateral arrangements built on cooperation and collaboration in favor of negotiating bilateral deals that overcome what Trump sees as "unfair" practices in order to protect US interests and promote American prosperity. Trump campaigned against the Obama administration negotiated Trans-Pacific Partnership (TPP), a free-trade agreement designed largely to thwart Chinese regional trade ambitions that, if ratified, would bind the US to Australia, Brunei, Canada, Chile, Japan, Malaysia, Mexico, New Zealand, Peru, Singapore and Vietnam. Trump withdrew the US from the TPP on his third day in office, citing it as a great victory for American workers and his America First promise. Trump has also taken aim at the North American Free Trade Agreement (NAFTA), preferring to renegotiate bilaterally with its two other signatories, Mexico and Canada. One of Trump's mantras while campaigning was that China was responsible for the economic and financial problems faced by the US. In a rally in Indiana in May 2016, he used controversially blunt language to condemn China's economic and trade practices toward the US as well as taking a swipe at the Obama administration's current policy: "we can't continue to allow China to rape our country. And that's what they're doing. It's the greatest theft in the history of the world."

Since the rapprochement of the 1970s, competitive engagement and cooperation designed to facilitate China's economic liberalization has been the approach pursued by US administrations. The rationale has been that forging an economic relationship is the most effective way to minimize China's threat potential and encourage democratic progress. This approach has come under pressure in recent years from across the political spectrum in the US, however, and from allies in the Asia-Pacific region as fear of the impending "rise" of China has grown together with Beijing's regional and global ambitions. Majorities in US public opinion have viewed China negatively, fueled by strong concerns over the quality and safety of some Chinese-made products, the nature of its industrial practices, its censorship of the Internet domestically and cyber threats internationally, the lack of protection for intellectual property rights and the long-held disquiet over Beijing's human rights record.

Candidate Trump's views on China were far from extraordinary. His advocacy of a strong regime of tariffs to force China to revalue its currency, the yuan, and reverse the large trade deficit with the US had permeated congressional attitudes for some time. As early as 2005, US Senators proposed a bill, albeit unsuccessfully, to levy a 27.5% tariff on all Chinese imports unless the yuan was revalued by the same amount. As president, Trump initially continued the policy of engagement undertaken by previous administrations, holding a summit in Florida with Chinese President Xi Jinping early in his presidency and then undertaking a state visit to China in November 2017. After months of threats, however, the Trump administration began a trade war with China in July 2018 as it imposed a series of extremely high tariffs causing China to retaliate with tariffs on US goods. Trump stated that: "My great friendship with President Xi of China and our country's relationship with China are both very important to me" but he insisted that "Trade between our nations, however, has been very unfair, for a very long time. This situation is no longer sustainable." By September 2018, Trump indicated that his trade policy toward China was following a similar strategy as the "peace through strength" approach adopted in security matters when he tweeted that "Tariffs have put the US in a very strong bargaining position." The implication was that China would be forced to the negotiating table by the Trump administration's resolve and projected strength enabling the president to negotiate a trade deal that from his perspective would initiate a fairer relationship. The leverage as strength approach that businessman Trump had advocated in *The Art of the Deal* was now being employed by President Trump on the world stage.

# 3    Orthodoxy and Principled Realism

Far from being revolutionary, the Trump administration's assumptions about international affairs and their approach to foreign policy have been rather ordinary in terms of their orthodoxy, drawing upon a highly conservative view of how the world works. The "peace through strength" strategy is rooted in what Trump has referred to as "principled realism." This idea at the core of the Trump administration's thinking about the international system was laid bare in successive annual speeches to the United Nations General Assembly in 2017 and 2018, written primarily by Stephen Miller, a fiercely loyal senior policy adviser who the *New York Times* described as the "surviving watchman on the president's right flank since the removal…of Stephen K. Bannon as chief strategist" (Flegenheimer 2017). The speeches assert a view of the world that firmly rejects ideas of global governance, interdependence and transnationalism. Sounding much like the opening postulations of a Realism 101 lecture, Trump's 2017 speech claimed that "the nation-state remains the best vehicle for elevating the human condition," called on all world leaders to "put your countries first," to protect their interests and "reject threats to sovereignty," because "there can be no substitute for strong, sovereign, and independent nations … that are home to patriots."

In the 2018 UN speech, Trump claimed that "America's policy of principled realism means we will not be held hostage to old dogmas" yet his approach appears to be exactly that. As he asserted elsewhere in the speech, his administration has no interest in engaging in the complexity and contingency of more progressive and critical understandings of the international system that have become increasingly influential in policymaking in recent decades: "We reject the ideology of globalism, and we embrace the doctrine of patriotism." This retrograde approach to international affairs has seen the Trump administration work to undo progress that has been made, particularly by Democratic administrations, on any number of collaborative and cooperative programs and agreements. Here again, however, rather than being extraordinary, the administration is largely reverting to Republican form, unpicking advances made by the Obama administration on combating climate change by withdrawing from the Paris Agreement, for example, much in the same way that the Bush administration reversed commitments made by the Clinton White House with the Kyoto Protocols.

The Trump administration foreign policy approach and the assumptions behind it are really quite ordinary, even if its delivery by its main protagonist projects a deliberate air of extraordinariness. Trump is far from the first US president to come to office with little or no experience of foreign affairs. When they have this lack of knowledge and experience, newly elected presidents do usually make more of an effort than Trump to draw on a wide range of expertise from the foreign policy elite, mostly from within their own party but sometimes from bipartisan sources also. When they do so, however, it is rarely in ways that avoid internal conflicts and they rarely pick a foreign policy team that acts in a unified manner with a clear grand strategy. The closeness and strategic unity between Richard Nixon and his National Security Advisor Henry Kissinger were extraordinary in this regard, though even in the Nixon administration this concentration of foreign policymaking created issues of breadth of advice with alternative perspectives from other principals failing to gain a hearing. In other administrations, divisions and rivalries have largely been the norm with significant advisory battles royale breaking out between National Security Advisor Zbigniew Brzezinski and Secretary of State Cyrus Vance in the Carter administration, Secretary of Defense Caspar Weinberger and Secretary of State George Shultz in the Reagan administration, and Donald Rumsfeld at Defense and Colin Powell at State under George W. Bush.

The Trump White House has been portrayed in various depictions, most notably that of seasoned *Washington Post* investigative journalist Bob Woodward, as chaotic with senior officials often making documents "disappear" from the president's desk or ignoring his demands in order to avoid embarrassing or even potentially dangerous policy decisions and changes from being made (Woodward 2018). Turnover has been high in the administration with Trump at times hiring and firing seemingly at a whim. His foreign and security policy team has seen a number of significant changes, with three National Security Advisors, two Secretaries of State and two CIA directors in just eighteen months in office. Only Secretary of Defense Jim Mattis retained his position throughout Trump's first two years. Trump's revolving door of political appointees and White House staff suggests that he is taking expertise no more seriously in office than he was on the campaign trail when he claimed he was only listening to his own advice on foreign affairs. His habit of shooting from the hip in his tweets, unscripted statements and press conferences also suggest his foreign policy is something of a one man show. Despite his extraordinary claims and untutored outbursts on the world stage, however, the policy documents issued by Trump's administration, such as the National Security Strategy, the National Defense Strategy and the Nuclear Posture Review, indicate that administration viewpoints are more expertly considered before publication.

Although Mike Flynn had to resign over his Russian liaisons less than four weeks into the job, both his successors as National Security Advisor—H. R. McMaster and John Bolton—have brought levels of expertise and strong advice, even if in the latter's case with a particular theoretical and ideological bent, that have steered the underlying direction of policy in relatively orthodox and more predictable ways than would seem apparent from Trump's public performances. Rex Tillerson was often sidelined and never seemed to get to grips with his leadership role at State or his contributions to the National Security Council. He was not helped by gaping holes in the appointment of senior staff in his department and his president's habit of contradicting his public statements just hours after he had made them. The movement of experienced legislator and policy maker Mike Pompeo from CIA Director to replace Tillerson as Secretary of State, like Bolton's appointment, is consequential in terms of certain policy preferences, not least toward Iran and China, but has also suggested a steadying of the ship in quite traditional ways. The consistent security policy voice-of-reason among Trump's closest advisors was Jim Mattis as Secretary of Defense. According to Woodward, Mattis' approach was admired within the White House and seemed effective with the president: "avoid the confrontation, demonstrate respect and deference, proceed smartly with business, travel as much as possible, get and stay out of town" (Woodward 2018, 227–228).

# 4 Accomplishments?

At the outset of the 2018 UN speech, Trump declared brashly that "In less than two years, my administration has accomplished more than almost any administration in the history of our country." Much to Trump's visible surprise, the claim drew derisive laughter from the floor of the General Assembly. Trump has certainly been a disruptive presence on the world stage, talking tough while reversing several of the previous administration's policy positions and agreements. The latter are "accomplishments" in so far as they have been carried into effect, but they do not warrant the conclusion that they have been successful in resolving the problems in international affairs that the United States faces. Despite Trump's confidence that he has achieved a remarkable amount of success since becoming president, his administration's "achievements" can readily be perceived as either resetting the US approach to approximately that taken by previous Republican administrations, making modest gains that are yet to be consolidated, or exacerbating the problems they are designed to address. In other words, they have been rather ordinary and not out of step with the levels of issue engagement and policy outcomes that might be expected at this stage of a presidency. It is far too early to assess their long-term effects.

Trump points in particular to the progress made in relations with North Korea as a vindication of his administration's "peace through strength" approach and also the crowning achievement of the first half of his first term in office. It is certainly significant that a US president sat down for direct talks with a North Korean leader for the first time and relations between Pyongyang and Seoul have shown a great deal of progress toward normalization in a remarkably short time. Normalization, however, appears to have been driven far more by the Koreans themselves rather than any direct intervention or facilitation by Trump or any of his advisers, though it could be argued that Trump's saber rattling stirred sufficient fear of war breaking out on the Korean peninsula that political leaders on both sides of the Demilitarized Zone decided it was time to talk. Even the summit meeting between Trump and Kim in Singapore in June 2018, however, was initiated by Korean diplomacy rather than the White House. Most significantly, there has been no concrete agreement let alone treaty signed by which North Korea will formally undertake "complete, verifiable, irreversible disarmament" as demanded by the US. While Trump declares confidently that North Korea has ceased its nuclear program with a halt to missile and nuclear testing as well as the destruction of some of its nuclear infrastructure, no time frame or systematic program of verified denuclearization has been set, North Korea has not indicated that it will rejoin the NPT, and only limited ongoing negotiations appear to be taking place with some shuttle diplomacy from Secretary of State Mike Pompeo and the suggestion of a second summit meeting. The situation has not been fully resolved and North Korea has made agreements previously on which it has reneged, so despite some advances the Trump administration is far from securing a nuclear-free Korean peninsula.

In quite opposite ways, the administration has failed to advance the cause of nuclear non-proliferation by withdrawing from the Iran Nuclear Deal. Rejecting the JCPoA, which all other signatories believe was working, and returning to a policy of sanctions and isolation that failed to rein in purported Iranian nuclear ambitions during the Bush administration has exacerbated rather than resolved the problems that Trump had with the deal. Trump objected to the lack of permanency of the agreement, its failure to address Iranian missile development and its lack of attention to what he perceives as regional aggression by Tehran. Yet the history of arms control, particularly with the Soviet Union and now Russia, demonstrates that time-limited agreements or treaties that focus on specific elements of nuclear programs are the established method of containing, reducing or eradicating nuclear weapons programs. A more comprehensive deal that covered broader non-nuclear issues was not and continues not to be a credible option. Trump may have succeeded in tearing up what he considers the "worst deal ever" but it is likely to stimulate calls for a renewed nuclear program in Iran and diplomatic disengagement that, as the Bush administration discovered, is unlikely to achieve a more cooperative relationship with Tehran.

Elsewhere in the Middle East, Trump has claimed that the administration's "new approach is...yielding great strides and very historic change," yet in sum it appears to be more like business as usual. Trump is correct that Islamic State is now all but defeated in Iraq and Syria, and the military successes did accelerate considerably since he came to office and loosened the tactical rules of engagement for US forces and their proxies, but the strategic approach to defeating IS has not changed significantly from that put in place by the Pentagon under Obama's watch and the risks of IS sponsored or inspired terrorism outside the region remain in place. In the complex wars in Syria and Yemen, the Trump administration has also shown an increased willingness to deploy force, especially air power but also special operations forces, including striking directly against Syrian government targets with its attack on the Shayrat air base and threats of further action should Assad again authorize the use of chemical weapons. Fighting has not abated, however, and in both situations the Trump administration has not managed to initiate a comprehensive plan for confronting the issues inherent in the conflicts and bringing the wars to an end. Although Trump signals a desire to bring stability to both situations, there appears to be no clear strategy for finding a political solution that satisfies all the parties involved in the fighting, a problem that is further complicated in Syria by broader issues in the relationships with the other deeply involved external powers of Russia, Iran and Israel.

Trump's efforts in securing a comprehensive Middle East peace agreement between Israel and Palestine have also failed to produce any significant progress. Trump continues to hint that he has a plan for negotiation that he believes will be successful, not least because he has great faith in his own skills as chief negotiator. By October 2018, however, it was no clearer what that plan might be or how he would intervene to break the current diplomatic deadlock and the deepening tensions that have been exacerbated by his own administration's actions over the moving of the US Embassy in Israel from Tel Aviv to Jerusalem and the ejection of the Palestinian Liberation Organization (PLO) from their Washington, DC offices. The impasse over the proposed two-state solution and the desire of the United States to broker a deal has been a priority common to every US administration since George H. W. Bush initiated the Madrid Conference in 1991. Given the intractable nature of the situation, expectations for success are always low so it gives US presidents a relatively risk-free opportunity to achieve a significant breakthrough. President Trump is no different than his predecessors in desiring a successful negotiation and his inability so far to achieve it is not at all out of the ordinary.

In other policy areas, successes in terms of resolving major issues, permanently fixing problems or comprehensively overcoming threats have been few and far between. Yet again, this is not unusual given the complexity and difficulty of contemporary international relations. Indeed, the relative lack of success also puts the Trump presidency so far very much in line with previous administrations which, despite the immense military, economic, political and cultural power of the US, for several decades have been ordinarily frustrated in their efforts to bring peace and stability to the Middle East; to tame the ambitions of other major powers such as Russia and China; to bring what they perceive as "rogue states" including Venezuela and Iran fully in line with US objectives and goals; to end the unpredictable threat posed by international terrorism; to use US military force quickly and effectively without getting bogged down in long-term intractable conflicts such as Vietnam, Afghanistan and Iraq; to stem nuclear proliferation and fulfill obligations under the NPT to make progress with nuclear disarmament; to ensure that allies undertake effective burden sharing and set trade and finance policies that do not seem to disadvantage US interests; let alone deal effectively with global problems that transcend territorial borders such as poverty, crime, trafficking, environmental disasters whatever the view of climate change, and the humanitarian effects of war.

# 5     Conclusion

Beyond the bluster of Trump's rhetoric and positioning, as well as the often equally hyperbolic condemnations of his approach and his style, lies a foreign policy that is rooted in long established conservative nationalist ideas about the relationship of the US to the world, a strategy that has been a staple of modern Republican presidencies. Far from instigating a revolution in US foreign policy, the Trump administration has so far followed an approach that draws upon highly orthodox realist ideas about the nature of the international system, is steeped in the deep-rooted Republican logic of "peace through strength" and is focused on areas of the world and issues of security and stability that are the usual fare of US foreign policy.

As with domestic issues and politics, there is a difference between the style of the president and the outcomes of his policymaking. Importantly in foreign affairs, there is often also a difference between the disruptive, extraordinary nature of the president's presentation of policy and the more measured, ordinary approach and policy implementation of his administration. President Trump says whatever he wants about foreign policy in his tweets, seems unconcerned about whether he gets details correct or understands the complexities of situations when he speaks without autocue about international affairs, and takes no issue with speaking plainly and often offensively either directly to or about other world leaders, regardless of whether they are his adversaries or his allies. Particularly in contrast to his immediate predecessor Barack Obama, he appears to be an extraordinary type of US president for whom the etiquette of diplomacy seems irrelevant. He is accused by his critics of either barreling through foreign affairs without a care for the consequences of his words and actions, or worse still deliberately attempting to dismantle the architecture of the international liberal order that his post-World War II predecessors had worked so hard to establish as the best way to protect and promote American interests. In these widely held portrayals, he is the stuff of nightmares with a pocketful of nuclear codes, making the world an extremely dangerous place due to his erratic behavior and unpredictable temperament.

Nonetheless, no matter how extraordinary the president's style and rhetoric in foreign affairs, the underlying logic of the administration's foreign and security policy strategy and implementation in most areas renders it far more normal and ordinary than its main protagonist often projects it to be. The Trump administration's policy focus is fundamentally concerned with problems and issues that do ordinarily occupy the minds of US presidents and their foreign policy teams, and in the modern era often with little short-term gain or long-term peace and stability. The Trump administration has not yet bucked the trend of recent US presidencies that have struggled to secure and promote US interests abroad, found intractable international problems are characterized that way for a reason, and had to realize that their priorities and goals do not always align with those of the allies they need cooperation with to achieve them. They have also discovered that adversaries will very often not bend to the will of the United States regardless of the size of its military or its willingness to threaten or use force, that international economic relationships are often complex and require a degree of compromise in order to secure the "best deal," and that the world has become increasingly globalized and interconnected in ways that mean there are limits to the power the US has to get its own way in foreign affairs. Whatever progress they might be making in bringing peace to the Korean peninsula, this is not yet a presidency that has enjoyed an unusually successful foreign policy. For all the extraordinary behavior of the president himself, in terms of overarching strategy and outcomes the Republican administration of Donald Trump is so far pursuing a rather ordinary foreign policy.

# References

America First Foreign Policy. 2017. White House Website. Accessed January 20, 2017. https://www.whitehouse.gov/issues/foreign-policy/.

Browning, Taylor. 2018. 1983: *The World at the Brink*. London: Little, Brown.

Flegenheimer, Matt. 2017. "On Trump's Right Flank, a Survivor Well Attuned to Resentment." *New York Times*, October 10.

Goldwater, Barry. 2007. *The Conscience of a Conservative*. Edited by C. C. Goldwater. Princeton: Princeton University Press.

Jones, Nate, and Thomas S. Blanton. 2016. *Able Archer 83: The Secret History of the NATO Exercise That Almost Triggered Nuclear War*. New York: The New Press.

Krauthammer, Charles. 2017. "Trump's Foreign Policy Revolution." *Washington Post*, January 26.

Laderman, Charlie, and Brendan Simms. 2017. *Donald Trump: The Making of a World View*. London: I.B. Tauris.

Michaels, Jeffrey, and Heather Williams. 2017. "The Nuclear Education of Donald Trump." *Contemporary Security Policy* 38 (1): 60–61.

National Security and Defense. 2018. White House Website. Accessed September 7, 2018. https://www.whitehouse.gov/issues/national-security-defense/.

National Security Strategy of the United States of America. 2017. The White House, December.

*New York Times*. 2016. "A Letter From G.O.P. National Security Officials Opposing Donald Trump." *New York Times*, August 8.

Plaskin, Glenn. 1990. "The 1990 Playboy Interview with Donald Trump." *Playboy*, March 1. https://www.playboy.com/read/playboy-interview-donald-trump-1990.

Reagan, Ronald. 1983. "Remarks at the Annual Convention of the National Association of Evangelicals in Orlando, Florida", March 8, 1983. Public Papers of the Presidents of the United States, Ronald Reagan. http://www.presidency.ucsb.edu/ws/?pid=41023.

Trump, Donald J. 1987. *Trump: The Art of the Deal*. New York: Random House.

Will, George F. 2004. "Goldwater's Grinning." *Pittsburgh Tribune-Review*, September 2. http://pittsburghlive.com/x/pittsburghtrib/opinion/column-ists/will/s_246932.html.

Woodward, Bob. 2018. *Fear: Trump in the White House*. London: Simon & Schuster.

Wright, Robin. 2017. "Trump Drops the Mother of All Bombs on Afghanistan." *The New Yorker*, April 14.

# 9

# Conclusion: Extraordinary President, Ordinary Presidency

There is a counterintuitive quality to the claim that Donald J. Trump's is an ordinary presidency. How can this most extraordinary president be judged to be conducting a presidency that is ordinary? Surely, if there's never been a president like him then that means his presidency is extraordinary? It does not, but to see why, it is necessary to recognize the distinction between the president and his presidency.

The president is the person himself. That includes the attributes that he (or surely soon, she) brings to the office in terms of personality, character, experience, knowledge, intelligence, temperament, honesty, integrity, trustworthiness, constancy, sociability, humor, friendliness, eloquence and, especially, persuasiveness. It also includes the way in which the president approaches this most difficult of jobs. How does the president organize the White House, who staffs the key positions and gives untrammeled advice? What are the media and legislative strategies, are they carefully entwined and mutually supporting? How does the president respond to criticism from within and without his own party? Is the president more idealist and ideologically driven or more realist and pragmatic? The decisions are not all self-evidently momentous, but can be crucial to success: Does the president make a point of

© The Author(s) 2019
J. Herbert et al., *The Ordinary Presidency of Donald J. Trump*,
Palgrave Studies in Political Leadership,
https://doi.org/10.1007/978-3-030-04943-0_9

speaking to a Member of Congress who has suffered a bereavement or whose daughter has won a little league title? The list is almost endless but collectively constitutes what we have called a president's methodology. It is about how the president approaches the job and the processes and strategies that are put in place (or not) to enhance the likelihood of success, or "winning" as Trump likes to say.

So, the president refers to the person in the White House, the attributes he brings to the job and the approaches or strategies adopted to maximize his influence and likelihood of success. On almost every aspect imaginable, Donald Trump is an extraordinary *president*. We do not claim or argue that President Trump himself is anything less than extraordinary or anything approaching ordinary. Instead, the preceding chapters lay out an innovative but straightforward argument: While Trump is an extraordinary president, his *presidency* is quite ordinary. We are also arguing that the distinction is extremely important and one that is often overlooked in assessments of any US administration. Since US politics is widely characterized as a presidential system, the person of the president is all too often conflated with the success or otherwise of his presidency. But distinguishing between them facilitates a more nuanced assessment of the presidency that any individual president leads.

If President Trump is extraordinary, in what ways is his presidency ordinary? The answer is that it is ordinary in its outcomes and accomplishments. First, the number and scope of his achievements are rather meager, and this is quite normal. Presidents of the United States are constrained by a constitutional structure that deliberately makes it very difficult to get things done. Indeed, the separation of powers and checks and balances were instituted specifically to hold ambitious and potentially tyrannical executives in check. They are the constitutional equivalent of a dog leash and muzzle. In addition to being leashed and muzzled by the Constitution, modern presidents must face an increasingly difficult governing environment in which a partisan and polarized polity are able to stifle reform. It is all very well to run on a promise to "drain the swamp," but how do you do that when the swamp is full of clever, very large and aggressive alligators and your lead is short and muzzle strong? Trump is ordinary in that, like most presidents, his accomplishments are few.

Second, he is also ordinary in the sense that the few accomplishments he can lay claim to are largely mainstream Republican ones. The Tax Cuts and Jobs Act (TCJA) that Trump signed in December 2017 is classic of the type. Not only did it award the largest tax cuts to big business and America's wealthiest individuals—like Trump, for example—and look very like nearly every other Republican tax bill in the last four decades, but it decidedly failed to address the economic precariousness of the "left behinds" that Trump had built his presidential campaign around. Another useful example is the North American Free Trade Agreement. The worse trade deal in history according to Trump was accused of destroying American jobs, of creating a wasteland in the industrial heartlands of the Midwest. NAFTA had to go. It did, but only in name. The new incarnation–the United States-Mexico-Canada Agreement–looks remarkably similar: a free-trade agreement between the three nations of North America. There is no rabid assault upon the international trade system and globalization. The notion that Trump is fighting the corner of the common man in Washington is fanciful. The alleged tribune of the working class has morphed into a classic Republican plutocrat, with the richest cabinet in history, cutting the taxes of the wealthy and the healthcare and social provisions of the poor, and striking free-trade deals that all but mirror those they replaced. If Trump had delivered on his promises to protect the economically precarious and insecure, it would have been a truly extraordinary accomplishment for a Republican president. But there is huge chasm between Trump's words and actions, his promises made and promises delivered. He is a faint-hearted revolutionary, talking the talk but not walking the walk—the people's tribune turned mainstream Republican.

One comparison that can give the impression that Trump is extraordinary is with the person who preceded him in the White House, Barack Obama. On the one hand, there are the obvious personal and methodological differences between the two presidents, but there are also important policy differences, especially on foreign policy as we argued in Chapter 7. While there have certainly been some continuities in terms of policy focus, Obama nonetheless seems to stand in complete contrast to Trump's approach to US foreign policy and its execution. The Obama administration emphasized the complex connections between policy areas, recognized the interdependence of nations in a globalized world and attempted to construct a sophisticated and reflective approach to foreign policy where the benefits of multilateralism were central. Trump's worldview is rooted largely in a far more orthodox set of realist assumptions that reject globalism, emphasize the role of nationalism and the sovereignty of nation-states in international affairs, are skeptical or even hostile to the relevance of international organizations and multilateral agreements, and sees the balance of power and interests in the world as a mostly zero-sum game. With Obama as a comparator, this appears to be an extraordinary, revolutionary change in direction. Yet as with much of Trump's domestic agenda, what his administration has done is to largely return the US to an emphasis on traditional Republican priorities, objectives and goals in foreign policy utilizing an underlying strategic approach that reverts to a long-established Republican idea of seeking "peace through strength." Compared with the line of Republican presidents who preceded Trump, going back through the two Bushes, Reagan and Nixon, the revolution looks far more ordinary and can be understood as a corrective to the Obama years that is setting the US back on the preferred Republican track. When compared against his own party's historical approach, rather than the Democrats, Trump's foreign policy looks much more ordinary.

Even Trump's election victory was standard Republican fare. Despite running the most extraordinary primary and general election campaigns (that is, the process or methodology) in the television age, the vote (that is, the outcome) split along the usual party lines. Moreover, our analysis shows that Trump did not win more votes from the white working class than one would expect given the historical trend of this group toward the GOP. And once in office, Trump has not realigned those deep-seated party identifications that structure America's party and electoral systems. There has been no political earthquake, no seismic shift in the tectonic plates, despite the many erupting volcanoes that peppered his campaigns.

Third, it is also the case that Trump looks especially ordinary next to the scale of his promises and the absurdity of his claims as to their delivery. America would be made great again, foreign nations would stop laughing at it, and the carnage would stop. Now in office, so numerous and extraordinary are his accomplishments in Trump's eyes that he feels able to compare himself to the greatest American presidents. The extent of Trump's achievements is of course more prosaic, but is made to look even more mundane when held up and judged next to his outlandish promises and grandiose self-assessments. This in part is a democratic problem. Presidents and others don't win elections by promising to limit their ambitions, to downscale the American Dream, and by striving for ordinariness. They win by promising that "Happy Days Are Here Again" (Roosevelt 1932), it is "A time for greatness" (Kennedy 1960), "It's morning again in America" (Reagan), or by "Building a bridge to the twenty-first century" (Clinton 1992), and "Let's Make America Great Again" (Reagan, not Trump, 1980). But none of these presidents, including the almost undisputedly extraordinary Franklin Delano Roosevelt, ever made the subsequent claim that theirs was one of the greatest presidencies in American history. Trump has. And maybe he really believes it. We cannot know for sure. His very high opinion of himself—a very stable genius with the best words and biggest brain and highest IQ and unrivaled deal-making skills—would suggest that he is at least capable of rationalizing that such extraordinary success is a natural consequence of his extraordinary talent. Trump has a hugely self-confident faith in his abilities to boss the political system, just as he did his real estate business and the contestants on The Apprentice. In contrast to his promise and bluster, however, Trump has so far delivered outcomes and accomplishments that appear all the more ordinary as a result.

In sum, the balance of evidence presented in this book strongly supports the conclusion that while Trump is an extraordinary president his presidency is rather ordinary. Having established that, we then asked the "why" question. How can a president so extraordinary inhabit a presidency so ordinary?

The first part of the explanation is outlined above and is fairly straightforward: the American constitution tethers and muzzles its presidents, just as it does the legislature and the judiciary. Power is separated, shared and limited. Trump has been constrained by the structures of power designed 230 years ago with people like him very much in mind. Those structures are a constant and explain why so many presidents achieve very little of note. Absent a tremendous crisis, it is unlikely that Trump will be afforded an opportunity for greatness by making deep political, social or economic changes, or to undo the fabric of the international system.

There are also deeper structural constraints that Trump has encountered as an outsider president. Bringing an unfamiliar and underdeveloped agenda to Washington to confront a highly partisan system, Trump has faced considerable challenges. He has lacked a network of people to call on, to staff his administration, to provide the intellectual capital to support the development of new policies and to deliver specific policy plans. Rather than an insider president leading a party with greater agreement over priorities and ideology, Trump has faced trying to build policies and coalitions not just opposed by one political party, but having to wrestle his own to win support. Amid Trump's hyperbole on how easy leading from the Oval Office would be, observers (and Trump himself) fail to recognize the scale of the challenge he has undertaken.

Given the formidable structural constraints, Trump's personal attributes and strategic choices need to be exceptional. But he confronts an irony: outsider presidents, facing the greatest leadership challenges, are usually the least well-equipped to govern. Bluntly, Trump is just not very good at the job of being president. He does not have the personal attributes or experience that a successful president requires and his strategic choices have further inhibited his prospects for success. The further irony is that it is precisely the attributes and methodology that make Trump an extraordinary president that also make his presidency ordinary, in terms of both the low number and narrow scope of his successes and their decidedly mainstream Republican flavor.

Trump is unable to make the system work for him. He cannot utilize the constitutional powers of his office to influence the outcomes of government. He is unable to overcome the constraints, divisions, barriers and entrenched interests that lie in his path. His dedication to media tactics, at the expense of effective governing in Washington, is self-defeating. Presidents have spent the best part of a century developing the White House as an institution to support their efforts; Trump's personalized version of leadership undermines the White House's work and with it his access to power. He has created a divided team around him, refuses to manage the divisions carefully and adds a layer of further chaos with his hyperactive Twitter thumbs. His administration has found it hard to stake out and support clear policy positions. He cannot even work effectively with potential allies: congressional leaders, including Democrats, genuinely want to know where President Trump stands on the important issues of the day, especially those such as immigration that helped define his campaign. His broader strategic vision is just as damaging. Trump has not understood how to mobilize the power of the presidency to pressure the key Washington players who make or break his agenda. His base strategy has failed to deliver action on his more radical proposals. His hostage politics, based on his supposedly world-class negotiating skills and understanding of leverage, are particularly suicidal. To put it mildly, this is not the methodology of great presidents. Trump's ignorance on the issues, lack of interest in the policy part of politics and poor management have created a policy vacuum. But politics, like nature, abhors a vacuum. And so other political leaders charge into the space abdicated by Trump. In a Congress where both chambers had Republican majorities for the first two years of Trump's presidency, the natural leaders of that charge were also Republicans. They strongly influenced what happened in Trump's voids. If the president managed to rally his ideas and offer a policy solution, it tended to wither without congressional Republicans offering it support and sustenance. Trump needed their support and thus his few triumphs are mainstream Republican triumphs. Trump did not run as a mainstream Republican—he was the outsider, the disruptor, the nationalist, the insurgent, the populist—but he certainly governs as one.

The final element of Trump's claim to being an extraordinary president is his appeal to the people and his skill as a communicator. His reality TV show, The Apprentice, commanded average audiences of 20 million viewers, his tweets are followed by upward of 54 million, and he delivers persistent reminders that almost 63 million people voted for him. He's a popular guy with an extraordinary media presence who can command an audience whether on television or in the flesh at a campaign rally. Yet this great sense of self, his projection of his affiliation with the common people, and his extraordinary reach on social media have failed to give his presidency either the legitimacy or the successes that he craves. Trump has maintained overall approval among Americans who identify as Republican, but their support appears to stem more from their rather ordinary partisanship than from any particular affinity with their party's president, a point reinforced by their more lukewarm support for his policy agenda. Trump's hostile attitude toward the traditional media again plays relatively well with his core supporters whose distrust of liberal elites extends to a hatred for the big media houses on the East and West coasts. But his visceral condemnations of the "fake news" media has made life more difficult for his presidency, quickly establishing an adversarial relationship akin to that faced by previous administrations such as Nixon's, and limiting opportunities for the president to spin the news cycle in his favor and use it as a tool to garner greater support among the public and fellow policy makers and legislators. Far from his presidency being marked by an extraordinary ability to communicate his message and persuade others to follow his lead, President Trump is experiencing ordinary levels of public support from his party's supporters coupled with persistent levels of opposition.

Looking forward from the midpoint in President Trump's first term in office, he may yet secure reelection and a further four years in which to press harder for the mantle of greatness that he craves and that his extraordinary attempts at disruptive politics demand. The evidence to date, however, suggests that he will be no more successful than other recent presidents who have struggled to master the complexities of Washington's system of checks and balances, have not been able to break the deeply divided and partisan nature of the electorate to build a new and more sustainable governing coalition, have failed to persuade even members of their own political party to wholeheartedly adopt their preferred policy positions, have not been able to dictate the direction of international relations or protect the United States from the plethora of threats and challenges that it faces globally, and have even when they have left the presidency with a fairly healthy final approval rating nonetheless not been able to climb into the upper echelons of the various league tables of most successful presidents that are regularly produced by journalists, political scientists and historians. The modern presidency has proven to be an extremely difficult office in which to be deemed a great success. Even this most extraordinary president is unlikely to break that mold. The presidency of Donald J. Trump has been and is likely to continue to be an ordinary presidency.

# Appendix

See Table A.1.

**Table A.1** Comparison of the Romney-Obama and Trump-Clinton vote margins among selected groups

|  | 2012 Republican margin | 2016 Republican margin | Change in Republican margin 2012→2016 |
|---|---|---|---|
| **Gender** | | | |
| Male | 7 | 11 | 4* |
| Female | −11 | −13 | −2 |
| **Race** | | | |
| White | 20 | 20 | 0 |
| Black | −87 | −81 | 6 |
| Latino | −44 | −38 | 6 |
| Asian | −47 | −38 | 9 |
| **Race × Gender** | | | |
| White men | 27 | 31 | 4* |
| White women | 14 | 9 | −5 |
| Black men | −76 | −69 | 7 |
| Black women | −93 | −89 | 4 |

(continued)

© The Editor(s) (if applicable) and The Author(s) 2019
J. Herbert et al., *The Ordinary Presidency of Donald J. Trump*,
Palgrave Studies in Political Leadership,
https://doi.org/10.1007/978-3-030-04943-0

Table A.1   (continued)

|  | 2012 Republican margin | 2016 Republican margin | Change in Republican margin 2012→2016 |
|---|---|---|---|
| Latino men | −32 | −31 | −1 |
| Latino women | −53 | −44 | 9* |
| **Education** (2 categories) |  |  |  |
| Non-college grad | −4 | 7 | 11* |
| College grad | −2 | −10 | −8* |
| **Education** (4 categories) |  |  |  |
| High-school grad or less | −6 | 5 | 11* |
| Some college | −1 | 8 | 9* |
| College grad | 4 | −5 | −9* |
| Postgraduate | −13 | −21 | −8* |
| **Education × Race** |  |  |  |
| White non-college grad | 25 | 37 | 12* |
| White college grad | 14 | 3 | −11* |
| Non-white non-college grad | −66 | −56 | 10* |
| Non-white college grad | −55 | −50 | 5 |
| **Income** |  |  |  |
| <$50K | −22 | −12 | 10* |
| $50–100K | 6 | 3 | −3 |
| >$100K | 10 | 0 | −10* |

*Source* 2012 and 2016 National Election Pool exit polls by Edison Research. Results reported by pool member CNN. 2012 $N = 26,872$, 2016 $N = 24,558$. Additional data from *Washington Post*, "2016 Election Exit Polls: How the Vote Has Shifted," November 29, 2016
*statistically significant at .05
All cell entries are percentage point differences between the two main parties

# Bibliography

Alberta, Tim. 2016. "The 'Diploma Divide' Explains Why Iowa Looks Better for Trump Than New Hampshire." *National Review*, October 24.

America First Foreign Policy. 2017. White House Website. Accessed January 20, 2017. https://www.whitehouse.gov/issues/foreign-policy/.

Anonymous. 2018. "Opinion: I Am Part of the Resistance Inside the Trump Administration." *New York Times*, September 5.

Bacon, Perry, Jr. 2018. "How the Freedom Caucus Learned to Love Trump." *fivethirtyeight.com*, July 31. https://fivethirtyeight.com/features/how-the-freedom-caucus-learned-to-love-trump/.

Bade, Rachael, Burgess Everett, and Josh Dawsey. 2017. "Trump Sides with Democrats in Debt Limit, Funding, Harvey Deal." *Politico*, September 6. https://www.politico.com/story/2017/09/06/schumer-and-pelosi-offer-support-for-harvey-aid-and-debt-limit-boost-242376.

Baker, Peter. 2017. "For Trump, A Year of Reinventing the Presidency." *New York Times*, December 31.

Barstow, David, Susanne Craig, and Russ Buettner. 2018. "Trump Engaged in Suspect Tax Schemes as He Reaped Riches from His Father." *New York Times*, October 2.

Bartels, Larry. 2016. "2016 Was an Ordinary Election, Not a Realignment." *Washington Post*, November 10.

© The Editor(s) (if applicable) and The Author(s) 2019
J. Herbert et al., *The Ordinary Presidency of Donald J. Trump*,
Palgrave Studies in Political Leadership,
https://doi.org/10.1007/978-3-030-04943-0

Bartels, Larry. 2018. "Partisanship in the Trump Era." Paper Presented to Center for the Study of Democratic Institutions, Vanderbilt University, February 7.

Benoit, William L., and John P. McHale. 2003. "Presidential Candidates' Television Spots and Personal Qualities." *Southern Communication Journal* 68 (4): 319–334.

Bernstein, Jonathan. 2018. "John Kelly's Problems Go Well Beyond Porter Mess." *Bloomberg.com*, February 14. https://www.bloomberg.com/view/articles/2018-02-14/john-kelly-s-problems-go-well-beyond-porter-mess.

Bowles, Nigel. 2005. *Nixon's Business*. College Station: Texas A&M University Press.

Brenan, Megan. 2018a. "Snapshot: 4 in 10 Still Strongly Disapprove of Trump." *Gallup.com*, August 29. https://news.gallup.com/poll/241787/snapshot-strongly-disapprove-trump.aspx.

Brenan, Megan. 2018b. "Record-High 75% of Americans Say Immigration Is Good Thing." *Gallup.com*, June 21. https://news.gallup.com/poll/235793/record-high-americans-say-immigration-good-thing.aspx.

Brooks, David. 2016. "The Week That Trump Won." *New York Times*, October 30.

Brownstein, Ronald. 2015. "The Billionaire Candidate and His Blue-Collar Following." *The Atlantic*, September 11.

Brownstein, Ronald. 2016a. "The Parties Invert." *The Atlantic*, May 23.

Brownstein, Ronald. 2016b. "The Class Inversion of American Politics Accelerates." *The Atlantic*, July 26.

Browning, Taylor. 2018. *1983: The World at the Brink*. London: Little, Brown.

Bruni, Frank. 2018. "Ann Coulter to Donald Trump: Beware the Former Trumpers." *New York Times*, March 30.

Bycoffe, Aaron. 2016. "The Endorsement Primary." *fivethirtyeight.com*, June 7. https://projects.fivethirtyeight.com/2016-endorsement-primary/.

Calamur, Krishnadev. 2017. "The International Incidents Sparked by Trump's Twitter Feed." *The Atlantic*, December 19.

Carnes, Nicholas, and Noam Lupu. 2017. "It's Time to Bust the Myth: Most Trump Voters Were Not Working Class." *Washington Post*, June 5.

Casselman, Ben, Maggie Koerth-Baker, and Anna Maria Barry-Jester. 2017. "Trump Keeps Derailing His Own Agenda." *fivethirtyeight.com*, August 18. https://fivethirtyeight.com/features/trump-keeps-derailing-his-own-agenda/.

Cassino, Dan. 2016. *Fox News and American Politics: How One Channel Shapes American Politics and Society*. New York: Routledge.

Cillizza, Chris. 2017. "Burning Every Bridge." *Washington Post*, August 24.

Clinton, Hillary Rodham. 2017. *What Happened.* New York: Simon & Schuster.

Cohen, Marty, David Karol, Hans Noel, and John Zaller. 2008. *The Party Decides: Presidential Nominations Before and After Reform.* Chicago: University of Chicago Press.

Cohn, Nate. 2016. "Why Trump Won: Working-Class Whites." *New York Times*, November 9.

Colvin, Jill. 2018. "Trump Shuffle: Suddenly Trade Guru Navarro Takes Spotlight." *US News and World Report*, March 7.

Comey, James. 2018. *A Higher Loyalty: Truth, Lies, and Leadership.* New York: Macmillan.

Cook, Nancy. 2017. "Trump Finds Success on Taxes Doing What He Knows Best—Selling." *Politico*, December 18. https://www.politico.com/story/2017/12/18/trump-taxes-sales-congress-302241.

Cost, Jay. 2016. "Why Neither Hillary Nor Trump Deserve My Vote." *The Weekly Standard*, September 10.

Costa, Robert. 2017. "Pressure Cooker." *Washington Post*, October 9.

Costa, Robert. 2018. "Pennsylvania Vote Shows That Trumpism Has Its Limits—Even in Trump Country." *Washington Post*, March 13.

Davis, Julie Hirschfield. 2018. "Trump Plans to Send National Guard to the Mexican Border." *New York Times*, April 3.

Dawsey, Josh. 2017a. "Fallout Grows as Trump Continues Attacks on Fellow GOP Members." *Politico*, August 25. https://www.politico.com/story/2017/08/25/trump-gop-attacks-fallout-grows-242051.

Dawsey, Josh. 2017b. "Inside a $100,000-Per-Person Trump Fundraiser: Chicken, Asparagus and 20 Minutes of Talk." *Washington Post*, December 7.

Dunn, Amina. 2018. "Trump's Approval Ratings so Far Are Unusually Stable—And Deeply Partisan." *Pew Research Center*, August 1. http://www.pewresearch.org/fact-tank/2018/08/01/trumps-approval-ratings-so-far-are-unusually-stable-and-deeply-partisan/.

Edsall, Thomas. 2016. "One Problem for Democratic Leaders Is Democratic Voters." *New York Times*, December 22.

Edwards III, George C. 2012. *The Strategic President: Persuasion and Opportunity in Presidential Leadership.* Princeton: Princeton University Press.

Ehrenfreund, Max, and Scott Clement. 2016. "Economic and Racial Anxiety: Two Separate Forces Driving Support for Donald Trump." *Washington Post*, March 22.

Enten, Harry. 2017. "The GOP Tax Cuts Are Even More Unpopular Than Past Tax Hikes." *fivethirtyeight.com*, November 29. https://fivethirtyeight.

com/features/the-gop-tax-cuts-are-even-more-unpopular-than-past-tax-hikes/.

Fahrenthold, David A. 2016. "Trump Boasts About His Philanthropy. But His Giving Falls Short of His Words." *Washington Post*, October 29.

Fahrenthold, David A., and Rosalind S. Helderman. 2016. "Trump Bragged That His Money Bought off Politicians. Just Not This Time." *Washington Post*, September 7.

Farhi, Paul. 2017. "Washington Post's David Fahrenthold Wins Pulitzer Prize for Dogged Reporting of Trump's Philanthropy." *Washington Post*, April 10.

Fernandez, Manny. 2018. "National Guard Has Eyes on the Border. But They're Not Watching Mexico." *New York Times*, May 15.

Fiorina, Morris. 2018. "The Meaning of Trump's Election Has Been Exaggerated." *RealClearPolitics.com*, January 10. https://www.realclearpolitics.com/articles/2018/01/10/the_meaning_of_trumps_election_has_been_exaggerated__135968.html.

Fiorina, Morris P., Samuel J. Abrams, and Jeremy C. Pope. 2004. *Culture War? The Myth of a Polarized America*. New York: Longman Publishing.

Fivethirtyeight. 2018. "Tracking Congress in the Age of Trump." *Fivethirtyeight.com*. https://projects.fivethirtyeight.com/congress-trump-score/. Accessed October 21, 2018.

Flegenheimer, Matt. 2017. "On Trump's Right Flank, a Survivor Well Attuned to Resentment." *New York Times*, October 10.

Funk, Carolyn L. 1996. "The Impact of Scandal on Candidate Evaluations: An Experimental Test of the Role of Candidate Traits." *Political Behavior* 18 (1): 1–24.

Funk, Carolyn L. 1999. "Bringing the Candidate into Models of Candidate Evaluation." *Journal of Politics* 61 (1): 700–720.

Gamio, Lazaro, and Dan Keating. 2016. "How Trump Redrew the Electoral Map, from Sea to Shining Sea." *Washington Post*, November 9.

Goldwater, Barry. 2007. *The Conscience of a Conservative*. Edited by C. C Goldwater. Princeton: Princeton University Press.

Gosling, Amanda, and Andrew Wroe. 2017. "De-industrialisation and the 2016 Presidential Election: A Spatial Analysis of Trump's Victory." Paper Presented at 2017 American Politics Group Conference, University of Leicester, January 5–7.

Graham, David A. 2017. "'As I Have Always Said': Trump's Ever-Changing Positions on Health Care." *The Atlantic*, July 28.

Green, Joshua. 2017. *Devil's Bargain: Steve Bannon, Donald Trump, and the Storming of the Presidency*. New York: Penguin Press.

Greenberg, Stanley B. 2018. "Riling up the Base May Backfire on Trump." *New York Times*, June 18.

Grynbaum, Michael M. 2018. "Trump, the Television President, Expands His Cast." *New York Times*, March 16.

Haberman, Maggie, Glenn Thrush, and Peter Baker. 2017. "Trump's Way: Inside Trump's Hour-by-Hour Battle for Self-Preservation." *New York Times*, December 9.

Harris, Mary. 2016. "A Media Post-mortem on the 2016 Presidential Election." *mediaQuant.net*, November 14. https://www.mediaquant.net/2016/11/a-media-post-mortem-on-the-2016-presidential-election/.

Harris, Shane, Felicia Somnez, and John Wagner. 2018. "'That's Going to be Special': Tensions Rise as Trump Invites Putin to Washington." *The Washington Post*, July 19.

Heinisch, Reinhard. 2003. "Success in Opposition—Failure in Government: Explaining the Performance of Right-Wing Populist Parties in Public Office." *West European Politics* 26 (3): 91–130.

Hetherington, Marc J., and Jonathan D. Weiler. 2009. *Authoritarianism and Polarization in American Politics*. Cambridge: Cambridge University Press.

Hohmann, James. 2018. "Under Trump, Americans Are Becoming More Supportive of Immigration." *Washington Post*, June 22.

Holland, Joshua. 2018. "In the Long Run, Trump Could Be a Huge Setback for the Anti-immigration Movement." *The Nation*, April 5.

Huetteman, Emmarie. 2017. "On Health Law, G.O.P. Faces a Formidable Policy Foe: House Republicans." *New York Times*, March 20.

Hulse, Carl. 2017. For McConnell, Health Care Failure Was a Map to Tax Success." *New York Times*, December 3.

Jamieson, Kathleen Hall, and Doron Taussig. 2017. "Disruption, Demonization, Deliverance, and Norm Destruction: The Rhetorical Signature of Donald J. Trump." *Political Science Quarterly* 132 (4): 619–650.

Johnson, Eliana, and Josh Dawsey. 2017. "GOP Despairs at Inability to Deliver." *Politico*, July 23. https://www.politico.com/story/2017/07/23/republicans-trump-despair-deliver-240868.

Johnson, Jenna. 2018. "Drain What Swamp? Trump's Supporters Embrace Kavanaugh, Member of a Class They Once Rebuked." *Washington Post*, October 6.

Johnstone, Ron, Charles Pattie, Kelvyn Jones, and David Manley. 2017. "Was the 2016 United States' Presidential Contest a Deviating Election? Continuity and Change in the Electoral Map." *Journal of Elections, Public Opinion and Parties* 27 (4): 369–388.

Jones, Charles O. 1998. *Passages to the Presidency: From Campaigning to Governing*. Washington, DC: Brookings Institution Press.

Jones, Charles O. 2005. *The Presidency in a Separated System*. 2nd ed. Washington, DC: Brookings Institution Press.

Jones, Jeffrey M. 2018. "Trump's Sixth Quarter His Best; Remains Weak Historically." *Gallup.com*, July 24. https://news.gallup.com/poll/237878/trump-sixth-quarter-best-remains-weak-historically.aspx.

Jones, Nate, and Thomas S. Blanton. 2016. *Able Archer 83: The Secret History of the NATO Exercise That Almost Triggered Nuclear War*. New York: The New Press.

Jordan, Miriam. 2017. "Without New Laws or Walls, Trump Presses the Brake on Legal Immigration." *New York Times*, December 20.

Jordan, Miriam. 2018. "U.S. Must Keep DACA and Accept New Applications, Federal Judge Rules." *New York Times*, April 24.

Karni, Annie. 2017. "John Kelly's Losing Battle with Trump's Twitter Feed." *Politico*, November 29. https://www.politico.com/story/2017/11/29/trump-twitter-fringe-websites-270490.

Karni, Annie. 2018. "Trump White House Recruits at a Hill Job Fair Amid Staff Exodus." *Politico*, June 13. https://www.politico.com/story/2018/06/13/white-house-hill-job-fair-645592.

Kernell, Samuel. 1997. *Going Public: New Strategies of Presidential Leadership*. Washington, DC: CQ Press.

Kim, Seung Min. 2017. "How McConnell Got a Win on Taxes." *Politico*, December 2.

Kinder, Donald R. 1983. "Presidential Traits." Report to the NES Board of Overseers, Center for Political Studies, University of Michigan.

Kinder, Donald R. 1986. "Presidential Character Revisited." In *Political Cognition*, edited by Richard R. Lau and David O. Sears. Hillsdale, NJ: Lawrence Erlbaum.

Klein, Ezra. 2018. "Trump Is Winning." *Vox*, January 29. https://www.vox.com/policy-and-politics/2018/1/29/16900646/trump-administration-tweets-media-polarization.

Kranish, Michael. 2018. "Trump's China Whisperer: How Billionaire Stephen Schwarzman Has Sought to Keep the President Close to Beijing." *Washington Post*, March 12.

Kranish, Michael, and Marc Fisher. 2016. *Trump Revealed: The Definitive Biography of the 45th President*. London: Simon & Schuster.

Krauthammer, Charles. 2017. "Trump's Foreign Policy Revolution." *Washington Post*, January 26.

Kristol, William. 2016. "Donald J. Obama." *The Weekly Standard*, April 29.

Kruse, Michael. 2017. "The Loneliest President." *Politico*, September 15. https://www.politico.com/magazine/story/2017/09/15/donald-trump-isolated-alone-trumpology-white-house-215604.

Laderman, Charlie, and Brendan Simms. 2017. *Donald Trump: The Making of a World View*. London: I.B. Tauris.

Lewandowski, Corey R., and David N. Bossie. 2018. *Let Trump Be Trump: The Inside Story of His Rise to the Presidency*. New York: Center Street.

Lewis, David E., Patrick Bernhard, and Emily You. 2018. "President Trump as Manager: Reflections on the First Year." *Presidential Studies Quarterly* 48 (3): 480–501.

Lind, Michael. 2016. "This Is What the Future of American Politics Looks Like." *Politico*, May 22. https://www.politico.com/magazine/story/2016/05/2016-election-realignment-partisan-political-party-policy-democrats-republicans-politics-213909.

Liptak, Adam. 2018. "Trump v. California: The Biggest Legal Clashes." *New York Times*, April 5.

Liu, Huchen, and Gary C. Jacobson 2018. "Republican Candidates' Positions on Donald Trump in the 2016 Congressional Elections: Strategies and Consequences." *Presidential Studies Quarterly* 48 (1): 49–71.

Machin, Stephen. 2008. "An Appraisal of Economic Research on Changes in Wage Inequality." *Labour* 22 (1): 7–26.

MacWilliams, Matthew. 2016. "Who Decides When the Party Doesn't? Authoritarian Voters and the Rise of Donald Trump." *PS: Political Science & Politics* 49 (4): 716–721.

Mayer, Kenneth R. 1999. "Executive Orders and Presidential Power." *Journal of Politics* 61 (2): 445–466.

Merry, Robert W. 2016. "Trump vs. Hillary Is Nationalism vs. Globalism." *The National Interest*, May 4.

Michaels, Jeffrey, and Heather Williams. 2017. "The Nuclear Education of Donald Trump." *Contemporary Security Policy* 38 (1): 60–61.

Mitchell, Amy, Jeffrey Gottfried, Katerina Eva Matsa, and Elizabeth Grieco. 2017. "Covering President Trump in a Polarized Media Environment." *Pew Research Center*, October 2. http://assets.pewresearch.org/wp-content/uploads/sites/13/2017/10/10164210/PJ_2017.10.02_Trump-First-100-Days_FINAL.pdf.

Moe, Terry M. 1985. "The Politicized Presidency." In *The New Direction in American Politics*, edited by John E. Chubb and Paul E. Peterson. Washington, DC: The Brookings Institution.

National Security and Defense. 2018. White House Website. Accessed September 7, 2018. https://www.whitehouse.gov/issues/national-security-defense/.

National Security Strategy of the United States of America. 2017. The White House, December.

Nelson, Michael. 2018. *Trump's First Year*. Charlottesville: University of Virginia Press.

Neustadt, Richard. 1990. *Presidential Power and the Modern Presidents: The Politics of Leadership from Roosevelt to Reagan*. New York: The Free Press.

*New York Times*. 2016. "A Letter from G.O.P. National Security Officials Opposing Donald Trump." *New York Times*, August 8.

Newmyer, Tory, Juliet Eilperin, and Sean Sullivan. 2017. "McConnell Says Trump Needs to Provide Clarity on Health Care." *Washington Post*, October 22.

Newport, Frank. 2018. "Americans Oppose Border Walls, Favor Dealing with DACA." *Gallup.com*, June 20. https://news.gallup.com/poll/235775/americans-oppose-border-walls-favor-dealing-daca.aspx.

Noonan, Peggy. 2016. "The GOP Establishment's Civil War." *Wall Street Journal*, January 8.

Noonan, Peggy. 2017. "Trump, ObamaCare and the Art of the Fail: What Happens When We Elect a President Who Prefers to Freelance Rather Than to Lead." *Wall Street Journal*, July 20.

Nuzzi, Olivia. 2018. "Donald Trump and Sean Hannity Like to Talk Before Bedtime." *New York Magazine*, May 14.

O'Connell, Anne Joseph. 2018. "After One Year in Office, Trump's Behind on Staffing But Making Steady Progress." *Brookings Institution*, January 23. https://www.brookings.edu/research/after-one-year-in-office-trumps-behind-on-staffing-but-making-steady-progress/.

Paletta, Damian. 2018. "China Joins a Growing List of Countries to Brush off Trump's Trade Threats." *Washington Post*, July 6.

Patterson, Thomas E. 2017. "News Coverage of Donald Trump's First 100 Days." Harvard Kennedy School Shorenstein Center on Media, Politics and Public Policy, May 18.

Peterson, Kristina, Siobhan Hughes, Richard Rubin, and Peter Nicholas. 2017. "How Tax Bill Emerged from a Late Night of Deal Making." *Wall Street Journal*, December 2.

Pew. 2017a. "The Partisan Divide and Political Values Grown Even Wider." *Pew Research Center*, October 5. http://assets.pewresearch.org/wp-content/uploads/sites/5/2017/10/05162647/10-05-2017-Political-landscape-release.pdf.

Pew. 2017b. "Partisan Identification Is 'Sticky,' But About 10% Switched Parties Over the Past Year." *Pew Research Center*, May 17. http://assets.pewresearch.org/wp-content/uploads/sites/5/2017/05/31163430/05-17-17-Longitudinal-partisanship-release.pdf.

Pew. 2017c. "Political Typology Reveals Deep Fissures on the Right and Left." *Pew Research Center*, October 24. http://assets.pewresearch.org/wp-content/uploads/sites/5/2017/10/31115611/10-24-2017-Typology-release.pdf.

Pew. 2018. "Voters More Focused on Control of Congress—And the President—Than in Past Midterms." *Pew Research Center*, June 20. http://assets.pewresearch.org/wp-content/uploads/sites/5/2018/06/22114930/06-20-2018-Political-release.pdf.

Pfiffner, James P. 1996. *The Strategic Presidency: Hitting the Ground Running.* 2nd ed. Lawrence: University Press of Kansas.

Pfiffner, James P. 2018. "The Contemporary Presidency: Organizing the Trump Presidency." *Presidential Studies Quarterly* 48 (1): 153–167.

Philips, Amber. 2016. "Why Even Lindsey Graham Might Be a Ted Cruz Voter Now." *Washington Post*, March 2.

Plaskin, Glenn. 1990. "The 1990 Playboy Interview with Donald Trump." *Playboy*, March 1. https://www.playboy.com/read/playboy-interview-donald-trump-1990.

Polsby, Nelson, 1984. *Political Innovation in America: The Politics of Policy Initiation.* New Haven, CT: Yale University Press.

Reagan, Ronald. 1983. "Remarks at the Annual Convention of the National Association of Evangelicals in Orlando, Florida, March 8, 1983." Public Papers of the Presidents of the United States, Ronald Reagan. http://www.presidency.ucsb.edu/ws/?pid=41023.

Rein, Lisa. 2016. "The Plum Book Is Here for Those Angling for Jobs in Trump's Washington." *Washington Post*, December 4.

Rein, Lisa, and Andrew Ba Tan. 2017. "How the Trump Era Is Changing the Federal Bureaucracy." *Washington Post*, December 30.

Resh, William G. 2015. *Rethinking the Administrative Presidency.* Baltimore, MD: Johns Hopkins University Press.

Restuccia, Andrew, and Nancy Cook. 2018. "This New Zealander Is Trying to Tame Trump's Chaotic Policy Shop." *Politico*, July 3. https://www.politico.com/story/2018/07/03/trump-foreign-policy-chris-liddell-692613.

Roberts, David. 2016. "The Most Common Words in Hillary Clinton's Speeches, in One Chart: They Weren't About 'Identity Politics'." *Vox*, December 16. https://www.vox.com/policy-and-politics/2016/12/16/13972394/most-common-words-hillary-clinton-speech.

Rudalevige, Andrew. 2006. *The New Imperial Presidency: Renewing Presidential Power After Watergate*. Ann Arbor: University of Michigan Press.

Sacchetti, Maria. 2018. "Federal Judge: Trump Administration Must Accept New DACA Applications." *Washington Post*, April 25.

Sargent, Greg. 2018. "Alarming New Revelations About Trump's Addiction to Fox News." *Washington Post*, May 14.

Schaffner, Brian. 2016. "White Support for Donald Trump Was Driven by Economic Anxiety, but Also by Racism and Sexism." *Vox*, November 16. https://www.vox.com/mischiefs-of-faction/2016/11/16/13651184/trump-support-economic-anxiety-racism-sexism.

Scherer, Michael, and Josh Dawsey. 2018. "Trump Cites as a Negotiating Tool His Policy of Separating Immigration Children from Their Parents." *Washington Post*, June 15.

Schmidt, Michael S., and Michael D. Shear. 2017. "Trump Says Russia Inquiry Makes U.S. 'Look Very Bad'." *New York Times*, December 28.

Shear, Michael D., and Julie Hirschfield Davis. 2017a. "Stoking Fears, Trump Defied Bureaucracy to Advance Immigration Agenda." *New York Times*, December 23.

Shear, Michael D., and Julie Hirschfield Davis. 2017b. "Trump Moves to End DACA and Calls on Congress to Act." *New York Times*, September 5.

Skocpol, Theda, and Vanessa Williamson. 2016. *The Tea Party and the Remaking of Republican Conservatism*. Oxford: Oxford University Press.

Skowronek, Stephen. 1997. *The Politics Presidents Make: Leadership from John Adams to Bill Clinton*. Cambridge, MA: Belknap Press.

Small, Andrew. 2016. "Trump's Rust Belt Bet." *CityLab*, November 11. https://www.citylab.com/equity/2016/11/trumps-rust-belt-bet/507353/.

Snell, Kelsey, and Mike DeBonis. 2017. "Republicans Set Aggressive Agenda on Health Care, Regulations and Tax Reform." *Washington Post*, January 25.

Sundquist, James L. 1968. *Politics and Policy: The Eisenhower, Kennedy, and Johnson Years*. Washington, DC: Brookings Institution.

Tankersley, Jim. 2016. "How Trump Won: The Revenge of Working-Class Whites." *Washington Post*, November 9.

Tenpas, Kathryn Dunn, Elaine Kamarck, and Nicholas W. Zeppos. 2018. "Tracking Turnover in the Trump Administration." *Brookings Institution*, March 16.

Tesler, Michael. 2016. "Views About Race Mattered More in Electing Trump Than in Electing Obama." *Washington Post*, November 22.

Thompson, Derek. 2016. "The Dangerous Myth That Hillary Clinton Ignored the Working Class." *The Atlantic*, December 5.

Thrush, Glenn. 2018. "Mulvaney, Watchdog Bureau's Leader, Advises Bankers on Ways to Curtail Agency." *New York Times*, April 24.

Trump, Donald J. 1987. *Trump: The Art of the Deal*. New York: Random House.

Trump, Donald J. 2016. "Full Draft: Donald Trump 2016 RNC Draft Speech Transcript." *Politico*, July 21. https://www.politico.com/story/2016/07/full-transcript-donald-trump-nomination-acceptance-speech-at-rnc-225974.

Trump, Donald J. 2017a. "The Inaugural Address, January 20, 2017." The White House. https://www.whitehouse.gov/briefings-statements/the-inaugural-address/.

Trump, Donald J. 2017b. "Remarks by President Trump Before a Briefing on the Opioid Crisis." August 8. https://www.whitehouse.gov/briefings-statements/remarks-president-trump-briefing-opioid-crisis/.

Trump, Donald J. 2017c. "Remarks by President Trump to the 72nd Session of the United Nations General Assembly, September 19, 2017." The White House. https://www.whitehouse.gov/briefings-statements/remarks-president-trump-72nd-session-united-nations-general-assembly/.

Trump, Donald J. 2018. "Remarks in a Meeting with Members of Congress on Immigration Reform and an Exchange with Reporters." January 9. http://www.presidency.ucsb.edu/ws/?pid=128934.

Tur, Katy. 2017. "'Come Here, Katy': How Donald Trump Turned Me into a Target." *The Guardian*, October 11.

Watson, Kathryn. 2017. "'You All Just Got a Lot Richer,' Trump Tells Friends, Referencing Tax Overhaul." *CBSNews.com*, December 23. https://www.cbsnews.com/news/trump-mar-a-lago-christmas-trip/.

Weko, Thomas J. 1995. *The Politicizing Presidency: The White House Personnel Office, 1948–1994*. Lawrence, KS: University Press of Kansas.

Wildavsky, Aaron. 1966. "The Two Presidencies." *Trans-Action/Society* 4: 7–14.

Will, George F. 2004. "Goldwater's Grinning." *Pittsburgh Tribune-Review*, September 2. http://pittsburghlive.com/x/pittsburghtrib/opinion/columnists/will/s_246932.html.

Williams, Luke. 2016. *Disrupt: Think the Unthinkable to Spark Transformation in Your Business*. 2nd ed. Old Tappan, NJ: Pearson.

Wolff, Michael. 2018. *Fire and Fury: Inside the Trump White House*. London: Little, Brown.

Woodward, Bob. 2018. *Fear: Trump in the White House*. London: Simon & Schuster.

Wright, Robin. 2017. "Trump Drops the Mother of All Bombs on Afghanistan." *The New Yorker*, April 14.

Wroe, Andrew. 2008. *The Republican Party and Immigration Politics: From Proposition 187 to George W. Bush*. New York: Palgrave.

Yglesias, Matthew. 2017. "Trump's Latest Big Interview Is Both Funny and Terrifying: POTUS Swings and Misses at the Softest Softballs." *Vox*, October 23. https://www.vox.com/policy-and-politics/2017/10/23/16522456/trump-bartiromo-transcript.

Zanona, Melanie. 2017. "Trump's 'Infrastructure Week' Goes off the Rails." *The Hill*, June 9.

# Index

© The Editor(s) (if applicable) and The Author(s) 2019
J. Herbert et al., *The Ordinary Presidency of Donald J. Trump*,
Palgrave Studies in Political Leadership,
https://doi.org/10.1007/978-3-030-04943-0